HOWARD CARTER
BEFORE
TUTANKHAMUN

HOWARD CARTER
BEFORE
TUTANKHAMUN
NICHOLAS REEVES AND JOHN H. TAYLOR

PUBLISHED FOR THE TRUSTEES OF THE BRITISH MUSEUM BY BRITISH MUSEUM PRESS

Published by British Museum Press
A division of British Museum Publications Ltd
46 Bloomsbury Street, London WC1B 3QQ

British Library Cataloguing in Publication Data
A Catalogue record for this book is available
from the British Library.

ISBN 0–7141–0952–5

Designed by Harry Green

Set in Gill Medium and Century Schoolbook
Printed and bound in Great Britain
by Butler & Tanner Ltd, Frome and London

FRONT COVER
Top: Howard Carter as Chief Inspector of Antiquities
for Upper Egypt, about 1900.
Lower left : Head of Tutankhamun emerging from a lotus
flower, a painted and gessoed wooden sculpture from
the king's tomb. H. 30 cm.
Lower right : King Tuthmosis I; copy by Howard Carter
of a painted relief in the temple of Queen Hatshepsut
at Deir el-Bahri.

FRONTISPIECE Howard Carter as a young man,
about the time of his appointment as Chief Inspector
of Antiquities for Upper Egypt in 1899.

Contents

Acknowledgements

Thanks are due to all those who have helped in various ways in the preparation of this exhibition – in particular the following institutions and individuals, who have loaned objects in their care and granted permission to reproduce some of them in this book: Robert Lunsingh Scheurleer and Willem M. van Haarlem, Allard Pierson Museum, Amsterdam; Angela Thomas, Bolton Museum and Art Gallery; Rita E. Freed and Peter Lacovara, Museum of Fine Arts, Boston; Janet Backhouse, Department of Manuscripts, The British Library; Richard Fazzini and Donald Spanel, The Brooklyn Museum; Luc Limme and Patrick De Smet, Musées Royaux d'Art et d'Histoire, Brussels; the Earl of Carnarvon; Anthony Carter; John E. Carter; Venetia Chattey; Chiddingstone Castle; Arielle Kozloff, The Cleveland Museum of Art; Mogens Jørgensen and Flemming Johansen, Ny Carlsberg Glyptotek, Copenhagen; William H. Peck, The Detroit Institute of Arts; The Egypt Exploration Society, London; Vronwy Hankey; Rosemarie Drenkhahn, Kestner Museum, Hanover; Arne Eggebrecht, Roemer- und Pelizaeus-Museum, Hildesheim; Christopher Lee; Neil Brown, The Science Museum, London; Valerie Mendes and Susan Lambert, Victoria and Albert Museum, London; Barbara Adams, The Petrie Museum, University College London; Dorothea Arnold and Catharine Roehrig, The Metropolitan Museum of Art, New York; Hugh Norwood; Margaret Orr; Jaromir Malek, The Griffith Institute, Oxford; Helen Whitehouse, Ashmolean Museum, Oxford; J-L De Cenival, Musée du Louvre, Paris; Anne Pemberton; Nicholas Reeves; Benjamin Ripper; Julia Rushbury; William Schenck; William Kelly Simpson; David Butters, Swaffham Museum; Eberhard Thiem. One of the principal pieces in the exhibition was generously loaned by a Japanese private collector. The documents quoted in this book are reproduced by courtesy of the owners, whose names appear in the List of Sources.

For valuable help and suggestions the authors would like to thank T. G. H. James, Renate Germer, Janine Bourriau and Huon Mallalieu. Special thanks are due to John Carter, great-nephew of Howard Carter, who allowed the authors unrestricted access to his extensive collection of papers and memorabilia.

A particular debt of gratitude is owed to Anne Pemberton. Without her infectious enthusiasm for Carter and his story, this exhibition might never have taken place.

Preface

This publication has been prepared to accompany the special exhibition 'Howard Carter: Before Tutankhamun', which has been mounted in the British Museum to coincide with the seventieth anniversary of the discovery in 1922 of the tomb of Tutankhamun by the British archaeologist Howard Carter. Unlike the previous anniversary celebration, 'Treasures of Tutankhamun', held in the British Museum in 1972, this present exhibition is concerned not with Tutankhamun's tomb and its content, but rather with Carter and with his other archaeological achievements, many and varied, which because of the spectacular nature and overwhelming importance of the great find of 1922 have not hitherto received the attention that they deserve.

The book is the joint work of Nicholas Reeves, who has acted as special consultant to the exhibition, and John H. Taylor, who is a curator in the Department of Egyptian Antiquities in the British Museum. The selection and arrangement of the text is largely the work of Dr Reeves, who has also contributed to the captions. A few sections of the main text have been written by Dr Taylor, who chose the illustrations, wrote the captions and saw the book through the press. The caption on page 37 was written by Mrs Vronwy Hankey. The maps are the work of Christine Barratt, Graphics Officer in the Department of Egyptian Antiquities. Peter Hayman took many of the photographs. The editing of the manuscript has been carried out by Rachel Rogers and Sarah Derry of British Museum Press.

W. V. Davies
Keeper of Egyptian Antiquities
British Museum

Introduction

When, on that November day in 1922, the flickering candle revealed the first glimpse of Tutankhamun's funerary treasures, Howard Carter took his place in the annals of archaeology as one of the most famous and successful Egyptologists of all time. It had been no easy journey. A self-made man of relatively humble origins, Carter had clawed his way to the top of the Egyptological tree by a combination of hard work, enormous flair and good fortune. By 1922 he had devoted thirty years of his life to Egyptology, working at many of Egypt's most important sites, making one exciting discovery after another. The reasons for his success are not hard to find. Possessed of tremendous energy, determination and personal courage, Carter was throughout his life a unique mix of man of principle and thoroughgoing pragmatist. This flexibility of approach did not make for popularity, and some of his exploits raise the hackles of more conventional archaeologists even today. Were Carter able to respond, it is doubtful whether (beyond the obligatory 'Tommy rot!', one of his favourite expressions) there would be any excuses; he would prefer his successes to speak for themselves.

It is the work of Carter's first thirty years — so often overshadowed by the famous find which marked the pinnacle of his career — which is the focus of the British Museum's exhibition 'Howard Carter: Before Tutankhamun'. This book, which has been prepared to accompany the exhibition, charts the life and achievements of Carter. It is, by design, less a biography than an anthology — of writings by and on this controversial man who carried an impossible dream through to reality. The aim has been not to judge with the benefit of hindsight but to present a picture of Carter as he projected himself, on and off public view, inaccuracies, exaggerations and all, and as he appeared to his contemporaries. Carter certainly had his faults, but even his sternest critics will find it difficult to suppress a grudging respect for this extraordinary individual — archaeologist, painter, draughtsman, photographer, connoisseur, dealer and benefactor — whose unswerving belief in himself and his cause was to so enrich the world's cultural heritage and put Egyptology on the map once and for all.

I

The Early Years
'It matters not whether
the artist is a gentleman'

'Miserably incomplete': the young artist

Born on 9 May 1874 at 10, Rich Terrace, north of London's Old Brompton Road in Kensington, Howard Carter was very much a product of his time. Though one would not guess it from the following account, his origins were relatively humble, a fact which, in his subsequent dealings with the late Victorian aristocracy, was a considerable handicap and one that, even in later life, he was never able to shake off fully. Another 'deficiency', of which Carter was made painfully aware by many of his colleagues throughout his career, was the lack of any formal education. His insecurity, reflected in the numerous exaggerations of the 'autobiographical sketches' he was towards the end of his life preparing for publication, was combined with a short-tempered intolerance of fools: the somewhat sickly, youngest son of a family of eleven children, Carter was terribly spoiled and early on became used to getting his own way. As Guy Brunton was to remark in Carter's obituary published in 1939: 'Much ... was no doubt due to his unusual upbringing, and to some extent to his state of health; the discipline and rough and tumble of a big school might have made him a really great man'.

From Carter's autobiographical sketches
I was born in the early seventies at my father's town house in Earl's Court. Attached to this house was a lovely garden with beautiful trees, and for the purpose of study large pens for animals. However, soon after my birth, for

The Market Place, Swaffham, as it appeared in Howard Carter's youth. Although Carter was born in London he came from a family which had its roots firmly in Norfolk. The small market-town of Swaffham, between King's Lynn and Norwich, always occupied a special place in his affections, for it was the birthplace of both his parents, and most of his childhood was probably spent there. Several of his siblings were born in a house owned by his father just outside Swaffham on the Sporle road. This relatively humble cottage, maintained by two of Howard's aunts, was the family's 'country residence' and served as a retreat and a holiday home.

Samuel John Carter, Howard's father, was born in 1835 and displayed a strong talent for drawing and painting at a very early age. When only ten years old he is said to have won the first prize at the Swaffham school of drawing, an institution reputed to have been supervised by the painter John Sell Cotman. Samuel John Carter pursued a successful career as a painter and illustrator, working in London as an artist for the *Illustrated London News* and in Swaffham, where he supplied the local gentry with family portraits and paintings of their pets, bloodstock and farm animals.

reasons which were never explained to me, I was taken in charge of a nurse to our home at Swaffham in Norfolk.

I can hardly find any trace of my father in myself, except an inborn faculty for drawing, which unfortunately, in my case, was never fully cultivated. I work extremely hard when it pleases me, and when it does not I can be extremely idle. Although I am a lover of books, my regret is that I never read sufficiently. I may as well say straight out that I have no liking for writing, and thus, I fear, never take sufficient pains over it. I have a hot temper, and that amount of tenacity of purpose, which unfriendly observers sometimes call obstinacy, and which nowadays, due to such idiosyncrasies, it pleases my enemies to term me as having *un mauvaise (sic) caractère*. Well, that I can't help!

My father, an animal painter of no little fame, was one of the most powerful draughtsmen I ever knew, particularly in the drawing of animals. His knowledge of comparative anatomy and memory for form were matchless.

Howard Carter belonged to a large family descended from yeoman farmers who can be traced back as far as the 18th century. His grandfather Samuel Carter (above right) served as gamekeeper to Robert Hamond, Lord of the Manor of Swaffham, and seems to have spent all his life in rustic surroundings. He married Frances Spinks (above left) in 1832. Their son Samuel John Carter drew these portraits.

Pencil sketch of an old cottage at Swaffham drawn by Samuel John Carter at the age of eleven. This remarkable performance by so young a child testifies to Samuel John's exceptional abilities as a draughtsman; the confident lines and attention to form and detail are features which were to characterise the best of Howard Carter's pencil copies from Egyptian monuments.

Swaffham Church and Keeper's Cottage, painted by Samuel John Carter. Keeper's Cottage, near Swaffham Manor House, was the Carter family's residence in the 1830s and Samuel John's birthplace. The picture, while providing a record of the family home, contains a strong element of pastoral idyll.

ABOVE *A Little Freehold*, engraving after Samuel John Carter. Samuel's work with animals displays a sympathy and sense of indulgence which sometimes bordered on the sentimental – a treatment which was becoming increasingly popular during the middle and later years of the Victorian era. The animal and bird specimens kept by his father for study fired the young Howard Carter with a keen interest in wildlife which he retained throughout his life.

He could depict any animal, in any action, foreshortened or otherwise, out of his head with the greatest ease, and be perfectly accurate both anatomically and specifically. However, if a son may criticize his father, this faculty was in many ways his misfortune. For by it he was not so obliged to seek nature as much as an artist should, hence his art became somewhat styled as well as period marked.

My mother, a small but most kindly woman, loved luxury. A liking I inherited together with a terrible habit of neatness. I will keep my correspondence with memoranda in the neatest order, but rarely write the necessary replies.

I was the youngest member of a large family, many brothers and only one sister. They, when referring to me, always spoke of me as their 'younger brother', using the adjective 'younger' more in the derogative sense than otherwise, and when mentioning themselves, always as 'senior brothers'. Be that as it may, I received from them a lot of good training, and at times sixpenny or threepenny bits if I allowed them to pick me up by my hair, or if I washed their paint brushes and scraped their palettes.

I have next to nothing to say about education. During my younger days I was a bad herniary case, and thus I was unable to go through a public school training, or join in sports, such as other lads did and still do. Again, being the youngest of an artist's family, I had to start earning my living at the early age of fifteen. It is said that nature thrusts some of us into the world miserably incomplete.

Carter's skills with pen, pencil and brush, though considerable, were those of a draughts-man and copyist rather than artist and innovator. He was trained by his father, for many years chief animal illustrator for the *Illustrated London News*, whose failings, as we have seen, Carter viewed objectively and determined to avoid. Observation was an important skill which Carter learned early and thoroughly. It would stand him in good stead throughout his archaeological career, setting him apart from the hangers-on he so detested and so cuttingly alludes to in the following extract.

From Carter's autobiographical sketches
I loved anything connected with ornithology and entomology, but was never allowed to follow up seriously those studies as drawing and painting were considered to be more profitable. Thus, for a living I began by drawing in water-colour and chalks portraits of pet parrots, cats and snappy, smelly, lap-dogs. Although I was always a great lover of birds and animals, in fact I was brought up with them, how I hated the particular species known as the lap-dog.

Lord Amherst and an opening in Egyptology

Carter might never have embarked upon an archaeological career without the influence and support of William Amhurst Tyssen-Amherst (later first Baron Amherst of Hackney), and particularly that of his wife who was responsible for the fateful introduction to the young Egyptologist Percy E. Newberry, then working for the Egypt Exploration Fund

FAR LEFT Martha Joyce Sands, Howard Carter's mother, was the daughter of a builder of Swaffham. This portrait, drawn by Howard's brother William, was exhibited at the Swaffham Fine Art Exhibition in 1882. It is probably identical with a drawing of 'the late Mrs Carter' which hung in Howard Carter's bedroom at 49 Albert Court, London, at the time of his death.

LEFT Portrait of Howard Carter as a boy, by his brother William. Howard seems to have had little formal education; by his own admission poor health prevented him from attending a public school and what little tuition he did receive seems to have been acquired in the undemanding atmosphere of a 'dame-school'. This portrait is similar in technique to that of his mother and was probably drawn when Howard was about eight years old.

RIGHT William Amhurst Tyssen-Amherst (1835–1909). Amherst, a keen enthusiast for ancient Egypt, assembled one of the finest collections of Egyptian antiquities in Britain at Didlington Hall, close to Swaffham. The youthful Howard Carter was given access to this private museum and from its contents received the spark which was to ignite his lifelong passion for Egyptology. Carter probably became acquainted with the Amhersts through his father, who had been commissioned to produce paintings for the family as early as the 1850s.

LEFT The Amherst Collection included a large number of *shabti*-figures–funerary statuettes which were supposed to perform any irksome tasks required of the deceased in the Underworld. Among the finest is the painted wooden *shabti* of a woman called Tamit. The figure holds a hoe in its right hand and has a basket of grain slung over one shoulder – necessary equipment for the onerous agricultural labour which Tamit hoped to delegate to her *shabti*. The magical spell to animate the figure (chapter 6 of the *Book of the Dead*) is inscribed in nine lines reaching from the waist to the feet. With its sensitive face and vibrant colours, this *shabti* typifies the pleasing work of the second half of the 18th Dynasty; on the evidence of stylistic features such as the almond-shaped eyes, it can be dated with probability to the reign of Amenophis III (*c*.1390–1352 BC). Carter himself was impressed by the piece and drew attention to its high quality in the sale catalogue of the Amherst Collection. H. 22.5 cm.

RIGHT Fragments of a painted wooden coffin of the late 21st or early 22nd Dynasty. The piece on the left, formerly in the Amherst Collection, shows the 'Opening of the Mouth' ceremony being performed before the mummies of a man apparently named Amenemope and a woman, [...] khons. The dead man's daughter, Mutenpermes, squats at the foot of his mummy in a traditional pose of lamentation. The second fragment, in the British Museum, shows part of a symmetrical scene centering on a complex depiction of the sunrise (a metaphor for rebirth): the sun-disc in its barque leaves the Underworld supported by the upraised hands of Nun (the primeval watery abyss), represented as a man whose body is covered with stylised ripples of water, to be received into the arms of the sky-goddess Nut. At each side is a seated mummiform god, that on the left receiving offerings from a man named Amenemope. The recurrence of this name on both the fragments, and the closely similar technique of painting, indicate that they formed parts of the same coffin. The piece from the Amherst Collection was purchased by Carter for the Cleveland Museum at the sale in 1921. The provenance of the second fragment is unknown. H. of fragment on left 61 cm; fragment on right 48 cm.

RIGHT Limestone statuette of a scribe, formerly in the Amherst Collection. Though belonging to a well-known category of private sculptures, this figure is a miniature masterpiece, providing an unusually lively depiction of one of the army of bureaucrats who handled the day-to-day running of state affairs in pharaonic Egypt. The scribe sits cross-legged, a papyrus unrolled on his skirt, which serves as a writing-desk. His right hand is poised to write (left-handedness seems to have been positively discouraged in ancient Egypt) and his head is bent slightly forward in concentration. Damage to the inscription around the base has resulted in the loss of the owner's name. Late 18th Dynasty. H. 17 cm.

The south front of Didlington Hall, Norfolk, home of the Amherst family, c. 1910. The seven statues of the goddess Sekhmet which commanded a view of the garden are reputed to have been found by Giovanni Battista Belzoni at the Temple of Mut at Karnak. They later formed part of the collection of Dr John Lee of Hartwell House, the source of many of Amherst's Egyptian antiquities, and were ultimately acquired for the Metropolitan Museum of Art, New York. The bulk of Amherst's collection was auctioned at Sotheby's, London, in 1921. Carter was closely involved in arrangements for the sale and prepared the detailed catalogue himself. The major European and American museums and private collectors competed vigorously for the choicest objects and Carter bought pieces on behalf of Lord Carnarvon and the Cleveland Museum of Art.

The trials of ancient tomb-robbers. One of the treasures of the Didlington Hall collection was the hieratic document known as the Amherst Papyrus, now in the Pierpont Morgan Library, New York. In fact it consisted of only the lower halves of four sheets; the missing upper portions came to light in 1935, concealed within a wooden funerary statuette. This had been brought from Egypt in the mid-19th century by the future King Leopold II of Belgium and was subsequently presented to the Musées Royaux d'Art et d'Histoire in Brussels. The complete document dates to Year 16 of the reign of Ramesses IX (c. 1126–1108 BC) and is one of a series of papyri recording the robbery of tombs in the Theban necropolis and the subsequent trials of the thieves. The text of the Leopold II-Amherst Papyrus includes the dramatic confession by the stonemason Amenpanefer of the plundering of the pyramid-tomb of King Sekhemre-shedtawy Sebekemsaf of the 17th Dynasty and his wife Nubkhaas. In the course of the confession, a (perhaps somewhat exaggerated) account of the trappings of the royal mummies is given: 'We ... found the noble mummy of this king equipped with a sword; a large number of amulets and jewels of gold were upon his neck, and his headpiece of gold was upon him. The noble mummy of this king was completely bedecked with gold, and his coffins were adorned with gold and silver inside and out ...'. H. 21.5 cm.

OPPOSITE Block-statue of Senusret-senebefny, one of the most important pieces of sculpture from the Amherst Collection. Block statues represent a man (rarely a woman) in a squatting position, wrapped in a cloak which conceals most of the shape of the body. They made their first appearance in the 12th Dynasty (c. 1985–1795 BC) and long remained one of the most popular forms for sculptures of non-royal persons. The shape may have religious significance; it has been argued that such statues represent the deceased emerging from a mound at the instant of rebirth, having been resurrected by the rays of the sun as it makes its nocturnal passage through the Underworld. This large block statue, made from brown quartzite, can be dated on stylistic grounds to the later years of the 12th Dynasty. The front of the statue served to accommodate a hieroglyphic inscription mentioning the owner, the Overseer of the Reckoning of Cattle Senusret-senebefny, and Itneferuseneb (perhaps his wife), whose small figure stands between the man's feet. It is among the finest examples of Middle Kingdom private statuary, notable particularly for the subtle suggestion of the bodily forms beneath the robe. The statue was brought from Egypt by Napoleon, who apparently presented it to the Empress Josephine. It entered the Amherst Collection in 1865; among its later distinguished owners was the American publisher William Randolph Hearst. H. 68.3 cm.

Percy Edward Newberry (1868–1949), sketched by Carter in about 1902. Newberry spent much of his career in Egypt and he and his brother John played an active role in the excavation and survey work carried out by the London-based Egypt Exploration Fund (EEF) in the 1890s. A shared interest in ancient Egypt and the history of English gardens brought him into contact with the Amherst family and when the EEF were seeking an artist to copy tomb paintings in Egypt under Newberry's supervision it was evidently the Amhersts who recommended Howard Carter. Newberry's association with Carter lasted throughout the latter's career and both Newberry and his wife were to lend valuable assistance in the clearance of the tomb of Tutankhamun.

RIGHT Francis Llewellyn Griffith (1862–1934) was a key figure in the history of British Egyptology. He made fundamental contributions to the understanding of hieratic and demotic writing and was the first to decipher the Meroitic script of the ancient Sudan. He was an enthusiastic supporter of fieldwork and himself directed excavations both in Egypt and the Sudan. He also advocated the recording of the standing monuments of ancient Egypt which, even in the 1890s, were rapidly deteriorating due to weathering, vandalism and the adverse effects of tourism; it was largely thanks to his efforts that the EEF organised a survey to remedy the situation. This was the enterprise which gave Howard Carter his first taste of work in Egypt.

(EEF). The young Carter came into contact with Egypt early through the great collection at nearby Didlington Hall, the Amherst family residence. Amherst had acquired the bulk of his antiquities from the Rev. R. T. Lieder in 1861 and from the executors of Dr John Lee of Hartwell House in 1865. These acquisitions were supplemented by purchases and finds made in Egypt by Amherst himself, by the Egyptologist W. M. Flinders Petrie, by Lady William Cecil (Amherst's eldest daughter) and, in due course, by Carter himself (see below). Carter's youthful exposure to this magnificent private museum would be crucial to the formation of his tastes and interests; objects like the *shabti* of Tamit introduced his eye to the compelling charm of Egyptian art and documents such as the Amherst tomb-robbery papyrus, with its description of an Egyptian kingly burial, opened his eyes to the possibilities of work in the field.

From Carter's autobiographical sketches
[It is] to Lord and Lady Amherst of Hackney ... [that] I owe an immense debt of gratitude for their extreme kindness to me during my early career ... It was the Amherst Egyptian Collection at Didlington Hall, Brandon, Norfolk, perhaps the largest and most interesting collection of its kind then in England, that aroused my longing for that country. It gave me an earnest desire to see Egypt.

Carter's introduction to Newberry, with whom he was to maintain a close friendship throughout his life, opened up vistas which would otherwise have been inappropriate to a young man of his relatively modest station. Carter's chance came in early 1891, when Percy's brother, John, was approached by Francis Llewellyn Griffith, a curator at the British Museum and a senior officer of the Egypt Exploration Fund. The latter body had found itself in need of an artist for its newly formed Archaeological Survey branch.

OPPOSITE BOTTOM Copy of a wall-painting in the tomb of Amenemhat (No. 2) at Beni Hasan, made in 1833 by the French lithographer A. Dupuy, a member of Robert Hay's expedition. Great care was taken to ensure accuracy; Dupuy's work was checked and corrected by Hay himself, whose marginal comments (in French) are visible at the left. The copies made by Hay and his co-workers in the 1820s and 1830s, besides being unsurpassed for completeness and accuracy, possess the additional advantage of having been made at a time when the monuments were in a far better state of preservation than they were at the time of the EEF's Archaeological Survey in 1890–1. In his study of the Hay papers in the British Museum, Carter found a standard of copying worthy of emulation and he was to be disappointed by the comparatively primitive techniques employed by his own colleagues in the field.

Letter from Francis Llewellyn Griffith to John E. Newberry, 2 February 1891
... If you come across a colourist (eye for colour must be the chief quali-fication added to drawing) who would like the trip [to Egypt] for expenses paid and nothing else, I should be much obliged if you would ask him to call at the Brit. Mus. or send specimens of work ... I am making enquiries again in two or three directions.

ABOVE One of a number of unconventional types of *shabti* developed during the late 18th Dynasty, represented the owner as a servant kneeling and grinding corn. The introduction of such *shabtis* marks the revival of a type of figure commonly placed in tombs of the Old Kingdom, but whereas these prototypes represented servants grinding corn to make bread for the tomb-owner, the New Kingdom milling *shabti* depicts the owner himself performing the task for Osiris or his mother the goddess Nut (as the inscriptions on several examples make clear). By preparing meals for the ruler of the Underworld, the deceased sought to obtain the enviable status of personal servant in the god's household, a position which would ensure for him perpetual sustenance. Although responsible for more specialised tasks, these statuettes were intended to function like ordinary *shabtis*, deputising for the owner when he should be summoned to work, and hence most examples are inscribed with the *shabti*-spell. On this limestone specimen, formerly in the Amherst Collection, the subject wears a panther skin, a pleated kilt and a short curled wig with sidelock. The owner was most likely an official of high rank; unfortunately the ink inscription around the plinth, which probably contained his name, is illegible. H. 10 cm.

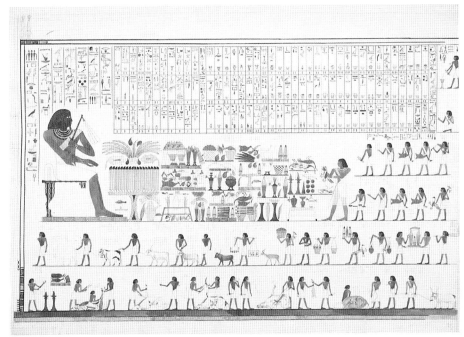

It seems to me that as cost is a great consideration it matters not whether the artist is a gentleman or not. Your brother [Percy E. Newberry] can fraternise with Fraser, and the artist need not find his time woefully dull. A gentleman unless of an economical turn of mind would run into extra expenses very likely, while if a non-gentleman were sent out P. E. N[ewberry] could take him under his wing and manage all his feeding etc. as his employer. In this way 2 or 3 shillings might be saved daily. So you see we shall at least value an economical turn of mind ...

Carter was evidently considered to fit the bill perfectly.

Letter from Mrs Margaret Tyssen-Amherst to Percy E. Newberry, 29 May 1891
... I am so glad that you have been able to get an appointment for Howard Carter. I am very grateful to you and I hope he will prove a useful help in every way. I told his mother that he ought to try and improve himself by study as much as possible during his leisure time....

Through his new if modest position with the Fund, Carter was given access to that intimidating shrine of nineteenth-century scholarship, the British Museum. Here he served a three month Egyptological apprenticeship inking-in the tracings Newberry had made in the previous season and taking notes on earlier copies of tomb-scenes in preparation and as a reference for the Egypt Exploration Fund's second season at Beni Hasan.

From Carter's autobiographical sketches
During the summer before I left England, I did some preparatory work, or perhaps I should say that I was hastily trained under F. Ll. Griffith M.A., the Superintendent of the Archaeological Survey, who with C. H. Read (afterwards Sir Charles Hercules Read, LLD.) was then in Sir Augustus Wollaston Frank's Department in the British Museum. These venerable people and this august building, with its associations, its resonant rooms, and my instructors, deeply impressed me and produced an awe that caused me to be in a mortal funk lest my boots squeaked. My main work there was studying and copying the MSS. (preserved in the British Museum folios) of Robert Hay, an explorer, and patron of explorers, who during the first part of the nineteenth century made a collection of detailed drawings, minutely accurate copies of inscriptions and plans of the Egyptian monuments, that put to shame most of the contemporary and later work in that country.

To Egypt in 1891 and a first encounter with Petrie

Carter's satisfactory 'trial-run' at the British Museum during the summer of 1891 opened the door for travel to Egypt that same autumn and to his first experience of work in the field – at Beni Hasan, in the company of what, to this gauche youth of seventeen and a half years, must have seemed an intimidating assemblage of elders and betters. It was his first experience of foreign travel, alone at that, and he must at the time have been in two minds about the wisdom of his actions; but he would never look back.

Minutes of the EEF Committee, 16 October 1891
[Resolved] that Mr Carter be appointed as Tracer to assist Mr Newberry at a cost not exceeding £50.

From Carter's autobiographical sketches

The complement of the expedition that I joined to Egypt comprised Mr. G. Willoughby Fraser for the surveying work, Mr. M. W. Blackden a painter and copyist, and Mr. Percy E. Newberry B.A., my immediate chief, for the Egyptological work. They were then working on the survey of the rock-tombs of the Eleventh and Twelfth Dynasty nomarchs of the Oryx nome (province) at Beni Hasan, situated about 150 miles south of Cairo. ...

HOWARD CARTER, OF SWAFFHAM.

A PHOTOGRAPH OF MR. HOWARD CARTER WHEN HE WAS 18 YEARS OLD.

Carter at about the time of his first visit to Egypt in 1891. This picture was published in a Norfolk newspaper in the 1920s, after the discovery of Tutankhamun's tomb had made Carter internationally famous.

How well I remember the depressed state of mind I was in when I left Victoria Station, and the nostalgia of the young and inexperienced when I crossed the Channel and found myself alone for the first time in a foreign country, the tongue of which I had no practical knowledge. Then the long tedious day at Marseilles waiting to embark upon an old fashioned half sail half steamship of the Messagerie Maritimes Cie., with its old fashioned cabins opening directly into a smelly dining-saloon. It was then that I discovered I was not physically fitted for a sailor; that an appetite for food oozy with oil, and the motion of the ship caused very adverse sensations

William Matthew Flinders Petrie (1853–1942). Petrie first visited Egypt in 1880 to conduct a survey of the pyramids of Giza. He excavated for the EEF for three years but soon became dissatisfied with the conduct of the Fund's activities and organised the Egyptian Research Account (later the British School of Archaeology in Egypt) as a basis for his work. In his long life he dug at over fifty sites in Egypt and the Near East, and produced over a hundred books and more than a thousand articles. He was one of the pioneers of modern 'scientific' methods of excavation and, unusually for the time, attached great importance to the value of pottery and small antiquities as evidence for the reconstruction of ancient chronology and cultural interconnections. Petrie met Carter shortly after his arrival in Egypt in 1891 and was to exercise an important influence over the younger man when they worked together at Amarna the following year.

which centered around the sensitive nerves of the solar plexus, and which in my case resulted in a complete 'knock-out'. My feelings, however, were solaced by my stable-companion, a kindly Franciscan priest, who by his sympathies and bubbling champagne helped me to bear the many days tossing upon the Mediterranean before I reached the port of Alexandria, where I was met by Percy E. Newberry.

Notwithstanding the struggle I experienced among a tumult of porters that swarmed the ship and screamed for passengers' baggage, what a bliss to the heart and body that landing was. In tar, rope and brine I had found no affinity. Thus it was with renewed youth and vigour I strode through Alexandria, noticing that her streets and public buildings still bore traces of the bombardment in July 1882. But I was there for only a few hours – we left for Cairo by the early train the following morning.

The driving force in Egyptian archaeology at this time was William Matthew Flinders Petrie, a legend in archaeological circles who, through his authorship of more than a thousand books, articles and reviews, exerts still an enormous influence on the subject. Later to become first Edwards Professor of Egyptology at University College London, Petrie was a strange combination of revolutionary and reactionary, an intense, complex individual whom few of his contemporaries truly understood or particularly liked. Following a disagreement in 1886, he had quit the EEF to work on his own. At the time of his first meeting with Carter, Petrie was preparing to dig at Amarna, the city founded by Tutankhamun's father, the 'heretic' pharaoh Akhenaten; it was a reign upon which Petrie's work would shed much important light. Little did the youthful Carter realise how intertwined in his own life these characters from past and present would later become.

From Carter's autobiographical sketches

At Cairo we put up at [the] very convenient Hotel Royal in the Ezbekîya quarter. An hotel then famous for its cooking, it being owned by the chef of Shepheard's Hotel. And there I met for the first time the famous archaeologist, Mr. W. M. Flinders Petrie, who was occupying his spare time by visiting native antiquity merchants in search of rare specimens to add to his collection of historical scarab-shaped seals – of which there is no better judge. I found him a man of simple tastes, at first a little puzzling for me to understand, but obviously a man endowed with wits which gave him both confidence and the power to solve problems – in archaeological matters a Sherlock Holmes. But what interested me most, as a son of an artist, was his recognition and love for fine art. It was, in fact, a delightful meeting and, although a good while ago, it still remains one of those impressible incidents of my early life. The few days that I had in Cairo were spent in visiting the Giza Museum, the pyramids and in the evenings, after seven o'clock dinner, in Petrie's room listening silently to his conversations. I say silently, for born more alive than most people, he suffered no fools.

Beni Hasan

The thirty-nine rock-cut tombs of Beni Hasan are situated on the east bank of the Nile south of Minya, the best and most important having been prepared for the 'princes' of the 'Oryx' nome (the 16th Upper Egyptian province) during the Eleventh and Twelfth Dynasties. Through his work at the British Museum, Carter was as familiar as anyone

Façade of the rock-cut tomb of one of the nomarchs of the Oryx nome (province), hewn out of the cliffs overlooking the Nile at Beni Hasan. The fluted columns, dubbed 'protodoric' by Jean François Champollion, occur only rarely in Egyptian architecture. The relief carvings and paintings in these tombs include exceptionally interesting scenes of daily life and it was these which were the object of the first expedition of the EEF's Archaeological Survey in 1890–1. The task was a formidable one; preliminary studies of the copies made by Robert Hay and his colleagues enabled Griffith to estimate that the painted scenes to be recorded covered no less than 1,115 square metres.

with their decoration; the magic of their setting, however, took him rather by surprise – as did the rather more mundane realities of life in the field.

From Carter's autobiographical sketches

The railway station for Upper Egypt was at that time at Bûlaq e'Dakrûr, about 4 miles outside Cairo, whence with Newberry I left by train at eight in the morning. In due course we arrived at Abu Qurqâs – the station for Beni Hasan. Alighting from a dusty train, stiff and dirty after a long journey, does not fill one with any particular enthusiasm. With our luggage and various impedimenta strapped upon donkeys, we rode through the cultivated fields to the river, crossed over to the east bank in an antiquated ferry-boat, and in the dusk we climbed up the slope of the desert escarpment to the terrace where the rock tombs are situated. And there, as the twilight fell swiftly and silently upon those dun coloured cliffs, my first experience was an aspect of dreary desolation which, I must admit, filled me with distrustful phantoms that sometimes haunt the mind on the eve of adventure.

We encamped in a large undecorated rock-tomb chapel, ourselves including the Nubian cook in one chamber, while the wee donkeys employed for bringing water and other necessary supplies, were lodged in unfinished chambers nearby.

Our abode was rough and ready, certainly not elaborate, but good enough for those who were not over-fastidious, and it was certainly healthy, if only from the point of view of the evenness of the temperature that prevails within those rock-cut chapels, with just the one doorway for ingress and egress, light and air.

The warm, dry and motionless atmosphere made me conscious of a strange sensation as I lay somewhat bewildered in my new surroundings, endeav-

Interior of tomb No. 16 at Beni Hasan which served as a dwelling for the members of the Archaeological Survey. Adaptability to uncomfortable surroundings and the willingness to improvise furniture and utensils were taken for granted; beds were made of palm sticks and equipment such as ladders constructed on the spot. The Huntley and Palmer's biscuit tins, seen here forming the supports of the bookshelf, were favoured by several excavators of the period for the packing of small finds. Compared with the spartan conditions Carter was to endure at Flinders Petrie's camp at Amarna in 1892, this was veritable luxury.

ouring to sleep upon a roughly made palm-branch bedstead. That first night I watched from my bed the brilliant starry heavens visible through the open doorway. I listened to the faint flutterings of the bats that flitted around our rock-chamber and, in imagination I called up strange spirits from the ancient dead until the first gleam of dawn when, from sheer fatigue I fell asleep. . . .

[When we awoke we discovered that] our daily supply of water had not arrived. In the East delays are considered but trifles, in fact, due to a lack of forethought they are the general rule. There was barely sufficient in our water jar for us to drink, therefore our ablutions had to wait until a later hour. But this was not the only trouble, for neither had the milk or food supplies arrived. A cup of tea, and the residue of yesterday's fare in the train, was all we had for breakfast.

After straightening out my things and making myself comfortable, the rest of the day I spent in examining the tombs and their chapels. At the time it struck me that what made the site really unique was not so much its tomb-chapels and their architecture, but its situation. Its height gave it the sense of security in the wilderness, and the vast stretch of landscape visible from its portals, its charm.

It did not take Carter long to settle into his new life.

Letter from Percy E. Newberry to F. Ll. Griffith, 18 November 1891
. . . Our time (Carter's and my own) has been spent from 7 morning till sunset entirely on tracing and we now have only a very little more to do here. I never reckoned on getting done so fast. It is astonishing how much can be done by *two* men working hard when the hands are *willing*. I believe that

Carter and I could almost trace all the tombs in Egypt in five years!!! On Sunday last I tried Carter at painting and found he could copy things here very well indeed – almost as well as Blackden ...

Letter from F. Ll. Griffith to John E. Newberry, 30 November 1891
... I have had a report today from Beni Hassan. The work is going capitally, and Carter seems to be working thoroughly well. They are going on far quicker than they had calculated, which is splendid ...

Nor did it take long for Carter to show signs of that impolitic challenge to authority which would become his trademark.

From Carter's autobiographical sketches
I never took much time to arrive at any conclusion, I generally make up my mind in a flash, I think mostly from instinct. The moment I first saw Egyptian

Copy of wall-decoration from the tomb of Khnumhotep II (No. 3). Khnumhotep was governor of the Oryx nome or province in the middle years of the 12th Dynasty and his tomb contains some of the most informative scenes and inscriptions to have survived at this site. The making of accurate facsimiles of the scenes and texts on ancient monuments was still a rare practice in the 1890s and early attempts left much to be desired. The technique of copying employed at Beni Hasan by Percy Newberry, in which figures, hieroglyphs and other details were inked in in solid black, resulted in the loss of much internal detail and was disapproved of by the young Carter. The figure of the cat stalking birds in the papyrus marshes was one of several details reproduced with great accuracy by Carter.

Colour facsimile by Carter of a detail in the tomb of Khnumhotep II at Beni Hasan, showing a cat hunting in the marshes. The original forms part of the large painting on p. 27 showing Khnumhotep fishing. This and the following painting were published (with small alterations made by the printer) in 1900 in *Beni Hasan* IV, a volume devoted to copies of details from the decoration of Khnumhotep's tomb. Carter's meticulous approach and his painstaking reproduction of the original colours on the tomb walls show how much he had learned from studying the papers of Robert Hay.

Colour facsimile by Carter showing a hoopoe perched in the branches of an acacia tree, a detail of a scene showing the snaring of wild birds in a clapnet, from the tomb of Khnumhotep II at Beni Hasan. The scene is notable for the ancient painter's minute attention to detail in the representation of the bird's plumage and the small leaves and characteristic flowers of the acacia.

ABOVE Following the completion of work at Beni Hasan, Newberry and his colleagues moved south to the vicinity of Deir el-Bersha. The Wadi el-Nakhla, which cuts through the eastern cliffs of the Nile at this point, contains some of the most interesting rock-cut tombs in Egypt in a situation unparalleled for its dramatic ruggedness. The finest of the tombs, dating to the 12th Dynasty, belonged to the nomarchs of the 15th (or Hare) nome of Upper Egypt and contained carved and painted scenes of great interest. Copies of some of these were made by early travellers such as John Gardner Wilkinson, but the survey by the EEF was the first systematic attempt to record them. Some of the tombs had possessed elaborate façades, now much weathered, and, as that of Djehutyhotep (shown here) illustrates, thrown into picturesque ruin by earthquake activity.

BELOW Fragment of painted relief from a wall in the tomb of Djehutyhotep at Deir el-Bersha. In its original state, the scene showed the tomb-owner, accompanied by members of his family, viewing agricultural activities and servants producing food, cloth and other essentials. This fragment shows a procession of retainers with a carrying-chair and a variety of weapons which are carefully delineated. Djehutyhotep lived during the middle years of the 12th Dynasty and was able to commission the most richly decorated of the tombs at the site. The reliefs illustrate the standard technique used in tomb decoration of high quality, by which the sculptor's outlines were supplemented with many internal details painted in colour, providing crucial information on the materials of which items such as the weapons and shields were constructed, and giving an added sense of realism to the hieroglyphic signs representing birds and animals. L. 165 cm.

art I was struck by its immense dignity and restraint. Indeed, from the moment I began to study that art, I was struck by the beauty of its line, and above all its deep understanding in interpreting character. It was for that reason, and for no other reason, that I was disappointed with the method I was obliged to employ to copy that art so dependent upon its purity of line.

To my horror I found the *modus operandi* in force was to hang large sheets of tracing paper upon the walls, and with a soft pencil trace the scenes upon them, no matter whether those scenes were painted on the flat, or sculptured in relief, and no matter whether the wall surfaces were smooth or granular. These completed paintings were then to be rolled up, transported to England, where they could be inked in with a brush, and all inside the outlines of the figure filled in black like a silhouette, as it proved afterwards, often by persons without any knowledge of drawing. These blackened tracings were then reduced to a very small scale by the process known as photo-lithography. Needless to say, from the point of view of Egyptian art, the results were far from being satisfactory. I was young, however, it was my first experience, and in the struggle for existence I had to obey and carry out this extra-ordinary method of reproducing those beautiful Egyptian records enhanced by the romance of an immense antiquity.

To my relief most of the tracings were completed during the preceding season, so of this particular work I had very little to do, and to my joy was soon set to work to make careful coloured drawings of the more interesting and important details among these mural decorations.

Deir el-Bersha

Moving upstream (for much of the way on foot, searching all the while for new tombs and inscriptions to copy), Newberry, G. Willoughby Fraser, a surveyor, and the young Carter arrived exhausted at Sheikh Ibada, proceeding to their final destination, Deir el-Bersha, by boat. Situated on the east bank, Deir el-Bersha was famous for its series of fine, rock-cut tombs, prepared for the Middle Kingdom overlords of the 15th or 'Hare' nome. Newberry's team, finding no suitable living quarters among the ancient city of the dead, pitched tent and proceeded with their work of recording. And it is here, at Deir el-Bersha, that Carter's influence on the work can for the first time be detected, at least in the published results. The crudely blocked-in figures of the Beni Hasan volumes are gradually abandoned in favour of what has today become the standard method of linear reproduction – outline filled with informative detail. Carter had begun to make his mark.

From Carter's autobiographical sketches
By the end of November the expedition moved on to Deir el-Bersheh, a site similar to Beni Hasan situated about 20 miles south, and opposite the modern town of Mellawi. ...

Behind the Coptic village of Deir el-Bersheh situated on the borders of the arable fields, some three miles across the sandy desert tract, is an extensive desert ravine called Wâdi Deir el-Nakhleh. The rock chapels and tombs here are of the 'Great Chiefs' of the Hare-nome, and contain the history of the nomarchs that flourished during the Middle Kingdom, their walls embellished with coloured reliefs and paintings. In one instance, the chapel of the nomarch Tehuti.hetep [Djehutyhotep], the workmanship is even finer than those at Beni Hasan. In this particular chapel there is a remarkable scene representing the transportation of a colossal statue that

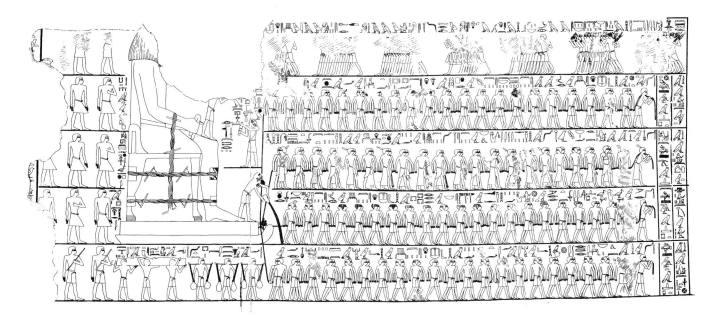

Carter's line drawing of a relief in the tomb of Djehutyhotep at Deir el-Bersha, showing the transport of a colossal seated statue of the tomb-owner, carved from calcite ('alabaster') which was obtained from the quarry of Hatnub. The scene is of unrivalled importance for the information it provides as to the methods used by the ancient Egyptians for transporting such huge pieces of sculpture. The statue is mounted on a wooden sledge, held securely in place by twisted ropes kept taut by means of sticks, and is pulled by four gangs each of forty-two men, hauling on ropes in time to the rhythmical clapping of the man standing on the statue's knees (this figure was partly effaced by the time Carter's copy was made). An accompanying inscription states that the statue was thirteen cubits in height (about 6.8m). The precision and attention to detail which Carter brought to his work is obvious in this copy, which is a much more faithful rendering of the original than the scene from Beni Hasan reproduced on page 27.

was hewn and brought from the quarries of Hat.nûb. It is practically the only scene in Egypt that pictures for us the method employed by the Egyptians when transporting on land their enormous monuments.

The accompanying inscription to this scene tells us that this seated figure of the nomarch Tehuti.hetep was 13 cubits in height, wrought out of a single block of alabaster (calcite). This means that it must have been over 19 feet high, and weighed something like 45 tons....

I passed many weeks, time enough for me to become accustomed to this new life, standing all day upon a ladder and tracing the mural decorations, rich and varied ...

The discovery of Hatnub

Petrie's excavations at Amarna (alluded to above and considered further below) reflected the burgeoning interest in all things related to that 'heretical' interlude of the Eighteenth Dynasty known as the Amarna Period. One of the principal Egyptological participation sports of the early 1890s was the search for the tomb of Akhenaten. Not only Petrie, but also Newberry and his team found themselves caught up in the race, with its strong nationalistic overtones, as Carter records in his unpublished memoirs. But they were to find themselves on the track of something quite different, a discovery the repercussions of which would break friendships and end more than one promising Egyptological career.

From Carter's autobiographical sketches
There were rumours abroad that the Bedu had discovered the long lost tomb of the famous heretic king Amenophis IV [Akhenaten], which from inscriptions was believed to be hidden somewhere in the desert hills behind the great plain of El-Amarna, south of Deir el-Bersheh ...

Encamped on the desert near us between the cultivated fields of Deir el-Nakhleh and the ravine in which we were working, there was a large Bedu family, of the Abâbda tribe who dwell in groups and haunt the solitudes of the eastern desert.... From these nomads we sought information:- Whether they had any knowledge of a large tomb in the desert east of El-Amarna. The chief man among them, called Sheikh Eid, professed to know of a place situated on the desert plateau east of a village at El-Amarna, called Haggi Qandîl, where there was a deep cutting in the rock, which he described as being much like the chapels of El-Bersheh. But as the Abâbda, who possessed an original language of their own, had exchanged it for bad Arabic, it was very difficult to understand the sheikh's description of the cutting excepting that it was 'written' (i.e. inscribed). The sheikh, however, volunteered for a remuneration and the hire of his camels to show us the spot ...

Early in the morning of 24 December, while M. W. Blackden, a painter and copyist, and Fraser were celebrating Christmas at Minya, Carter and Newberry set off on Sheikh Eid's camels.

From Carter's autobiographical sketches
We crossed the desert tract of El-Bersheh, skirted along the base of the perpendicular cliffs of Sheikh Saïd that reach down to the river bank, whence we gained, at about noon, the great open desert tract of El-Amarna. Here lie the picturesque ruins of the city of Akh.en.Aten, bordered by palm-groves that grow along the narrow strip of cultivated land beside the river. From there we trailed across desert tract in a south-easterly direction, our guide obviously following an old beaten track of the Bedu. This path led to an open spacious valley, situated on the south-eastern corner of the plain, and which winds away amid the Arabian desert. At the entrance of this valley, along its bed, we struck the remains of an ancient Egyptian road. This we followed over undulating ground for about an hour, when it took a sharp turn to the left (eastward), and wound up a pass on to the higher desert plateau. On this barren boulder bestrewn plateau the track of the ancient road became very distinct. It was swept clear of boulders, confused masses of broken rocks, and in parts it looked as fresh as if it had been made quite recently. We continued to follow it over hill and dale for at least another two hours, until it reached some extensive mounds of debris, which were obviously refuse dumps from some ancient excavation. Here we dismounted, stiff and tired from the rolling gaits of the camels. In the midst of these dumps were two deep and extensive cuttings in the rock of the plateau; not the tomb of Amenophis IV but the famous Hat.nûb quarries, their existence hitherto unknown save from records upon the ancient monuments.

These quarries were cut deep into a stratum of alabaster (calcite), where immense blocks of that material could be procured. Engraved upon their vertical sides was a multitude of inscriptions, from which we learn that the quarries were opened during the Old Kingdom ... It was no less than the road and quarry whence came the famous colossal statue of the Nomarch Tehuti.hetep (mentioned above) that was dragged upon a sledge by nearly two hundred men during the eighteenth century B.C. ...

Newberry and Carter's discovery of the Hatnub quarries and their rock-cut inscriptions, though quite fortuitous, was nonetheless of great archaeological significance and one to which, for the discoverers, no little prestige promised to attach itself upon publication. Fraser and Blackden, already proving to be thorns in Newberry's side, were eager to make a name for themselves and leapfrogged their companions in a most ungentlemanly manner by visiting the site, copying the texts and identifying the name of the quarry.

The entrance to the ancient quarries of Hatnub, situated on the desert fringe south-east of Amarna. The quarries are important not only for what they reveal about the techniques used by the ancient workmen to extract stone, but also on account of the numerous inscriptions and graffiti on the rocks—the records, both official and unofficial, of expeditions to obtain fine white calcite for statues, offering tables and vessels. These range in date from the reign of Khufu, builder of the Great Pyramid, to the New Kingdom, and among them are the inscriptions of the rulers of the Hare nome with whose tombs at Deir el-Bersha Carter was already familiar. It was from these quarries that the stone for the colossal statue depicted in the tomb of Djehutyhotep was obtained.

Their actions caused a furore in the Bersha camp. Newberry wrote to Amelia Edwards, the novelist and joint-secretary of the EEF; he resigned his position and threatened never to return to Egypt. Carter, not unnaturally, sided with him.

From Carter's autobiographical sketches
Fraser and Blackden returned to El-Bersheh the following evening full of the Christmas amenities at Mînia. When we told them of our exploit they seemed somewhat crest-fallen, and did not take it in the light we expected. After a day or so, they disappeared hastily at the break of dawn from the camp, taking with them their servants and tents. We were puzzled to know why. But, later, we learnt, from the Bedu, whose camels they had taken, that they had gone with Sheikh Eid to the selfsame Hat.nûb quarries. And when after five days' absence, they returned, in a somewhat lofty manner informed us that they had succeeded in making a complete survey of the quarries, and had made copies of all the more important inscriptions therein.

I think it is only fair to add that in our adventure there was not the slightest idea of winning discovery by selfish competition with our colleagues, nor getting the advantage over others. We merely proposed to make an exploration and to offer up any result of the adventure for the advancement of general knowledge, with the strictness of the mutual bond among fellow workers. But in all such archaeological research, there is one recognized un-written law: the right of first publication being that of the discoverer. In short, this matter brought about an unpleasant feeling in our camp – an atmosphere far less genial than heretofore.

Secondment to the Petrie camp, 1892

Every cloud has a silver lining. Blackden's 'dishonourable' conduct over the Hatnub discovery put paid to plans for him to be seconded to Flinders Petrie to learn the rudiments of field archaeology. In his stead, thanks in large part to the influence of Mr Tyssen-Amherst, Carter was despatched, arriving at the Petrie camp on 2 January 1892. It was a wonderful opportunity for the young man, but, in spite of Carter's enthusiasm, Petrie's initial assessment hardly augured well.

From Petrie's journal, entry for 3–9 January 1892
Mr. Carter is a good-natured lad whose interest is entirely in painting and natural history; ... it is of no use to me to work him up as an excavator.

From Carter's autobiographical sketches
Although I was unaware of the fact, at that moment my fate was turning on a pivot. In a week's time I was to leave the expedition. By a mutual arrangement I had been seconded to Flinders Petrie, under whom I was to work on behalf of Lord Amherst. His lordship had taken over a part of Petrie's concession at El-Amarna and wished me to try my hand in excavating.

In this way began another phase in my career. A transformation from a draughtsman to an excavator. Although I had always had a longing to excavate, it was in fact one of my day dreams in life, I must admit that I had sad misgivings regarding this new undertaking. The vagueness of the project, for which I had not the least experience – my knowledge of Arabic still embryonic – caused my brain to be in a hopeless dilemma. At the moment I felt like one of the order of insects known as Lepidoptera, or rather what I imagined those insects must feel, when going through its life-cycle. However, in spite of this, in the morning I arose earlier than usual and set myself with some enthusiasm to arrange my things and pack.

Petrie was an idiosyncratic personality, little interested in the frills and fripperies of life, who followed a harsh and rather humourless regime with which many of his assistants found it difficult to cope. Carter was no exception. Arriving at the Amarna camp in Petrie's absence, he surveyed his new surroundings.

From Carter's autobiographical sketches
While waiting I wandered about the establishment. Among other things I noticed behind his own particular dwelling a large stack of sun-dried mud bricks, and a mortar-bed full of freshly prepared mud mortar. This intrigued me not a little. Half an hour had hardly elapsed when Petrie came from the works. He received me very kindly, and suggested that we sat down to lunch immediately. For about an hour after lunch, he explained to me my various future duties, of which I only took in but a vague conception. I gleaned, however, that I was to spend a week watching him at work, and then, with a number of workmen that he would hand over to me, I was to start upon digging in the section of the ancient town he had portioned off for Lord Amherst. One of the first questions he asked me was: 'Had I any money with me?' When I told him that I had received fifty pounds to start with, he said 'Then wait until it is dark and bury them!'

We spent rather an incommunicative first evening. Petrie hardly said a word, unless addressed. Then, indeed, he would make the briefest reply, and betake himself back into his thoughts in mind. He was absorbed, I imagined, in some abstruse problem in connexion with his investigations. 'Take my advice,' he said eventually, 'and get to bed as soon as you can. I shall be rooting you out at day break, so that you may build a room for yourself'. Thus ended my first evening at Haggi Qandîl. The puzzle regarding those bricks and mortar that I had noticed before lunch was solved. The great open desert tract was shimmering in the moonlight. I looked at it for a few moments before retiring, feeling somewhat miserable.

The following morning, before I could make out exactly why, I had entered into the spirit of building my own room, where, in accordance with the simplicity of my new life, my bed and supper-table were to be spread, though not by necessity, nor by choice. It was the first practical trial of my theories in building. When I had finished, I felt as if something had been accomplished towards making me an excavator. But I did not refrain from questioning, in secret, whether it would not have been better to have employed the village bricklayer, who would have done the job much quicker and certainly more skillfully (sic).

For the roof, I was given a number of deal boards and a mass of dhurra-stalks with which to form a kind of thatch. This thatch was held in place by pieces of string and heavy stones. For a door a native rush-mat was also supplied, to be suspended from the wooden lintel by nails. But, to my sorrow, the inner surfaces of the walls were not to be plastered; thereby, the interstices between the bricks afforded perfect hiding places for beetles, spiders – big fat spiders as time proved – and scorpions.

For chairs and tables, empty boxes and packing cases were provided. A small paraffin lamp for cooking. A number of cases containing each a complete month's tinned stores were also handed over to me, and debited to my account. With these provisions I received strict instructions to keep the empty tins for the storage of antiquities. Sheets, table-cloths and napkins were disapproved [of], but the luxury of a substitute – newspapers – was allowed. Another peculiarity that I discovered to my dismay, was that no servant of any kind was permitted within the domain. One had to make one's bed, clean up the slops, prepare and cook one's meals, and wash up.

Digging at Amarna

Flinders Petrie had long recognised the immense historical importance and archaeological potential of the vast area of ruins at Amarna, the site of Akhetaten, 'Horizon of the solar-disc'. This city was founded during the middle years of the fourteenth century BC as the focus of worship of the Aten, or sun-disc, by Akhenaten, who had proscribed the worship of Amun, the principal state deity under his predecessors. Petrie's desire to dig at Amarna, however, had been given an added urgency by the recent discovery by locals of a unique hoard of cuneiform tablets from the ancient state diplomatic archives, the so-called 'Amarna Letters'. It was at this exciting site that Carter was to learn the rudiments of excavation – and under the watchful eye of a master. Despite Petrie's initial lack of enthusiasm for Carter, the two got on tolerably well and the younger man's abilities soon became apparent – as Petrie records in his published memoirs: 'I little thought how much he would be enabled to do'. The area Carter had been assigned to explore on behalf of Amherst, who wished to supplement his Egyptian collection from among the finds of the season, turned out to be one of the most productive on the site – the Great Temple of the Aten. He began work on 12 January 1892.

From Carter's autobiographical sketches
My cocoon thus completed, minus any silken lining, now for the meta-

Ruins of the city of Akhetaten ('Horizon of the Aten') at Amarna. The city was founded in the reign of Akhenaten, the 'heretic' pharaoh of the 18th Dynasty, as his capital and the principal centre of the new religion he promoted, based on the worship of the sun-disc. The city was abandoned soon after Akhenaten's death and the surviving ruins give an exceptionally clear picture of the layout and composition of a major ancient Egyptian settlement. Flinders Petrie's excavation, in which Howard Carter participated on behalf of Lord Amherst, brought to light the remains of several of the main official buildings at the site, including the Great Temple of the Aten, the Great Official Palace, and the Records Office in which the hoard of cuneiform tablets known as the Amarna Letters had been found in 1887.

morphosis ... from draughtsman to excavator. ...

For a week, early each morning we walked over to the excavations, which in some cases were three to four miles distant. I had to run almost to keep up with Petrie's long quick strides. Once I murmured that a donkey would be useful. My suggestion was received by a dead silence. It temporarily upset the mutual equanimity. But no man is wise at all times, perhaps least of all when he is tired ...

During our inspections of the works, Petrie took great pains to point out to me the main features exhibited by the ancient mounds and exposed ruins of the town, as well as explain the features of a discovery, no matter how small. He explained and extolled the importance of studying the history of pottery, century by century; and how the history of an ancient site may be read from the masses of sherds that are distributed over it. 'An old rubbish heap,' he said, 'was most useful for reading the past history of a place or building; for by cutting a section through a heap of rubbish, thus exposing its successive layers, one could then by study deduce a sequence of events that had taken place during its formation'. In short, he explained the all important requirements for an excavator and his outfit, adding that the difficulty lies in the fact 'not a single living person combines all the requisite qualities that make up for complete archaeological work'. ...

The great Temple of the Aten, and parts of the town were portioned off to me.

My chief gave to me one or two of his older trained men and a number of the local workmen that had worked under him some little time. With these workmen I started. At first a great deal of my efforts were wide of the mark and to little or no purpose. Eventually, however, I was lucky, as most beginners are, and I succeeded in finding interesting archaeological material. Besides minor objects of antiquity of great beauty, I found specimens of an

Group of Mycenaean potsherds found during Carter's excavations in the city ruins at Amarna. Small flasks and stirrup (false-necked) jars containing perfumed olive oil, and pots filled with a thick unidentified substance were part of a vigorous Mycenaean trade with Cyprus, the Levant and Egypt during the reigns of Amenophis III and IV (Akhenaten). The pots, 10–20 cm high, are of fine buff to pink clay, evenly fired, with smooth shiny slip and standardised red to orange decoration. 1,329 sherds of this pottery were found at Amarna during Petrie's work and he claimed that their use at Akhetaten (officially occupied from Year 6 of Akhenaten to Year 3 of Tutankhamun) provided a close Egyptian date for the contemporary Mycenaean period. The latest support for this correlation with the period known as Late Helladic IIIA2 comes from excavations by Dr Alain Zivie at Saqqara, 1976–80; a stirrup jar and a piriform jar identical with Amarna types were buried with Aper-el, vizier to Amenophis III and IV. Largest piece 8.3 × 5 cm.

early style of Aegean pottery, which proved it not only to be coeval with the Egyptian New Empire, but it suggested a mutual intercourse at that period between the Egyptian and Aegean civilizations. I was also fortunate enough to find the remains of obsolete glass-factories, which threw light upon the methods employed in that manufacture. In the same quarter I discovered a sculptor's workshop which contained interesting and fine examples of their experimental studies. In the town proper, although the private houses proved to be remarkably bare, merely the substratum preserved, I was able to procure some knowledge of their general design. The great Temple of the Aten proved to have been completely destroyed, only the cores of its walls remained; but in a sort of fosse, just outside its temenos wall, I discovered portions of seventeen statues of the king and queen. These had been ruthlessly destroyed by the victorious sectarians when the reaction in favour of Amun triumphed. These were wrought of a pure white semi-crystalline limestone and were of the finest workmanship. With them were also fragments of beautiful blue-glazed votive tablets that some of those statues supported.

In the course of my work, I often perplexed myself with conjectures, and

The sculptural fragments found by Carter in a rubbish-heap to the south-east of the Great Temple at Amarna belonged to figures of Akhenaten and Nefertiti and must once have stood in the courts and colonnades of the temple itself. Like all other visible traces of Akhenaten's hated regime, the figures were mutilated after his death by the erasure of the cartouches of the Aten and the deliberate damaging of the facial features. The statues may have remained standing until the 19th Dynasty when the Great Temple evidently became a quarry for building materials, at which time they were probably smashed and thrown down. All the fragments were ceded to Lord Amherst in return for his financial support to the excavation and they remained in his possession until the sale of his collection in 1921.

RIGHT Torso of a statue of Akhenaten in indurated limestone. The king was represented standing. The full breasts are characteristic of the exaggeratedly effeminate depictions dating from the early years of his reign, a dating supported by the early form of the names of the Aten which appear in the three pairs of cartouches on the breast and originally upon the arms. H. 33.3 cm.

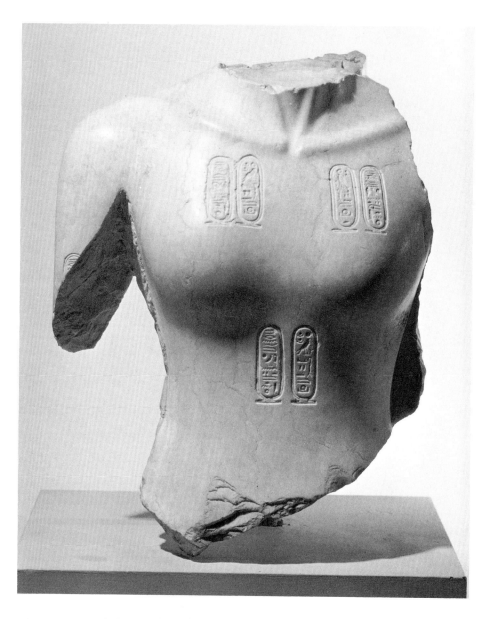

RIGHT Face of Akhenaten from a statue carved in indurated limestone. The confidence of the sculptor is readily apparent even in so small a fragment; the long nose and prominent lips mark it as a product of the early years of the reign when the royal sculptors were working under the personal supervision of Akhenaten himself. Following the sale of the Amherst Collection the piece entered the possession of Lord Carnarvon. H. 8.1 cm.

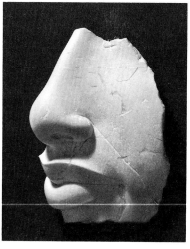

OPPOSITE TOP LEFT Among the finds made by Petrie and Carter in the city ruins at Amarna was this small fragment of a relief depicting a queen, almost certainly Nefertiti, with the very exaggerated facial features which mark depictions of the royal family in the early part of Akhenaten's reign. In addition to the long nose, fleshy lips and pendulous chin, the modelling of the eye in high relief without a clear outline is a hallmark of work produced in the first years of the new regime. H. 12.5 cm.

BELOW RIGHT Plaster cast found at Amarna during Petrie's excavation. It belongs to a group of sculptor's models of human faces made as preparatory studies for the carving of statues. A large number of these faces, which probably represent members of the royal family and officials at Akhenaten's court, were discovered by the German expedition at Amarna in 1912. The example found during Petrie's work, however, was the first of its kind to be discovered. Petrie, learning that Carter was 'accustomed to casts', asked for his opinion on the piece and together they came to the exciting (but erroneous) conclusion that it was nothing less than a cast of the face of Akhenaten himself, taken after death. In consequence it enjoyed special status for a number of years (appearing as the frontispiece to Petrie's *Tell el Amarna* in 1894). H. 26 cm.

ABOVE Another striking piece of sculpture which came to light during Carter's time at Amarna was this relief carved on the surface of a cylindrical piece of limestone which formed part of a column of composite construction. Nefertiti is shown presenting a bouquet to the Aten, whose rays shine downwards. One ray is visible, ending in a hand which touches the uraeus on the queen's brow. She wears the tall cap-like crown familiar from other depictions (most notably on the famous painted bust now in the Berlin Museum), but here modified by the addition of horns, sun-disc and tall plumes. Behind Nefertiti stands one of her daughters (probably Merytaten) shaking a sistrum–part of the traditional paraphernalia of divine worship in ancient Egypt which survived Akhenaten's proscription. Besides the exceptional form of the queen's crown, the relief is interesting for the exaggerated carving of her figure, typical of Akhenaten's early years, although the inclusion of the epithet Neferneferuaten in the cartouche indicates that it must date to after Year 5. H. 36.2 cm.

I had to appeal to Petrie to disentangle them. Under his acute perspicacity my ideas, sometimes, no doubt, very original, generally melted into thin air, especially when he pointed out to me that there was not the slightest foundation for them. But intuition, the subtle recognition of facts, develops slowly; [with] experience knowledge also develops, and thus the progress of true observation. Petrie's training during those months transformed me, I believe, into something of the nature of an investigator, [teaching me] to dig and examine systematically.

The tomb of Akhenaten

At the end of December 1891 the whereabouts of the tomb of Akhenaten was at last established by the Egyptian authorities. Within a matter of weeks, Petrie, in company with Carter and the famous orientalist Rev. Professor A. H. Sayce, visited the site to see this long sought-for monument. Carter carried with him pencils and drawing-pad; the results, two topographical sketches and a drawing of one of the scenes in the tomb, appeared as illustrations to a note contributed by Petrie to *The Daily Graphic* in March 1892. It was to be Carter's first appearance in print.

From Carter's autobiographical sketches

The rumour that [the tomb of Akhenaten] had been found by the Bedu proved to be correct. The officials of the Department of Antiquities had succeeded in extracting from them the secret. Its situation in relation to the town proved to be essentially the same as in the case of the Tombs of the Kings at Thebes, and is in many ways similar in construction to those Theban royal tombs. It varies insofar that it is more of the nature of a family

Two of the sketches made by Carter at the tomb of Akhenaten at Amarna and published in *The Daily Graphic* on 23 March 1892. The sketch on the left is a view of the entrance to the tomb; that on the right is a copy of a relief sculpted on a wall of one of the burial apartments, showing Akhenaten and Nefertiti mourning the death of their daughter Meketaten. The figure of the princess (or possibly a statue of her) stands within a structure perhaps representing the special pavilion in which she had recently given birth to a child. Carter's copy, his first published archaeological drawing, is in several respects more accurate – notably in the rendering of the forms of hieroglyphic signs – than that made for the 'official' record of the tomb published by Bouriant, Legrain and Jéquier in 1903.

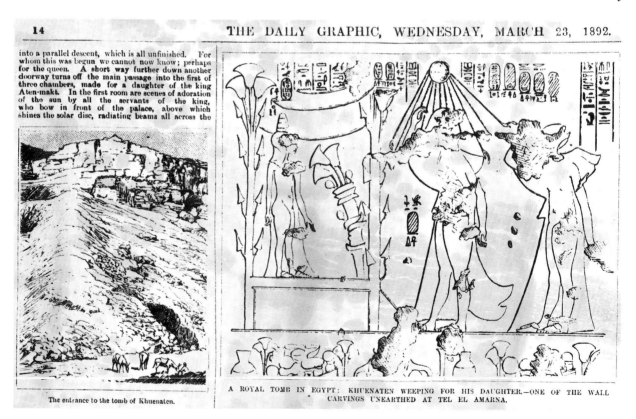

14   THE DAILY GRAPHIC, WEDNESDAY, MARCH 23, 1892.

into a parallel descent, which is all unfinished. For whom this was begun we cannot now know; perhaps for the queen. A short way further down another doorway turns off the main passage into the first of three chambers, made for a daughter of the king Aten-makt. In the first room are scenes of adoration of the sun by all the servants of the king, who bow in front of the palace, above which shines the solar disc, radiating beams all across the

The entrance to the tomb of Khuenaten.

A ROYAL TOMB IN EGYPT: KHUENATEN WEEPING FOR HIS DAUGHTER.—ONE OF THE WALL CARVINGS UNEARTHED AT TEL EL AMARNA.

Faience model throw-stick thought to come from the tomb of Akhenaten at Amarna. Akhenaten's tomb was thoroughly plundered in ancient times but a number of pieces from the burial equipment have come to light. These show that in spite of his unorthodox religious beliefs the 'heretic' king was buried with many of the traditional trappings of an Egyptian pharaoh, including *shabti* figures. Model throw-sticks of faience were a standard part of royal burial furnishings in the 18th Dynasty; examples have been found in the tombs of Amenophis II and Tuthmosis IV and throw-sticks almost identical to this one were provided for Tutankhamun. It is decorated on each side with a *wedjat* eye, lotus and palmette motifs at the ends, and the two cartouches of Akhenaten—prenomen on one side, nomen on the other. L. 38.5 cm.

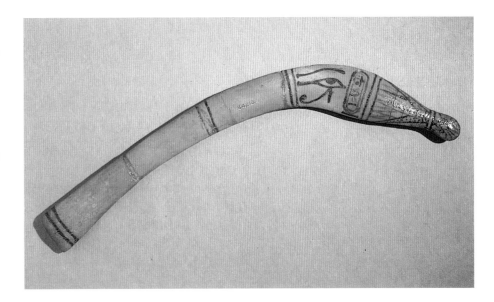

tomb, and thus presents a more human element than those austere Theban hypogea made solely for the Pharaoh. It is situated eight miles from the town, in an easterly direction, and is hidden in a mountain ravine called by the Bedu, Darb el-Melek, or 'The Valley of the King'.

At the invitation of a museum official then in charge of the discovery, we spent a most interesting day inspecting this sepulchre. We were accompanied by Professor Sayce, who was at that time paying a visit to Petrie. To reach the tomb we had first to cross the extensive desert tract of El-Amarna which afforded more than enough room for Akhenaten's city at the edge of the higher plateau, four miles distant from the river. This desert plateau, or highland, is furrowed out with deep ravines, which are evidence of the great rainfall that took place in pre-historic times. The ravine in which the tomb of the king is situated runs back for many miles, winding in a fantastic manner between steep sides, cut into vertical cliffs, at the turns of the stream. Immense fallen masses of rock and boulders lie in every variety of attitude in its stream course, sand is heaped around them. The ravine remains but a dried-up skeleton of conditions and forces that existed long since past. We had to clamber over these rocks and boulders for another four miles, until we reached a small side valley; turning up this, and round a corner we saw a square sharp cut opening steeply sloping down into the heart of the rock. It was the entrance of the king's tomb.

Unhappily, the fanatic zeal with which the monuments of this king were defaced during the religious revulsion that succeeded his death, had extended to this sepulchre. It was empty. It had been sacked by the ruthless victorious sectarians. Only portions of its once finely engraved granite sarcophagus and fragments of its funerary statuettes remained. Its passages and chambers were heaped with the rubbish of past ages. But it still contains many interesting scenes engraved upon its walls. The most striking to us was a pathetic picture depicting the obsequies of the king's second daughter, Maket.Aten, who apparently died at the tender age of five to six years. In that scene we see the royal family and the household lamenting over the body of this little child – weeping and casting dust in the air, like the bereaved in a modern Egyptian funeral. Here, too, were inscribed the

While Carter was convalescing after a bout of illness in 1892 he was visited at Amarna by the Reverend Greville John Chester (1830–92). Chester was a keen traveller and explorer who regularly spent the winters in Egypt and Palestine where he conducted explorations, sometimes in regions virtually unknown to Europeans. He had known Carter's father and was an enthusiastic antiquary, forming large collections of antiquities which enriched the British and the Ashmolean Museums besides many smaller institutions. He was a larger-than-life character: broad-minded, a religious reformer and an ardent champion of learning; argumentative but never ill-humoured. On his visit to Amarna, Chester's characteristic warmth and kindness helped raise the spirits of the young Carter, who remembered the occasion with gratitude in later years.

thoughts, the feelings, the outgushings from the hearts of a people long gone. What a contrast as we came out to look through the doorway and catch a glimpse of the bright blue sky beyond....

Death of a much-loved father – and closing down at Amarna
The unexpected death on 1 May 1892 of his father, the fount of all his skills and the one parent to whom he felt particularly close, struck Carter like a thunderbolt.

From Carter's autobiographical sketches
As time passed, and I was gradually gaining the sunny side of experience, Petrie became more and more pleased with the results of my efforts for Lord Amherst. This naturally gave me a lively sense of exultation. With success, however, there is often misfortune, or shall I say broken fortune. Sundry letters from home were the forerunners of gathering clouds. My father had a stroke. It was the second attack with the inevitable results. A cablegram posted from Cairo, followed by a deep black-edged letter conveyed the sad news. These were handed to me by Petrie. With a few friendly words he advised me to go to my room. There was a shade of inexpressible sadness in his utterance – for the moment the excavator existed no longer; it was the man speaking from out of his soul. It was in my father's studio and largely under his tuition I received my early training. We parted in Victoria Station, whence I left for Egypt. With kindly admonitions and a last farewell he gave me permission to smoke, and presented a tin of suitable tobacco together with a number of packets of cigarette papers, as the train slowly rolled away.

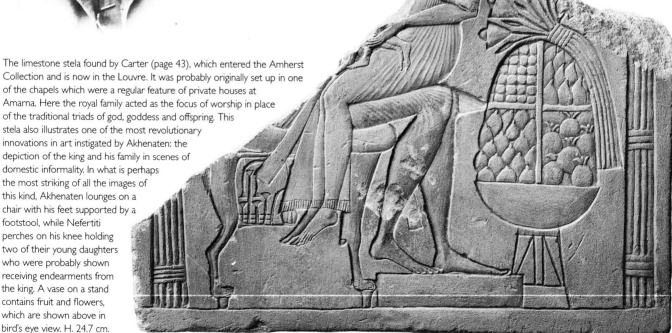

The limestone stela found by Carter (page 43), which entered the Amherst Collection and is now in the Louvre. It was probably originally set up in one of the chapels which were a regular feature of private houses at Amarna. Here the royal family acted as the focus of worship in place of the traditional triads of god, goddess and offspring. This stela also illustrates one of the most revolutionary innovations in art instigated by Akhenaten: the depiction of the king and his family in scenes of domestic informality. In what is perhaps the most striking of all the images of this kind, Akhenaten lounges on a chair with his feet supported by a footstool, while Nefertiti perches on his knee holding two of their young daughters who were probably shown receiving endearments from the king. A vase on a stand contains fruit and flowers, which are shown above in bird's eye view. H. 24.7 cm.

Like many others who laboured under the exacting conditions of a Petrie excavation, Carter, still grieving from his loss, fell ill. 'Valentine's meat-juice, champagne and oranges', a unique prescription he owed to the doctor accompanying Lord and Lady Waterford, who were then visiting the dig, pulled him through. By the time he was fit enough to resume work, the long task of packing the finds was under way.

Letter from Carter to Percy E. Newberry, 7 April 1892
... The work is coming to an end now, and we are hard at work packing. I found a very interesting tablet, with Khuenaten [Akhenaten] seated upon a throne dancing the Queen upon his knee with the two Princesses upon her lap. I am sorry to say that the heads are broken off; Petrie says he does not know of anything like it in Egypt ...

Return to Beni Hasan

Carter's time at the Petrie camp had been a great success, marred only by the loss, 'in the post', of an annotated topographical map of the city he had been asked to produce for Petrie. He had learned a great deal. The death of his father had effectively severed his links with home; the relationship with his widowed mother seems to have been dutiful and somewhat forced and he was, henceforth, to be constantly chided, albeit gently, for his erratic correspondence.

But, for the moment, he was faced with a question: where to now? This was to be resolved by Newberry who, having settled his differences with the EEF, was returning to Beni Hasan to complete the task already in hand. The man he invited to accompany him was his young friend, Howard Carter, who recorded his impressions.

From Carter's autobiographical sketches
In the autumn of 1892, I returned with Percy E. Newberry to Beni Hasan, to complete a collection of coloured facsimiles that were considered necessary to finish the survey of that site. The party this time consisted of Mr. John E. Newberry, for the architectural features; Mr. Percy Buckman, who made a series of water-colour drawings of the locality; myself, for making coloured facsimiles from the mural decorations of those chapels; while Newberry, in charge of the expedition, collated various texts and reproductions made during the former expeditions.

As a whole, it was a fellowship such as has seldom met together; we were of all opinions, on every imaginable subject, but generally tolerant of all. We camped as before in the uninscribed rock chamber. I do not know of a more beautiful or healthier aspect. The view over the Nile valley from that rock terrace was always interesting to observe. It changed every hour. At times, when the land is subdued in tint and cool in contrast to the golden after glow of the evening sky, it made a veritable picture of 'The Promised Land' ...

We were, however, soon to quit Beni Hasan, and to move south to the tombs of the grandees at El-Amarna, excavated in the foot-hills east of the ancient town. But in this particular project of the survey there was an unfortunate hitch. For unknown reasons we were unable to obtain the necessary permit from the Department of Antiquities. Hence we remained there for a few days only, and struck camp for the cliff-tombs at Sheikh Saïd, a site slightly north of El-Amarna, where permission to work was given.

Fig. 1

Fig. 2

The rich and exotic fauna of Egypt was always a strong temptation to a young man of Carter's artistic leanings. At Sheikh Said and other sites he took time off from archaeological work to sketch and paint the local wildlife. Some of his studies reveal a keen interest in the techniques used by the ancient craftsmen in representing different species of birds in the wall-paintings of tombs and temples. In this pair of watercolours (perhaps made during Carter's later years), the hieroglyphic sign for the sound *3* (aleph) – an Egyptian vulture – is juxtaposed with a study of the actual bird painted from life.

Sheikh Said

More than eighty tombs are known at the site of Sheikh Said, though a mere seven, prepared for the ruling elite of the 'Hare' nome during the Sixth Dynasty, are inscribed. The Archaeological Survey's programme of work in 1892–3 required Carter to prepare copies of the more obvious scenes, Percy Newberry to take notes on the inscriptions and John Newberry to plan the individual tombs. As it turned out, none of the team would be involved in the final publication; this was undertaken by Norman de Garis Davies, a later copyist with the EEF, in 1901, though two of Davies' drawings would be based upon Carter facsimiles. Carter's description of his time at the site – the development of his copying technique and his observations on the wildlife – is preserved:

From Carter's autobiographical sketches
The rock chapels here belonged to the Old Kingdom nomarchs of the Hare province. They were the predecessors of those 'Great Chiefs' of the Middle Kingdom, whose chapels are excavated in the side of the ravine of Deir el-Nakhleh, at El-Bersheh ...

A man who loves his work, and joyfully invests his energies in the prosecution of it, needs to have a fair and suitable method by which to carry it out. At the commencement of this particular undertaking, to make records of the mural decorations in these chapels, I was more than anxious to get away from the unsatisfactory system of tracing them. Here, for example, most of the scenes were either carved in high relief, or incised upon the native rock. To attempt to trace them would be absurd. As a compromise, I introduced a new and what I thought a far better method. In place of the tracing paper, to employ a suitable tough white linen paper, and by the application of careful pressure, by pressing the paper with thumb and finger on to the reliefs, ... thus obtain an impression – a sort of dry squeeze – of the reliefs, sufficient to guide the eye and the hand while making full-sized completed copies in pencil direct from the originals.

My recreation, from the drudgery of every day work tracing, was to watch the wild life that surrounded me. At Sheikh Saïd wild friends were fairly abundant, though diverse in character. Some scaly, a few furred like the desert-hare, but mostly feathered. Among them were several kinds of vulture, long-legged buzzards, ravens, blue rock pigeons, sand partridge and other desert birds which delight in eking out a precarious existence in desolate solitude. ...

Before too long, however, Carter's employers had found other uses for him.

From Carter's autobiographical sketches
But hardly had I commenced this work, when it was brought quickly to an end. I was sent off to the Delta, to a place called Tell Timai el-Amdîd, where a mass of burnt papyri had been found. The discovery was said to be the remains of a Greek library that had been destroyed anciently by fire. My touch, my fingers and my thumbs, were apparently considered sufficiently subtle to handle such delicate material, about which I knew nothing.

Tell el-Timai, 1893

The Egyptologist's chief passion has traditionally been the discovery of inscriptional material, and a report by Edouard Naville, the EEF's principal excavator, on the discovery of a classical 'library' at the Graeco-Roman site of Tell el-Timai in the Delta (close to modern Simbellawein) caused the collective pulse of the Fund's executive committee to race. But there were problems.

Edouard Naville, in Egypt Exploration Fund Archaeological Report 1892–3
... [The papyri] are most difficult to take out, they crumble to pieces when they are loosened from the earth which covers them, but by looking sideways the characters are still discernible; they generally are Greek in good hand-writing ... I tried to see whether some of the carbonized papyri, well packed in cotton, would stand a journey, but the contents of the five boxes which I sent to London are nothing but crumbs of charcoal and ashes ...

Naville suggested that something be done to rescue the remaining portion of the archive. On 7 February 1893 by special order of the Committee, Carter was sent down to the Delta to join another Fund worker, the shadowy Guthrie Roger; he would remain there until 13 April. Although permission to work at the site was eventually refused, Carter put his time to good use learning Arabic.

From Carter's autobiographical sketches
I was ordered to go to Cairo, where I was met by a strange being who had been sent out to assist me in extricating these documents; his archaeological attributes, I discovered, comprised athletics on a horizontal bar and lifting heavy weights. In Cairo I procured the necessary camp outfit; with these we descended the Delta, and pitched our camp on the Tell Timai el-Amdîd – the site of ancient Thmuis and Mendes of the sacred rams. But as far as it concerned salving burnt Greek papyri, matters did not turn out quite so favourable as had been anticipated. When I arrived, I discovered from the local authorities that the society I represented had completely omitted to procure the necessary permission to carry out such an operation. My cablegrams and letters were of no avail. But it mattered little. The sky had assumed a mask behind which she mysteriously hides herself from ordinary mortals; for weeks it rained almost unceasingly, making it, in any case, impracticable to extricate anything of the nature of burnt papyri from under masses of mud bricks and earth now sodden with rain water. This inclement weather, not unusual in the Delta in January, terminated in a tempestuous night, the force of which caused our tents to collapse and expose us to the elements, like wet and bedraggled crows. Upon this, my esteemed assistant began to weep profusely. So I hastily packed up ...

I had spent a great deal of time uselessly, but it was hardly my fault. If there was a fault, it lay with those endless committees, that sit in comfortable chairs in committee rooms, and arrange the destinies of others.

The progressive disintegration of the Simbellawein dig – which would have been amusing had its results not been such an archaeological tragedy – is chronicled in the surviving correspondence.

Letter from Carter to Percy E. Newberry, 10 February 1893
... I got alright to Simbellawin and had a good look all round Timai el andid [sic] and found two extensive mounds each covering about a square $\frac{1}{4}$ of a mile. I went all over these mounds with Roger but [Naville's] description

is so very vague that we were unable to make out which place it is. As far as I can see there are 3 or 4 places that might be it, but either [*sic*] of them would take at the very least 2 or 3 months to excavate. So I conclude that neither [*sic*] of them cannot [*sic*] be the place wanted.

I hope that if Mr Petrie's letter is found it will have some better description of the site, so that it will enable us to find it, or otherwise I shall have to wait till I can obtain information from the [EEF] committee.

During that time don't you think it would be advisable to see about the permit, in case it has not been already got? I don't exactly know how it would be best for me to obtain it. I should be very glad if you would kindly let me know ...

Copy, in Percy E. Newberry's handwriting, of a letter from W. M. F. Petrie, undated
... As for the library the facts are the following. I did not discover it. It has been known for several years to the fellaheen, and I have seen boxes of these carbonised papyri two years ago at Zagazig. I wished to see how and where they were found and I had the place pointed out to me by a Turk &c. &c. It is very easy to get at them (the chambers), it requires no serious excavation, the chambers are contiguous to each other, there are large and small ones, those of the large ones have been cleared ...

Letter from Carter to Percy E. Newberry, 1 March 1893
... I have found the chambers and they seem very promising. I have not yet received the permit, so I am unable to start work as the Sheikh will not let me start work till I show him it.

This is a very bad place for tenting as there is no guard for the wind and the ground is so soft that the pegs will not hold properly ...

P.S. Camping out is beginning to affect Roger's eyes.

Letter from Carter to Percy E. Newberry, 22 March 1893
... I cannot get any letters from M. de Morgan. I have written twice to him but have received no answer. This is the 4th week since I left Cairo and have not done a stroke of work. It is what I call – .

I am going to Cairo tomorrow to see what I can get out of Brugsch ...

Letter from Percy E. Newberry to Miss Paterson, Amelia Edwards' personal secretary, at the EEF, 9 April 1893
... from what I could judge of M. Brugsch's behaviour and what I have heard from other people I do not think that there is the least likelihood of the permission being granted. I therefore telegraphed to Mr Griffith saying that I am recalling Carter to join the Survey again. It is very important that I should have him back at once to do the water-colour drawings that are needed to complete El-Bersheh ...

Letter from Carter to Percy E. Newberry, 6 May 1893
... [P.S.] Awful joke about Roger [– he] should like to sue the Fund.

Loose ends – to Bersha again

The fiasco of the papyrus reclamation project was at last laid to rest – in practice, at least, if not in the minds of the EEF committee in London – and Carter returned, via

Deir el-Bahri on the west bank of the Nile at Luxor, showing the funerary temple of Hatshepsut, built during her reign as king in the 18th Dynasty. Until the 1890s, this temple, unique in the annals of pharaonic architecture, was in a very ruinous state and more than two-thirds of its area were covered with mounds of rubble and debris. Systematic clearance operations were carried out by the EEF under the direction of Edouard Naville in 1893–9, enabling the plan and architectural features of the monument to be fully understood for the first time. During this six year period, Howard Carter was employed to copy the wall-reliefs in the temple, besides assisting in the clearance of debris and the restoration of loose blocks and fragments. He looked back on this as one of the most rewarding phases of his career, in which he developed his understanding of Egyptian art and consolidated his skills as a copyist and watercolourist, rejoicing alike in the interest of the work and the beauty of the setting.

Sheikh Said, to more familiar work at Bersha where he would work alone on Newberry's behalf for a little longer. Despite Simbellawein, Carter was now seen as a trustworthy, immensely versatile and wholly dependable servant of the Fund. His reward came at a meeting of the Committee on 7 April 1893, with the appointment 'as Fund artist during the ensuing year, commencing on Nov 1st, 1893, at a salary of £100 a year, all authorized travelling expenses to be defrayed by the Fund, and £2.2.0 a week to be paid to him for living expenses while in Egypt'.

From Carter's autobiographical sketches
[Following the papyrus episode, I] returned to the milder climes of Sheikh Saïd, where I found my bugbear, the old familiar tracing paper, reigning with a strong upper hand ... [But] the expedition at Sheikh Saïd soon broke up, and I was left on my lonesome to finish up the work. After that, I was to go to El-Bersheh and complete some colour work there ...

Letter from Carter to Percy E. Newberry, 6 May 1893
... I am now getting on with the colouring [at El-Bersha] as fast as I can. The inspector at Roda is kicking up a row about me working here without any permit so I am working on the quiet, at the same time to shut him up I have written a note to Brugsch, but by the time any thing is done I shall have pretty well finished the work ...

The Swiss Egyptologist Edouard Naville (1844–1926) was one of the EEF's first field directors and had excavated at numerous sites before he was appointed to supervise the clearance of Hatshepsut's temple. His methods were very different from those of Petrie, from whom he received harsh criticism, particularly of his crude techniques of clearance and his lack of interest in small antiquities and their value for understanding the history of a site. Petrie protested in the strongest terms that Naville should be allowed to work at such an important and technically demanding site as Deir el-Bahri. Petrie had found Carter an able disciple during their work at Amarna, revising his original estimate of the young man's worth, and he suggested that Carter and the Newberry brothers might be trusted to carry out the work successfully on their own, without the interference of Naville. Petrie's attack almost succeeded in preventing Naville from working at Deir el-Bahri. In some respects his apprehension was justified for huge quantities of debris were cleared without proper records being kept and with scant attention to small finds; however, accurate plans were made and detailed facsimiles of the temple reliefs and inscriptions produced, in which work Howard Carter played a major role.

The exterior of the hypostyle hall of the chapel dedicated to Anubis, at the northern end of the temple of Hatshepsut before clearance – photograph taken by Howard Carter. This chapel, with its unusual polygonal columns, was for many years one of the most celebrated sites of Thebes. The seated figure is probably Verney Carter, one of Howard's elder brothers, who joined the EEF team as a copyist in 1894. Photography was another skill which the young Carter seems to have mastered rapidly; he made a large series of excellent negatives of the work at Deir el-Bahri and some of his 'beautiful photographs' were used to illustrate Naville's lecture on the excavations, delivered at the EEF's annual general meeting in London in October 1894.

Deir el-Bahri, 1893–9

Carter's future appeared increasingly uncertain when in 1893 it was decided to call a temporary halt to the fieldwork of the Archaeological Survey because of the considerable expense of the enterprise and an accumulating backlog of unpublished monuments. Carter could have found himself unemployed but his luck held. Thanks in large part to Newberry's support and intervention, his future was secured by appointment as principal artist to Naville at Deir el-Bahri, the magnificent temple of Hatshepsut built into the cliff face in front of the Valley of the Kings at Thebes. Carter devoted the next six years of his life to the work here, with spectacular success, as the published results show. He was joined in February 1894 by his brother Verney who, however, owing to a dislike of the heat, abandoned his nascent archaeological career at the season's end, leaving his brother to find another co-worker – Percy Brown, who himself resigned in 1896 to be followed by Charles Sillem.

Letter from Carter to Percy E. Newberry, December 1893
I dare say you will think it rude of me for not writing to you before and also for not thanking you for your kindness in recommending me for this work which I am very pleased with. I think M. Naville is a splendid man and his method of working could not be better for this kind of job . . .

From Carter's autobiographical sketches
This magnificent structure, of terrace form, is situated under the impressive cliffs at the head of the Deir el-Bâhari valley. A finer site for a mortuary temple could not be found, and, as Professor Naville's excavations proved, it was the Queen's greatest work. . . .

Before Professor Naville's excavations, very little of the temple was visible. My task was to copy, for the purpose of reproduction, all the important sculptures and inscriptions this temple contained. . . .

I felt that if I attempted to copy the scenes sculptured upon the walls of

ABOVE Work in progress at the temple of Hatshepsut, Deir el-Bahri, as photographed by Howard Carter. The actual clearance of the temple was completed in the winter of 1894/5. Subsequent seasons were occupied with the restoration of fallen and scattered blocks to their original locations and with the copying of the relief-decoration. The brick tower formed part of the Coptic monastery which gave the site its modern name ('Monastery of the North'). This structure was held by Naville to be of little interest, and since it incorporated many fragments of 18th Dynasty relief work, it was unceremoniously demolished, some of the bricks being reused in the building of a new house for the excavators.

OPPOSITE Carter's pencil copy of a relief at Deir el-Bahri showing the miraculous conception and birth of Queen Hatshepsut. This exceptionally interesting series of reliefs expounds the dogma that Hatshepsut was fathered by the god Amun, the principal state deity of Egypt, on the wife of the ruling king Tuthmosis I, whose physical form the god had adopted for the purpose. The divine paternity of the pharaoh is commemorated in reliefs of similar type in Amenophis III's Luxor temple, but is of special significance at Deir el-Bahri, as its depiction there was probably intended to lend divine sanction to the unorthodox claim of a woman to rule Egypt as king. On the left, the creator-god Khnum is shown before Amun-Ra; in the centre Khnum, assisted by the frog-headed goddess Heqat, models the child Hatshepsut and her *ka* (or spiritual counterpart, represented here as a 'double' of the queen) on a potter's wheel; on the right, the god Thoth stands before Hatshepsut's mother, Queen Ahmose. Carter's copies of the Deir el-Bahri scenes are a triumph of epigraphic skill; they are made from originals which abound not only with copious detail but also with erased and superimposed inscriptions and figures. His method of copying involved the tracing of the decoration directly from the walls and the subsequent reduction of the copies to a smaller scale on sheets of drawing paper, using a grid of reducing squares. The drawings were then carefully checked for accuracy against the originals. This painstaking approach marked a significant advance on the method used earlier, by which 'squeezes' or hand-copies, made on the spot, were prepared for publication in Europe, without reference to the originals.

OPPOSITE The excavators of Deir el-Bahri and their servants, in about 1893. From left to right: Howard Carter, John Newberry, Edouard Naville, Abdul Maleik (?) (servant), Said Gaddis (cook) and Shehate ('scribe'). Social niceties were observed in Naville's camp, as in those of many other archaeologists at this period. The composition of the group recalls 19th-century photographs of the occupants and staff of English country houses – the servant holding a bottle and glass and the cook a knife (?) as emblems of their duties.

Hat.shep.sut's mortuary temple by the prevailing system of tracing, the essential charm of those beautiful reliefs would have vanished in my copy. And as Professor Naville had given to me a free hand in the matter, I felt bounden to study the problem, to find a means to attain the best results. I tried many expedients; but they resolved in the simple solution: to first observe the fundamental laws of Egyptian art, how it eliminates the un-essential, to copy that art accurately and intelligently, with honest work, a free-hand, a good pencil, and suitable paper. Looking back I have always a cheerful reminiscence in connection with that piece of work; I think, perhaps, because in that undertaking I enjoyed liberty of action.

All my life I have looked back on Deir el-Bâhari as a place having a charm of its own, though it cannot be said to have been a perfect place to live in, except for the winter months. The surrounding cliffs which formed a sun trap made it impossible to live there in the warmer months. But artistically the site was a continual joy. The temple setting, the delicate sculptured reliefs upon its walls, were always a feast for the mind. In those six years, although full of hard work, I learnt more of Egyptian art, its serene simplicity, than in any other time or place. I had several colleagues to help me; there were tragedies, professional jealousies, and often amusing

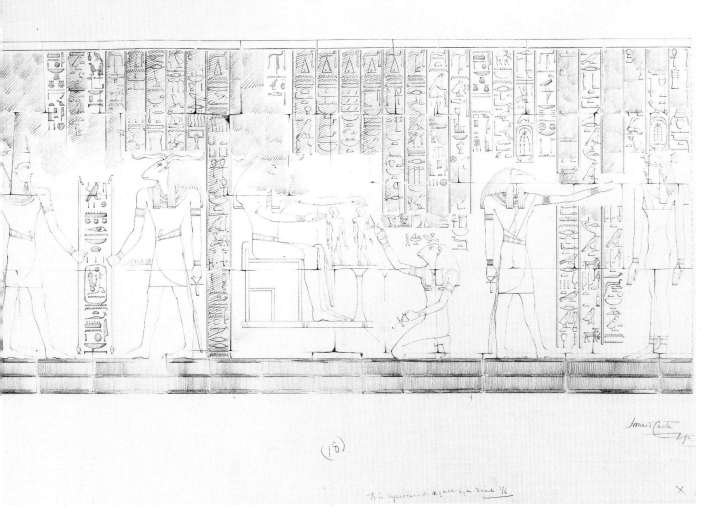

ABOVE Watercolour painted by Howard Carter in 1899 showing the temple of Hatshepsut at Deir el-Bahri, one of several versions of this subject which he produced at around the turn of the century. Over the next twenty years Carter was to make many paintings of Egyptian subjects – landscapes, copies of tomb and temple decoration and studies of wildlife. Some were given to friends and colleagues, others sold to tourists passing through Luxor. Occasionally, the contacts Carter established in this way, such as his introduction to Theodore Davis, were to prove valuable to him.

LEFT Carter had a keen eye for the unusual touch which lends a picture individuality and increases its appeal to potential buyers. This imaginative view of a hoopoe nesting under the protective wings of the vulture-goddess Nekhbet, painted on a wall of Hatshepsut's temple, illustrates his unerring ability to marry techniques required for naturalistic painting with those appropriate to mechanical copying to create a composition of great charm.

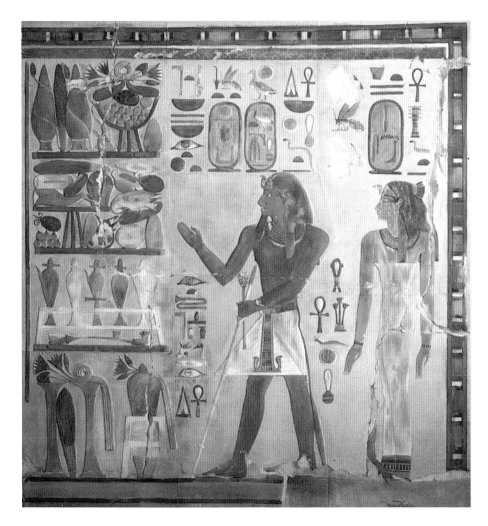

Besides making large-scale pencil copies of the wall decoration at Hatshepsut's temple, Carter painted several details which were reproduced in colour in the published volumes describing the monument. Among these were figures of Tuthmosis I and his mother Seniseneb (right) and a head of queen Ahmose (below). Carter made several copies of these and other royal heads as gifts for friends and as tourist souvenirs, and in 1906 or 1907 a portfolio was published under the title *Six Portraits of the Thothmes Family*. The head of Ahmose is based on a scene in which the queen is conducted by Khnum and Heqat to the chamber in which she is to give birth to Hatshepsut. The original relief is one of the great masterpieces of 18th Dynasty sculpture; indeed, Naville thought the queen's figure 'perhaps the finest piece of work in the whole temple'. Versions of the portraits illustrated were commissioned from Carter in 1899 by Emma Andrews, a relative and travelling-companion of Theodore Davis.

During the clearance at Deir el-Bahri a number of interesting finds were made. Hatshepsut's temple had served as a burial place for Theban priests and officials and their families during the Third Intermediate Period (c. 1070–664 BC) and continued to be used in this way as late as the Roman Period. Large numbers of fine painted coffins, mostly disturbed by robbers, had been discovered there in the 1850s and 1860s and Naville was fortunate in finding a group of three intact burials under the pavement of the Hathor chapel, besides others hidden in the debris which covered the middle platform in front of the Anubis chapel. Among the latter was the fine painted wooden coffin of a lady, which can be dated on stylistic grounds to the 25th Dynasty. The mummy, though not provided with amulets, was enclosed in a one-piece cartonnage mummy-case elaborately decorated with religious scenes. Carter took photographs of the cartonnage which, together with the coffin, was later ceded to the Bolton Museum. Curiously, the name of the owner appears in a different form on the two cases: as Tentkhaykhetes on the coffin and as Takhenmes on the cartonnage. H. 170 cm.

comedies. But I was lucky. For several years I had the great fortune of having Percy Brown's good assistance – a sincere and admirable draughtsman who helped me to earn my wages.

Letter from Edouard Naville to Edward Maunde Thompson, of the British Museum, 11 January 1894
... I have been able to judge what Mr. Carter can do. He certainly has much talent, his drawings are very good, and in this respect I do not think we could have a better artist. His copies when reproduced in colour or in black will make very fine plates ...

Carter's talents were found not to be confined solely to the artistic sphere. He was equally proficient at reconstruction ...

From Edouard Naville's Report to the EEF Committee, 27 February [1898]
... It is certainly quite remarkable how well that difficult work of rebuilding is done by Mr Carter [who has carried out also] the whole of the execution ... [He] has done the work admirably. He has a very quick eye for finding the places where the stones belong to; besides as he has a thorough command of Arabic, he can direct and superintend the men, or rather teach them what they are to do ...

... and fund-raising.

Letter from Edouard Naville to H. A. Grueber, 22 January 1896
... We had yesterday Mr. Horniman's [of Horniman's tea fame] visit, he had luncheon with us. Carter took him over the temple, and he was so much interested and struck by the beauty and the size of the work that he said at once that he would give us one day's profit, £100, and an annual subscription of £5. He immediately took out his cheque book, and wrote out the enclosed cheque ... I am bound to say that it is to Carter that the Society is indebted for that gift. It is he who made Mr Horniman acquainted with the Fund, and who took him over the temple yesterday ...

Carter was also proving to be useful with a camera, even if his table manners left something to be desired.

Letter from John E. Newberry to his brother Percy, 31 December 1893
... Carter's manners ... continue to be much as they were; he doesn't hesitate to pick his last hollow tooth with a match stalk during dinner, bite bread that is so hard you can hardly cut it with a chopper, and help himself to whisky in an absent minded fashion, emptying half the bottle into his tumbler, then laugh and say he wasn't thinking and pour it back again into the bottle, spilling a lot. However he works well, and has taken a lot of interesting photographs, which are very successful, and on the whole we get on all right ...

Howard Carter had, in one way or another, made his mark at Deir el-Bahri, carving a significant niche for himself on the Fund's epigraphic team, reflected in the increase in his salary from £100 a year to £275. But he was becoming restless; 'due possibly to Petrie's training, my great desire was to be an excavator. To me that calling had an

extraordinary attraction. I am now proud to acknowledge that the devoted kindness of many friends eventually led me to that occupation'.

An introduction to Theodore M. Davis, 1899

Around 1899, Carter began to paint an increasing number of delightful watercolours of Deir el-Bahri subjects, as gifts for friends and for sale to passing tourists of eminence. The introduction to Theodore M. Davis, a wealthy American amateur who would play a significant part in Carter's later career, came from Percy Newberry in 1899. Davis' companion, Emma B. Andrews, wished to have watercolour copies of two details of the Deir el-Bahri wall decorations – portraits of Queens Ahmose and Seniseneb – and these Carter promised to supply.

Letter from Carter to Percy E. Newberry, no date [1899]
Dear Newberry
   A thousand thanks to you. Mrs Davies [*sic*] has been here today and has very kindly given me the commission for £31-10-...
      Again I thank you
      Yours
      Howard Carter ...

ABOVE Fragment of painted limestone relief showing the head of a soldier equipped with shield and axe, from Howard Carter's private collection. Stylistically, this fragment almost certainly comes from the temple of Hatshepsut at Deir el-Bahri, though its precise location within the extensive wall-decoration of the monument has never been determined. H. 14cm.

RIGHT Theodore Davis, dressed in the flamboyant style of the archetypal 'explorer', poses outside the entrance to the tomb of Ramesses IV in the Valley of the Kings. Between 1902 and 1914, Davis funded work in the Valley which resulted in the discovery or clearance of over thirty tombs, including those of Tuthmosis IV, Hatshepsut, Yuya and Tjuyu, Horemheb and the puzzling tomb KV 55, believed by many scholars to have contained a reburial of Akhenaten, following removal from his tomb at Amarna. The excavations were supervised from 1902 until 1905 by Howard Carter and James Quibell, in their capacity as inspectors for the Egyptian Antiquities Service; during the later seasons Davis employed first Edward Ayrton and later E. Harold Jones and Harry Burton to conduct the fieldwork under the nominal supervision of the inspector. During their last season in the Valley in 1914, Davis' team excavated to within two metres of the tomb of Tutankhamun before work was halted. In this photograph, taken in January 1907, Davis stands between Ayrton (right) and Arthur Weigall (then Chief Inspector for Upper Egypt) and his wife Hortense.

2

Chief Inspector of Antiquities
'For that is an Inspector's life'

Appointment to 'the Service', 1899

Carter's star was in the ascendant. The reappointment, for a second term after a gap of thirteen years, of Gaston Maspero to direct the Service des Antiquités de l'Egypte brought in its wake a major reorganisation of the department and its personnel. Henceforth, there would be two Chief Inspectors – one in the north and one in the south. To the northern Inspectorate Maspero appointed James E. Quibell, a former Petrie student, while to the south, to the surprise of many and presumably on the recommendation of Naville, went Carter at a comfortable salary of £E400 per annum.

Minutes of the EEF committee, 7 November 1899
... telegrams were read from Mr. Howard Carter, stating that he had been offered the appointment of Inspector of Antiquities to the Egyptian Government, and asking if the Committee would permit him to resign his employment under the Fund from next January 1. Mr. Carter was congratulated on his new appointment, and the permission asked for was given, it being understood that he would make arrangements for the completion of the work at Deir el-Bahari ...

Letter from Carter to Edouard Naville, 14 November 1899
... You will be glad to hear that the Inspectorship has been offered me and I have accepted it, and shall start Jan. 1st – the date that the Committee has let me off the work here ... When in Cairo a few days back I saw Monsieur Maspero whom I found an exceedingly nice man. I believe [it] will be a pleasure to work with him. I cannot do otherwise than thank you for your kindness – as he said he knew me well through you ...

Letter from Gaston Maspero to Edouard Naville, 5 January 1900
... I have been at Luxor since 26 December and I have installed Carter. ... I find him very active, a very good young man, a little obstinate, but I believe that things will go well when he is persuaded of the impossibility of securing all the reforms in one go: the only misfortune is that he doesn't understand French, but he is learning it ...

Duties

In theory, and to a great extent in practice also, any archaeological work undertaken in Upper Egypt fell to the lot of the Chief Inspector of the area to supervise and safeguard. The first five years of the twentieth century witnessed a great deal of archaeological activity, with important work being carried out at several sites. The following extract reflects the breadth of Carter's duties during a single season.

Towards the end of 1899 Carter was offered a post with the Service des Antiquités de l'Egypte as Chief Inspector of Antiquities for Upper Egypt. Delighted, he took up his duties on 1 January 1900 and was soon enthusiastically travelling up and down Egypt, supervising excavations, arranging repairs to monuments and reporting on new discoveries. He was based on the west bank at Luxor in a house close to Medinet Habu, very conveniently situated for carrying out excavations of his own in the Theban necropolis and for closely supervising the work of Theodore Davis and others in the Valley of the Kings. In this photograph, Carter, sitting with Mr Cole on the steps of 'Castle Carter', his inspectorate house, holds the reins of his horse Sultan, through whose agency he discovered the subterranean chamber containing the seated statue of Nebhepetre Mentuhotep (page 65). Also visible in the photograph is one of the pet gazelles whose sad fate Carter could not bring himself to describe when writing to his mother (p. 59).

From the Egypt Exploration Fund Archaeological Report, 1903–4
Work in 1902–3 [scil. 1903–4], including repairs etc.

MR. HOWARD CARTER kindly contributes the following memorandum of work done in the Upper Egypt Inspectorate:–

ABU SIMBEL. Electric light installed in the temple of Rameses II.

ASWAN. The most important tombs at Qubbet el Hawa cleared of sand. Small excavations at Qubbet el Hawa by Lady WILLIAM CECIL. Complete excavation of the small Ptolemaic temple behind the town, and building of an enclosure wall to protect it. Discovery of Aramaic documents dated in the reigns of Artaxerxes I. and Darius II.

KOM OMBO. Repairs to the end enclosure wall in progress.

EDFU. Repairs to the west enclosure wall continued and nearly completed.

EL KAB. Excavations of Professor SAYCE and Mr. SOMERS CLARK.

THEBES. Karnak ... [continued work of restoration and reconstruction by GEORGES LEGRAIN; discovery of several hundred statues and other votive objects in the so-called *cachette*].

Tombs of the Kings. *(a)* The tomb of Queen Hatshepsut has been completely explored by the Service des Antiquités on behalf of Mr. THEO. M. DAVIS ... *(b)* The tomb of Merneptah has been completely excavated ... *(c)* The repairs to the tomb of Sety I. are completed.

Tombs of the Queens. SS. SCHIAPARELLI and BALLERINI have found the tombs of Queen Nefertari-Merimut, Prince Praherunamf, Prince Setherkhepshef, and Princess Aamest, daughter of King Seqenenra. The tomb of (queen?) Isis was also opened.

Deir el-Bahari. Excavations of the Egypt Exploration Fund [at the temple of Nebhepetre Mentuhotep].

Sheikh Abd el Qurneh. Mr. ROBERT MOND has cleared twelve tombs already known: namely, those of Neferrenpit, Tehutiemheb, Khamhat, Userhat *(a)*, Imhotep, Amenemhat, Roy, Userhat *(b)*, Neferhotep, Apity,

Nebuah, Menkheperra-senb; also two inscribed mummy pits of User and Minnekht.

Ramesseum. The excavation of the subsidiary buildings has been continued; large numbers of inscribed potsherds, contemporary with the temple, have been found.

QUFT. A naos of Nectanebo and the lower part of a sarcophagus, of Harsiêsi, have been obtained from sebakh-digging.

Letters home to mother

Behind-the-scenes glimpses of Carter and of his day-to-day life as Chief Inspector are contained in a short series of informal letters Carter wrote home to his mother in England between 1900 and 1902.

Letter from Carter to his mother, 24 August 1900

My Dear Mater

... With my new 6/- camera I can perhaps illustrate my letters when I can make time. Here are a few snaps from 'Castle Carter' to start with.

'*My Play Mates*' and '*Messy Mates*'. It's a wonder the cook did not put his face out the door at the time – this, exactly opposite you, being the kitchen. The pigeon on the right of the post, on top, is a particular kind, and makes or rather has [a] mournful note different to ordinary pigeons.

Here is their Mansion, in which eggs are laid and quarrels occur. Behind is where the Geegee [horse] lives. The ladder is for the small ones whose flight is not yet perfect.

This is not unsightly – but an important corner in my abode. No. 1 is taken on the edge of the verandah; no. 2 from Dining Room; no. 3 from my Bedroom.

To be continued in my next.

The Nile has risen and now when I used to ride I go by boat – between me and Luxor is one sheet of water.

Though yesterday was hot the weather is much cooler. I am now flooding the garden ready for seeding and am imagining in different plots peas, beans, cabbages, etc. 'Ah will it be true.' I am looking forward to those seeds....

Now with love to all and every wish

Your loving son

Howard ...

TOP LEFT 'My Play Mates' and 'Messy Mates'.
FAR LEFT 'Here is their mansion ...'.
LEFT 'This is not unsightly ...'

Letter from Carter to his mother, 12 September 1900

My Dear Mater

Yesterday I returned from an Inspection up country at a place called Edfu with the great pleasure of finding a letter from Mater dated Sept. 2nd and also a much needed ½ doz: prs of socks that caused great joy – to show my pleasure I work[ed] hard and developed photos in the evening and hence the prints. Tomorrow I am off again north, to Keneh and Baliana on Inspection and look into a case between subinspector and guards, either of which having taken palm-oil for settlement of some Antiquity land.

Having other negatives I printed them and herewith carry on the second Chapter of 'Castle Carter'. Now that the inundation comes up to the desert, beside the garden, the water is carried to it by 'Shadoof' and channels that run to each separate basin, the ground being divided into basins to receive the water. But to the kitchen it goes in pails, as here below photo.

The Sheikh and Sultan here below send you 'neighs' and 'salams' and prosperous life, with winnies and licks to the aunts and all. The stones behind are parts of a large colossal statue at a temple called the Ramesseum built by Ramesses II in Thebes to appease the gods and give life to his soul. 'And may it be so.'

No my Dear Mater all that remains of my poor Gazelles are 2 tomb stones on a cairn in the desert – the story being too sad to repeat. ...

It is only a short time since I wrote my last so have hardly anything to say – my flying visits to unexpected places make a few days seem weeks ago. It is a curious life – a letter may come in the morning and I go in quite an opposite way or perhaps must stay where I am – for that is an Inspector's life.

Now with a thousand thanks, ringing of bells and love to you and all I send this short note with apologies

from your Son

Howard ...

One of the letters sent by Carter to his mother in England during his period as Chief Inspector of Antiquities for Upper Egypt. The photographs show (from top to bottom): the court of the Temple of Horus at Edfu (Ptolemaic Period, 305–30 BC); a *shaduf*, the traditional means of raising water from the Nile; the kitchen of 'Castle Carter'; the horse Sultan.

During his years as Chief Inspector, Carter made occasional visits to England, spending time with his relatives. This photograph, taken in the summer of 1901, shows him on holiday with his sister Amy Walker and her family. Amy's daughter Phylis was Carter's favourite niece and acted as his companion and unofficial nurse in his declining years.

Letter from Carter to his mother, 15 April 1902
My dear Mater,

As you will see by the above I am back again from Cairo, after a very jolly week of civilization and cool air of the north. I left Cairo on Monday the 7th 6.30 pm arriving Luxor the following morning 9. am and put up at the Hotel for the day, to give the men time to go over and get the house ready against one coming the following day, when Mr Cole and I came. Now a days we journey up in a modern train in the one night, not as in the old days, by means of a house boat, taking three weeks and purely depending upon the wind. A more delightful mode of travel could not be imagined, but only now, for those to whom time is no object. With a good wind some 80 miles can be covered in the day, but a reverse wind means many hours and sometimes days of toil with the towing ropes. Still there is a charm that will never be superseded by the screeching train and nothing could be finer than a dahabeah in full swing during a cool moonlight night. When tying up in the day, the neighbouring hamlet turns out to look at the strangers travelling in their country and are willing to sell their goods for a very few piastres, the children keeping up a continual cry of 'Backsheesh' until the boat is once again to weigh.

As you will remember Mr Cole stayed with me some two years back and acted stepfather to my gazelles; but alas! they are dead and gone, now lying beneath the acacia tree in the garden of the compound. It is now 'San-Toy' who takes their place but I fear his ways and manners do not surpass them and his voice [is] far from elegant. His talents tend towards gardening, 'He reaps but never sows', a habit that runs in the family and I fear not annulled[?] by his guardian. Still let us hope that time will teach and that 'San-Toy' will carry his master ...

Well my dear Mater I will end with love and best wishes from your loving son
    Howard
        Please remember me to all at Swaffham.

The fate of Carter's beloved donkey San-Toy, referred to above in the letter to his mother, is recorded by Emma B. Andrews.

From the diary of Emma B. Andrews, 10 January 1903
... Poor little San Toy, Carter's young donkey, in whose education and development we all took such an interest, met his death in a tragic way this summer. He was wandering about the drive, when he encountered a cobra, and was dead in 3 hours, bitten in the mouth. The men called Carter, who went out with his gun and blew the cobra to pieces – but the donkey was already swaying about on his legs and nothing could save him. He used to go through the house looking for Carter, and when he found him he would bray with delight ...

The tomb of Amenophis II, 1900–1 – robbers!

The Valley of the Kings was to be the scene of Carter's greatest triumph – although that still lay twenty years in the future. His introduction to the royal burial-ground was itself not uneventful, however, and followed almost immediately upon his appointment as Chief Inspector.

From Carter's autobiographical sketches
In 1898, acting on information supplied by local officials, M. Loret, Director General of the Department of Antiquities, opened up several new royal tombs in the Valley of the Kings; these included the tombs of Tuthmosis I, Tuthmosis III, and Amenophis II. This last was a very important discovery. [In] the Twenty-first Dynasty some of the royal mummies had found sanctuary in this Amenophis' tomb, and here in 1898 thirteen were found. It was but their mummies that remained. The wealth, which in their power they had lavished on their burials, had long since vanished, but at least they had been spared the last indignity. The rewrapped mummy of Amenophis himself, still lay within its own sarcophagus, where it had rested for nearly three thousand three hundred years. On his breast were a few flowers and some foliage of the olive-tree. ...

Very rightly the Egyptian Government, at the representation of Sir William Garstin, the Under Secretary of State for the Public Works Department, decided against their removal. M. Loret, however, did not think this prudent. He disregarded these orders, carefully packed the mummies, embarked them upon his dahabîyah, and took them to the Museum at Ghiza. In consequence an administrative question arose, and he received orders to replace them in the tomb. This he did, but left them still in their packing cases. Here they remained for two years. Under the directorship of M. Maspero, I replaced the mummy of Amenophis II in his sarcophagus, with the flowers and foliage upon him as they were originally discovered; the three naked mummies I put back in the side treasury where they were found; and the mutilated mummy upon the frame of a model boat, in the Antechamber. With regard to the other nine mummies the original plan was changed. It was decided to transport them on a special government steamer to the Ghiza Museum, near Cairo. I was then ordered to fit up the tomb with protective barriers and make it accessible to the public, who were naturally eager to see this new discovery. The tomb I made secure with a steel gate and I placed a special guard over it ...

The tomb of Amenophis II was duly opened to the public and was an instant success with the tourists – the Tutankhamun of its day. Within a short time of the opening, however, on 24 November 1901, the tomb was entered by tomb-robbers. Both in subject-matter and style, Carter's 'procès-verbal' of the incident reads remarkably like the famed tomb-robbery papyri of the Twentieth Dynasty.

From Carter, Annales du Service des Antiquités de l'Egypte 3 (1902)
Nov. 24th 1901. – The night-guards of Biban El Moluk, Mohamed Abd El Ad, Taha Bogdadi and Ahmed Owad say that:- 'On the 24th of November, slightly after sunset, whilst they were sitting down, eating their food, in the tomb No. 10, they were suddenly surprised by thirteen armed men with covered faces and that they were threatened to be shot if they moved or attempted to make an alarm. Six men remained over them whilst seven apparently went and robbed the tomb of Amenophis II and got away together with their plunder ...' ...

Nov. 25th 1901. – The following morning the police were informed; the [relevant officials] went and inspected the tomb, this being about 3 p.m.;

they took the necessary precautions and a special man for tracking spoor was set to work.

The guards having stated that they recognized three men out of the thirteen robbers – namely Abd El Rasol Ahmed, Abdrachman Ahmed Abd El Rasol and Mohamed Abdrachman, – of Goorneh, – these men were arrested by the Ombdeh the same night ...

Nov. 27th 1901. – The following morning [having been summoned from Kom Ombo where I was on inspection], I ... went to the tomb of Amenophis II ..., and found that the bandages of the royal mummy had been ripped open, but the body not broken. This had evidently been done by an expert, as the places where objects are generally found had only been touched. I carefully examined the wrappings to see if there were any signs of their having contained jewellery, but could find no traces whatever and concluded that no jewellery had been found or stolen. The small chamber, containing the three bodies, had not been touched. The boat in the antechamber had been stolen; the mummy that was upon it, was lying on the floor, and had been smashed to pieces ... The marks on the iron gate and the lock, now in the hands of the parquet [prosecuting magistrate], shew that it had been broken by a lever....

Nov. 28th 1901. – The following day I again went to the tomb of Amenophis II ... It had been reported to me formerly by the parquet that the padlock of the tomb had been stuck together and made to look all right by means of little pieces of lead paper ... I found more small pieces of lead paper beneath the door and a little round piece of resin, probably from a sont-tree. This piece was the exact size of the socket for tongue in the padlock and gave me a small clue; for, on the 11th Nov., I had found that the tomb of Yi-ma-dua – No. 88 at Sheikh Abd El Goorneh – had been broken into, the lock being forced by a lever and made to look all right by the means of resin that stuck it together, the material and method in both cases being exactly the same ...

I must add before going on further that I had grave suspicions against Mohamed Abd El Rasol in the case of the Yi-ma-dua tomb, and I watched this man whenever possible, he being a well known tomb plunderer and his house being quite near the tomb.

... I carefully compared the footprints in both tombs and found them to have a strong resemblance. In both cases, *the foot prints, being prints of bare feet, are of one person only....* I then took photographs, to scale as near as possible, of the foot marks of bare feet, and measured them up very carefully.

During the mean time the spoor-man tracked foot prints from Biban El Moluk to the village of Goorneh and to the house of Soleman and Ahmed Abd El Rasol. These men were arrested....

30th Nov. 1901. – I went to the parquet and ... requested leave to inspect the footprints of Mohamed Abd El Rasol. This I did at Markaz, and found them to agree totally with my photographs and with the measurements which I had taken in the tomb of Amenophis II and Yi-ma-dua. The measurements agreed to a millimetre.

In consequence of these constatations Mohamed Abd El Rasol was locked up separately....

Carter was energetic in trying to bring to justice thieves and pilferers who stole and damaged antiquities, and his methods were sometimes reminiscent of those of Sherlock Holmes. In 1901 the recently discovered tomb of Amenophis II in the Valley of the Kings was broken into, almost certainly with the complicity of the official guards, and the mummy was torn open in a search for valuables. Carter strongly suspected Mohamed Abd el-Rassul, a member of the Egyptian family who had discovered the cache of royal mummies at Deir el-Bahri in the 1870s. In connection with his investigation, he measured footprints found in the tomb of Amenophis II and took a series of photographs, one of which is illustrated here. Although the prints of the naked feet matched exactly those of Abd el-Rassul, the court did not find the evidence persuasive; Carter maintained that the photograph produced at the trial was too small to carry the point.

From the diary of Emma B. Andrews, 17 January 1902

... Carter dined with us – always so pleasant – in spite of his dominant personality. His taste for all natural things is so charming to me and how he draws and paints. He is very much absorbed now in trying to bring on the trial of the thief who broke into the tomb, and robbed the body of the great Amenhotep II. The administration of justice is in this country administered in a very funny and desultory fashion. The thief of whose identity everyone is convinced, is at large on bail at the magnificent sum of £1. and the five gaffirs, or watchmen who are suspected of complicity, are contentedly reposing in prison having now no work to do, and more to eat than they usually have, and although Carter has offered £100 to anyone who will tell him the truth, the natives stand in such fear of each other that they all swear total ignorance. Carter, who is Inspector of Upper Egypt has proved himself a most efficient officer – is absolutely fearless – carries no arms – and rides about quite unattended at all hours of the night ...

[We went] with Maspero and Carter into the raided Amenhotep II tomb – what a sad change we found! It has not been shown since the robbery, and M. Maspero was to make his official examination of the body. No one but Carter and the head police officer had been in it. On his first visit Carter found certain footprints belonging to one pair of feet, which he instantly photographed, and on reaching home found they agreed with photos he had lately taken of suspected footprints in another raided tomb – and on an official examination of the suspected man, these photos *matched* perfectly in lines and size, his feet! We found the coffin of cartonnage had been lifted from the sarcophagus, laid on the floor, and the wrappings ripped from the feet to the head – and in a state of utter ruin – and the mummy which had been on the boat, in a neighboring (*sic*) room, was smashed to pieces and the boat taken away ...

The boat was later acquired for the Cairo Museum from a Giza antiquities dealer who had purchased it from Mohamed Abd el-Rassul. Abd el-Rassul himself, though brought to trial, was not convicted for the court considered the evidence, though ingenious, rather too circumstantial.

An auspicious find: the tomb of the horse, 1900–1

Carter's early years in the Luxor Inspectorate were particularly active and, as he explored his new domain, he made several interesting discoveries. One of these was the lost tomb of Pashedu (TT 3); another was the famed 'Tomb of the horse', Bab el-Hosan, the entrance to which Carter had stumbled upon (literally) in 1898 while trekking across the desert in the service of Naville and the EEF.

From Annales du Service des Antiquités de l'Egypte 2 (1901)

Some two years ago, I obtained the knowledge of the existence of this tomb, when riding home after some rain had fallen, for, on nearing my house, the ground gave way under the horse's legs bringing both of us down. Afterwards, on looking into the small hole there formed, I saw traces of stone work, from which I concluded that there must be something and most probably a tomb. I commenced excavating on the 20th January 1900, in order to find out what really was there, and, in a short time, I was able to trace the three sides of the stone work, the fourth side, to the east, being open. From this

The entrance to the Bab el-Hosan ('Tomb of the Horse') at Deir el-Bahri. In 1898, while he was still working for Naville, Carter's horse had stumbled in a depression in the sand in the unexplored area to the south of Hatshepsut's temple. A brief examination revealed stonework and Carter had high hopes that he had found a hidden tomb. At the time nothing further could be done since the spot lay beyond the limits of the EEF's excavation permit, but within a month of taking up his post as Chief Inspector of Antiquities in 1900 Carter had begun an excavation to clear the tomb of sand. After almost two months' work a doorway with its original sealing of mud bricks was revealed. As the photograph shows, this blocking was partially dismantled by Carter in order to gain access to the tomb's entrance passage. The clearance of the rest of the tomb proved extremely laborious and, although it was undisturbed, it contained only a large sandstone royal statue, an empty coffin and a few funerary offerings. These items seem to have constituted a ritual deposit associated with the funerary temple of King Nebhepetre Mentuhotep of the 11th Dynasty, situated beside Hatshepsut's temple but still covered with debris at the time of Carter's investigations.

state of the east end, I concluded that, if it was a tomb, the entrance would be below the western end, so I at once set the men to work there ...

After working down some 17 metres, on the 10th of March, I found the door which had its original mud brick sealings intact. ... I made a small hole at the top of the door and entered, finding myself in a long arch[ed] passage having a downward incline of about 1 in 5 ... Inside the door, a head of a calf and portions of a leg were lying on the floor. I descended the passage, which was quite clear and 150 metres long, ending in a large lofty chamber, the roof again arched ...

... In the left hand corner [of this chamber], lying on its side, was a seated statue about two metres high, completely wrapped in linen of a very fine quality: beside it lay a long wooden coffin which was inscribed but bore no name ... The style of the work shewed that the tomb was of the early Theban empire. Along the end wall and in the centre of the chamber, pots with mud sealings, a dish and many small saucers, all of rough red pottery, together with the skeletons of two ducks? and two forelegs of a calf which still had on them the dried up flesh, were lying on the floor. Having tested the ground

The sandstone statue of Nebhepetre Mentuhotep found in the Bab el-Hosan and now in the Cairo Museum. It represents the king wearing the Red Crown of Lower Egypt and a short white cloak similar to the garment worn by Egyptian kings at the *sed*-festival. The skin is painted black, a colour associated with death in the minds of the ancient Egyptians. At the time of its discovery no comparable sculptures were known, but seated and standing figures of similar type came to light in the course of excavations at the funerary temple of Mentuhotep by the Metropolitan Museum of Art in the 1920s. These differed only in the red colouring of the skin; indeed it is possible that the statue from the Bab el-Hosan originally had red skin also and that it too was set up in the temple. The painting of the skin black perhaps took place as part of a ritual in which the figure underwent a symbolic 'death', after which it was wrapped in bandages like a mummy and buried in the tomb. It has been suggested that the interment of the statue may have been connected with the *sed*-festival, an event which was celebrated at least once in Mentuhotep's reign. H. 183 cm.

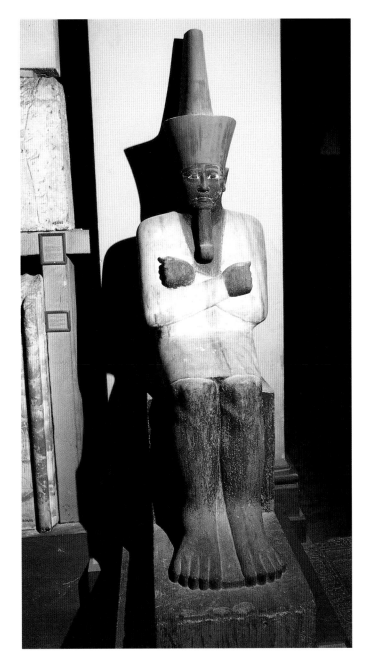

No photographs of the interior of the Bab el-Hosan at the time of discovery are known and this watercolour by Carter is the only illustration which shows the appearance of the wrapped statue and the empty wooden coffin as found. The statue lay on its left side, the position in which the bodies of the dead were laid to rest at this period. The coffin was in all probability intended to serve symbolically as a receptacle for the statue, even though the figure was too large to be placed inside it.

with a piercing rod, I found that there was a shaft leading down from the chamber.

... On the 16th of March 1900, [I] started the men to open the shaft; but on the 20th of April, the shaft proved to be so deep, the rock so bad and becoming so dangerous that I was obliged to stop the work until the next season ...

Letter from Carter to Lady Amherst, 19 December 1900
... I am hard at work trying to get to the bottom of the tomb I found at Deir el-Bahari last year. I trust to manage it soon though under difficulties – the men have now got down 97 metres vertical drop and still no end, but cannot help but think the end will come soon; then there are chances of perhaps a good find, it being untouched ...

From Annales du Service des Antiquités de l'Egypte 2 (1901)
... [On] the 31st of December, ... the men found the first signs of a doorway, a little less than 30 metres from the surface, closed with slabs of limestone.

On January 1st 1901, I opened this doorway in the presence of Viscount Cromer [British Consul-General in Egypt] and M. Maspero, finding the chamber to be very small and full of rubbish. The only objects found in it were three very rough wooden boats, and pots like those in the upper chamber ... After thoroughly cleaning out the chamber M. Maspero and I we went down, and, after examining closely the rough wall of rock, we found that we had come to the end, the shaft going no further and there being no signs whatever of the existence of another chamber.

I then set the reis [foreman] to investigate the rest of the upper chamber and passage, and, in the middle of the latter, half way down, he found another shaft which again raised our hopes, but only to be disappointed as before, as it turned out to be but two metres deep and leading nowhere. In it was found a small wooden box ..., and this [by its inscriptions] gave us the only clue to the name of the person for whom the tomb was made ...

If we may rely on the testimonial of this inscription, the newly-discovered tomb had belonged to one of the first kings of the XIth Dynasty, Mentuhotep I. It may be doubted whether we have found the real rooms, and perhaps we may be entitled to conjecture that there is, somewhere in the passage or elsewhere, another shaft which would lead us to the place where the mummy of the king is to be found. Possibly, the shaft or entrance to the real tomb may be found outside the door, but there is such an immense amount of rubbish to clear away before one can see, that I have postponed further work until a future date ...

What Carter had found was a part of the elaborate funerary temple of King Nebhepetre Mentuhotep of the Eleventh Dynasty, constructed in the bay of Deir el-Bahri immediately south of the spot on which Queen Hatshepsut was to build her temple six hundred years later. Mentuhotep's monument was almost completely hidden by debris until Edouard Naville cleared the site on behalf of the EEF in 1903–7. More recent work there by the Metropolitan Museum of Art, New York, and the German Archaeological Institute has enabled the structural evolution of the building to be understood. The Bab el-Hosan probably belongs to an early phase of the temple's design and may originally have been intended to receive the mummy of the king. Changes in the overall conception of the monument led the architects to abandon this plan and to construct a new burial chamber at the end of a long passage leading under the cliffs. This sepulchre, plundered in antiquity, was found during Naville's excavations. The Bab el-Hosan was ultimately used for the ritual burial of the statue found by Carter, wrapped and laid to rest like a human body, with a coffin, funerary models and food offerings. The discovery of the statue, under any other circumstances, ought to have been regarded as a triumph, but by comparison with Carter's expectations of finding an intact royal burial it was a bitter disappointment.

Letter from Gaston Maspero to Edouard Naville, 8 January 1901
... [Carter] had announced his discovery too soon to Lord Cromer. Lord Cromer came to be present at his success and he is now very saddened at not having been able to show him anything of what he foretold. I console him as best I can, for he truly is a good fellow and he does his duty very well ...

The lesson was a hard one for the young Chief Inspector but he learnt it well. When Tutankhamun's tomb came to light, he would make absolutely sure of his facts before venturing any opinion on what he had found.

The tomb of Hatshepsut-Meryetre, 1900

Tomb KV 42 was Carter's first tomb-clearance in the Valley of the Kings (the second would be the reused Eighteenth Dynasty tomb KV44), carried out during November and December 1900 on behalf of two private individuals, Chinouda Macarios and Boutros Andraos. Odds and ends from tomb KV 42 had been brought to light during extensive clearance work two years earlier by Victor Loret, Director-General of the Antiquities Service 1897–9, although the sepulchre itself had evidently not been found or entered at that time. Later, in 1921, Carter was to discover a group of foundation deposits at the entrance to the tomb inscribed with the name of Hatshepsut-Meryetre, principal wife of Tuthmosis III and mother of Amenophis II. There can be little doubt that the tomb had originally been prepared for this queen, though she seems in actual fact to have been interred with her son and the tomb passed on, as a kingly favour, to one or more members of the Sennefer family. In the following report, prepared by Carter for the 'house journal' of the Antiquities Service, may already be discerned the sober, logical analysis which, in matters archaeological, characterised his writings from the very beginning and would serve him so well during his work at the tomb of Tutankhamun two decades later.

From Carter, Annales du Service des Antiquités de l'Egypte 2 (1901)
... Only the lower part of the original sealing of the [tomb] door was intact, the upper part being filled up by stones fallen from above. On entering, I at once saw that the tomb had already been plundered in early times, and that, during heavy rains, it had been filled to a considerable depth with water which probably entered by the breach made by the early robbers. On inspecting the interior, the former plundering of this tomb was only too evident, for the funereal furniture, vases and Canopic jars, were smashed and lying about on the ground of the passages and chambers, evidently just as the former robbers had thrown them ...

The sarcophagus had, leaning against its side, the lid which had been thrown down and was resting upon a piece of timber ...

The small chamber was evidently intended for the offerings, for here, upon a higher level than the rest of the floor, I found some twenty or thirty, whole

Carter's photograph of the sarcophagus in tomb 42 in the Valley of the Kings, a sepulchre which he cleared in 1900. The name of the individual for whom the tomb was originally designed was not found at this time, though several features indicated clearly that it was a royal personage – notably the right-angled bend in the plan and the cartouche-shaped burial-chamber. The sarcophagus appeared never to have been used and its lid was found supported by an ancient piece of timber. A note in Carter's hand on the reverse of this photograph reads: 'The two stones under corner of lid I put because the air getting to the old wood began to give way (sic)– note white mark made by lid on corner of coffin due to movement of the same'. The foundation deposits which indicated that the tomb was cut for Queen Hatshepsut-Meryetre did not come to light until 1921. Before this discovery it had been suggested that the tomb was that of Tuthmosis II, an attribution which has persisted to the present day in the face of all evidence to the contrary.

Cartonnage mummy-case of the lady Tentkerer discovered by Carter in a small tomb in the Valley of the Kings in 1901 and now in the Cairo Museum. The tomb (KV 44) apparently dated to the New Kingdom but had been reused in the 22nd Dynasty for the interment of three individuals, buried in black-painted wooden coffins. The mummy of Tentkerer bore leather straps impressed with the cartouches of Osorkon I (c. 924–889 BC) in whose reign she had died. Her finely painted cartonnage case is of an unusual type, representing the dead lady in the dress of daily life and adorned with several highly coloured religious motifs: various deities, the sun-disc on the horizon, and Isis nursing Horus in the papyrus marshes. Some of these figures are shown suspended from Tentkerer's shoulders on strings of beads.

and broken, rough earthen jars, some with their sealings still intact: these probably contained liquids, etc., for the *ka* [spirit] of the owner...

Although it is not absolutely certain that this tomb is of Sen-nefer, the evidence in favour of its being so is very strong. One set of Canopic jars was found in a more or less perfect condition, and on them appears the name of Sent-naï, whom we know to have been the wife of Sen-nefer. Another set of these jars was found in a somewhat fragmentary condition, and on them occurs the name of a lady, Bakt-Râ. Lastly, a complete set of bearded heads only; is it not probable that these belong to the Canopic jars of Sen-nefer himself?

... I think that it is evident that this tomb was broken into and robbed by the metal robbers of the 22nd Dynasty, as, a short distance along the passage at the entrance, under the rubbish, the reis found some gold leaf

RIGHT Tomb KV 42 was eventually used for the burial of the Royal Nurse Senetnay, wife of the Mayor of Thebes Sennefer, to whom it was probably given as a special favour by Amenophis II. These two limestone canopic jars found by Carter in the tomb formed part of the set of four vessels made to hold the embalmed viscera of Senetnay. The lids represent the head of the decreased wearing a wig and with her eyes painted black. The incised inscriptions on the walls were originally filled with blue pigment. One is an address to the goddess Isis to 'spread your arms around that which is in you; provide protection around Hapi who is in you ...' The other invokes Nephthys to protect Qebhsennuf, who in turn guarded one of the visceral packages. To ensure a correct matching of the lids with the jars the names of Isis and Nephthys were scratched on the tops of the heads as well as appearing in the formal texts on the sides. H. of larger jar 44 cm.

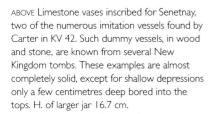

ABOVE Limestone vases inscribed for Senetnay, two of the numerous imitation vessels found by Carter in KV 42. Such dummy vessels, in wood and stone, are known from several New Kingdom tombs. These examples are almost completely solid, except for shallow depressions only a few centimetres deep bored into the tops. H. of larger jar 16.7 cm.

and an exquisite gold inlaid rosette, probably the bottom part of a menât wrenched off, these having been dropped by the robbers when hurriedly leaving the tomb, as might well be the case ...

Unfortunately all the wood had decayed by the water, but the fragments show that there were sledges and wooden coffins, the latter showing signs of ivory inlay, which it was impossible to preserve, as, on being touched, it instantly fell to pieces ...

Letter from Carter to Lady Amherst, 19 December 1900
... Last week I allowed some excavations to be made in the tombs of the Kings by a native, resulting in the finding of the tomb of Sen-nefer, Mayor of Thebes during Amenhotep II; there are many antiquities in it mostly inscribed vases of good work. As my agreement was with the native that

either half value or half antiquities shall be the finder's property and there are many duplicates, I am advising Newberry to purchase one for you. Would willingly do so myself but feel that I ought not to under one's present circumstances ...

Restoration and conservation

Carter took his job as Inspector very seriously and one of the prime duties of the position, as he saw it, was to ensure the preservation of the monuments in his charge. In this respect he had perhaps been influenced by his years with the Archaeological Survey of the EEF; to achieve his ends, moreover, he was not above chasing – and securing – outside sponsorship.

Letter from Carter to Mrs Goff, Luxor, 21 March 1902
Dear Mrs Goff
In reply to your very kind letter of the 21st inst: I must, in acknowledging the receipt for cheque for £10- you so kindly enclosed, thank you on behalf of the Service des Antiquités. The sum shall be spent on preserving a special monument and a report shall be duly sent to you.
    Believe me
    Yours sincerely
    Howard Carter

A contemporary photograph showing the mummy of Amenophis II after its reinstallation by Carter in the original sarcophagus. In addition to making good the damage wrought by the modern tomb-robbers, Carter installed an electric light at the head of the sarcophagus, illuminating the king's exposed face to striking effect.

Mrs Goff's funding enabled Carter to undertake the clearance of the tomb of Sety II (KV 15) between 1902 and 1904. Other restoration work had been undertaken in 1901/2 within the tombs of Amenophis II (KV 35), Ramesses I (KV 16), Ramesses III (KV 11), Ramesses VI (KV 9) and Ramesses IX (KV 6); Carter also cleared the entrance to the tomb of Ramesses X (KV 18) at this time. Restoration work in the tomb of Sety I, 'Belzoni's tomb' (KV 17), was to be carried out under Carter's supervision in the winter of 1903/4, the year in which Carter cleared the inner chambers of the tomb of Merenptah (KV 8). All highly commendable – but what would catch the public's imagination was Carter's installation of electric lighting, thanks to which the full splendour of the hitherto gloomy, torch-lit 'grottoes' would now be seen for the first time.

From the diary of Emma B. Andrews, 13 January 1903
… We entered Amenhotep [II]'s tomb – now lighted with electricity, showing arrangement and decoration delightfully. The rifled mummy has been restored to his sarcophagus, and decently wrapped with the torn mummy cloths – and Carter has arranged the whole thing most artistically. A shrouded electric light is at the head of the sarcophagus, throwing the fine face into splendid relief – and when all the other lights were extinguished, the effect was solemn and impressive. Carter has done wonderful work over there [in the Valley of the Kings] in a dozen different ways – all the tombs, the principal ones, are lighted – no more stumbling about amongst yawning pits and rough stair cases, with flickering candles dripping wax all over one.

Theodore Davis and the tomb of Tuthmosis IV, 1903

In 1902 Theodore Davis, the successful New York lawyer whose enthusiasm for Egyptology was already well-known, obtained permission to excavate in the Valley of the Kings. Carter was to supervise the work.

From Carter's autobiographical sketches
… Mr. Theo. M. Davis of Newport, U.S.A., as everyone knows, took a great interest in Egyptian archaeology as well as in Egypt. He came out every year and spent his winters on the Nile in his dahabeyeh 'The Bedouin'. He often told me that he would like to have some active interest during his sojourns in Upper Egypt. Thus, with Maspero's consent, I put the following proposition to him. The Egyptian Government would be willing, when my duties permitted, for me to carry out researches in the Valley of the tombs of the Kings on his behalf, if he would be willing on his part to cover the costs thereof, that the Egyptian Government in return for his generosity would be pleased, whenever it was possible, to give him any duplicate antiquities resulting from these researches. At the same time I told him of my conjecture regarding the possibility of discovering the tomb of Tuthmosis IV. The Government offer he accepted …

From the diary of Emma B. Andrews, 17 January 1902
… After lunch, Maspero and Carter walked about with Theodore to fix upon the site of an exploration, which Theodore under Carter is to make in the Valley of the Tombs …

Carter's first major find for Davis was tomb KV 45, the 18th Dynasty tomb of one

RIGHT One of the two leather loincloths of Maiherpri found by Carter in a hollow in the rock above his tomb in the Valley of the Kings in 1902. It is made from a piece of gazelle skin which, with the exception of the outer edge and a small patch covering the buttocks, has been converted to a net by the laborious cutting out of tiny squares of leather with a small fine tool. The two lateral flaps were intended to fit around the hips and the larger central flap passed between the legs and was secured at the waist. The other loincloth was of similar design, differing chiefly in the larger pattern of the network. Such network loincloths are frequently shown in Theban tomb-paintings being worn by soldiers, sailors and labourers; the examples belonging to Maiherpri appear to have been intended for ceremonial occasions, since the delicacy of their construction would have made them impracticable for everyday use. H. 85 cm.

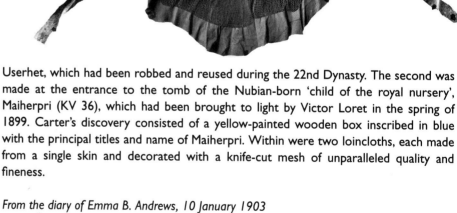

ABOVE The yellow-painted wooden box which contained the loincloths described above. It is made from cypress wood, carefully fitted together with dovetail joints. Both lid and box are inscribed in hieroglyphs with Maiherpri's titles and name. His mummy shows that he was of Nubian extraction and, since he was given the rare privilege of burial in the Valley of the Kings, it may be assumed that he enjoyed the favour of one of the kings of the mid-18th Dynasty – probably Amenophis II or Tuthmosis IV. Maiherpri's title, Child of the Royal Nursery, indicates that he was brought up with the king's children in the palace. Possibly he was the son of a Nubian chief brought to the Egyptian court in accordance with the New Kingdom pharaohs' practice of indoctrinating the sons of foreign rulers to promote good relations with Egypt in the long term. H. including lid 13.5 cm.

Userhet, which had been robbed and reused during the 22nd Dynasty. The second was made at the entrance to the tomb of the Nubian-born 'child of the royal nursery', Maiherpri (KV 36), which had been brought to light by Victor Loret in the spring of 1899. Carter's discovery consisted of a yellow-painted wooden box inscribed in blue with the principal titles and name of Maiherpri. Within were two loincloths, each made from a single skin and decorated with a knife-cut mesh of unparalleled quality and fineness.

From the diary of Emma B. Andrews, 10 January 1903
... We saw at Carter's, the two wonderful leathern aprons that he found in the tomb he opened last year for Theodore – the most wonderful work I have seen in Egypt ...

Carter continued the search for Tuthmosis IV and the clues began to mount up

From Carter's autobiographical sketches
... The work in the minor valley began to reveal other fragments of glazed-ware that obviously came from Tuthmosis' burial. By making a chart of

these fragments I eventually got a hint as to the probable direction whence they came. What was even more pleasing, at a point where the small valley forked, where there might have been a doubt as to which of the two tributaries should next be taken, at the beginning of the right-hand tributary a portion of a fine alabaster (calcite) vase bearing an engraved cartouche of the king was found....

Work continued the following season. Carter was on the right track, but was temporarily diverted by the discovery of a small corridor-tomb, KV 60, containing two mummies – one a wet-nurse of Queen Hatshepsut called In. In January 1903, the first positive indications of Tuthmosis IV's tomb were revealed.

From Carter's autobiographical sketches
... Just above [KV 60], on the southern side of that tributary valley, was a long shelf-like projection. This rock ledge attracted me. It looked like a tempting place for an Eighteenth Dynasty royal tomb ... [W]hen the men reached the further end of the ledge, they discovered two small holes cut in the rock ... They contained a number of ceremonial objects – miniature tools, etc. – each bearing the names and titles of Tuthmosis IV ... A very little more digging revealed the four sides of a much larger cutting in the rock, and a further day's work sufficed to clear this sunken stairway entrance to the tomb sufficiently to permit of entry. ...

Since Davis had sailed for Aswan two days before, Carter decided that it would be wise to examine the tomb in more detail before unduly raising his sponsor's hopes. This he did on 18 January 1903 in company with the American Robb de Peyster Tytus, who had been digging with Newberry at the Malqata palace ruins of Amenophis III. The tomb had been plundered in ancient times but the excitement of the discovery was none the less for that.

From Carter's autobiographical sketches
... A few eroded steps led us down to the entrance doorway partially blocked with stones. We crept under its lintel into a steep descending corridor that penetrated into the heart of the rock. As we slithered down the mass of debris that encumbered this corridor the stones under our feet rolled with a hollow rumbling sound, echoed, re-echoed, in the depths of the tomb. At the end of this corridor we came came to a steep flight of steps with a shallow recess on either side. These steps, sixteen in number, led down to another descending corridor which brought us to the brink of a large gaping well. We looked down into dusky excavated space. At the edge of this abyss we waited until our eyes became more accustomed to the dim light of our candles, and then we realized in the gloom that the upper part of the walls of this well were elaborately sculptured and painted. The scenes represented the Pharaoh Tuthmosis IV standing before various gods and goddesses of the Netherworld. Each of these scenes was accompanied by explanatory inscriptions. Here was final proof that I had found the tomb of Tuthmosis IV, which, as you may conceive, gave me a considerable degree of satisfaction....

As we stood on the edge of this 'Protective-well', we could see the [exit] in the opposite wall, wide open. Just as the last dynastic tomb-robbers had left it. Dangling from it and reaching to the bottom of the well was a stout palm-fibre rope which the last intruders employed when they quitted the

One of the most important discoveries made by Theodore Davis in the Valley of the Kings under Carter's supervision was that of the tomb of Tuthmosis IV, great-grandfather of Tutankhamun, found in 1903. Although plundered, the tomb yielded a substantial quantity of pieces of funerary furniture and provided new information about types of objects which formed part of the burial equipment of a New Kingdom pharaoh. The most impressive piece was the wooden body of a chariot (seen here as it was found), richly decorated outside and inside with reliefs and inscriptions. The king's chariots seem to have been stored at the southern end of the burial chamber, which also yielded fragments of harness.

'tomb-proper'. It had kept this attitude for more than 3000 years. Whatever its use, it made us realize that we would require rope and ladders if we desired to penetrate any further . . .

After a short delay, Carter procured the necessary equipment and the explorers bridged the well, to find themselves in a small undecorated room which gave access, by means of a short staircase and a corridor, into a second chamber, this time decorated with scenes showing pharaoh being welcomed into the afterlife by the gods. A hieratic graffito on one of the walls recorded that, in Year 8 of Horemheb, the damage done by the tomb robbers had been restored by the necropolis official Maya and his assistant Djehutymose.

From Carter's autobiographical sketches
Leading from this decorated room, a comparatively small doorway, showing signs of having been twice closed with masonry and twice carefully sealed, admitted us into a large and lofty sepulchral hall, which by the dim light of our candles looked immense and mysterious. Its rock surfaces were left

quite plain. A double row of massive columns supported its roof. The central aisle, nearly 45 feet in length, was united to the open crypt at the end by a flight of 5 steps. In the centre of this crypt stood an immense quartzite sarcophagus, superbly engraved with texts of religious nature.

As we stood in this venerable sepulchre it was impossible not to be struck with the extraordinary scene that surrounded us. It required no great exercise of imagination to see that the tomb-plunderers had held an orgy here. The floor of the hall was literally strewn from end to end with splinters from the original funerary equipment. Everything had been broken to bits and thrown helter-skelter by those ruthless vandals, who in their thirst for gold had spared nothing. Even the immense quartzite sarcophagus stayed not their impious hands: its massive lid weighing many tons had been prised-off and thrown to the ground, its contents despoiled.

At the edge of the flight of steps that led to the crypt was the body of a war chariot; the king's gauntlet lay at its side. With the exception of the sarcophagus, these were the only objects that had any resemblance to their pristine state.

 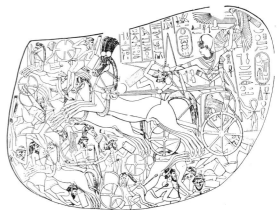

Drawings of the decoration on the chariot body, made by Carter for Davis' publication of the tomb of Tuthmosis IV. The scenes on the exterior show the king in his chariot plunging masses of Asiatic warriors into a confused rout. The images reflect the tendency at this period to depict the King as a super-hero: unequalled in athleticism, in the arts of war and in the handling of horses. The falcon-headed god Montu, who gave the king support and success in battle, guides Tuthmosis' hand in shooting arrows, while the king controls his team without the aid of a charioteer, the reins tied around his hips. The interior panels show the king again, this time as a sphinx, trampling enemies underfoot while Montu, with outstretched winged arms, extends a sickle-sword and religious emblems towards him. The chariot body is of wood, covered with linen, gessoed and perhaps originally silvered; the carving of the scenes is of the highest quality.

It now only remains to notice the four small chambers, two on each side of the sepulchral hall, that are called 'treasuries'. They served as storerooms for the purpose of storing prepared meats, grain, water, precious oils and cosmetics. They, too, had been completely ransacked, everything in them broken to atoms. In one of them was a ghastly sight: the nude mummy of a boy prince propped against the wall with the abdomen ripped wide open by a sharp knife. . . .

From the diary of Emma B. Andrews, 21 January 1903
. . . Carter appeared unexpectedly while we were at breakfast, and announced the thrilling news that he had found the tomb of Thothmes IV and that he and Robb Tytus went into it – finding a splendid sarcophagus, beautiful wall decorations and floor strewn with blue pottery . . .

From the diary of Emma B. Andrews, 8 February 1903
. . . We went to see the things from the tomb – all spread out in one of Carter's rooms – a really splendid show. I was enchanted. The wonderful chariot – which is of the finest and most spirited work – the entrancing blue things – many unusual and unique things . . .

RIGHT Limestone canopic jar made for the King's Son Amenemhet, one of a set of four found in the tomb of Tuthmosis IV. The prince evidently died young and was buried in his father's tomb in the Valley of the Kings. The stopper is carved in the form of a human head and the hieroglyphic inscription is the standard formula guaranteeing the protection of the goddess Neith over Duamutef, the deity responsible for the safety of the jar's contents. The carving of the face is particularly fine, the almond-shaped eyes, arched eyebrows and prominently-outlined lips foreshadowing some of the most typical features found on the statuary of Amenophis III a few years later. H. 37 cm.

ABOVE Ankh (sign of life) in blue faience from the tomb of Tuthmosis IV, inscribed with the king's cartouche. Objects of this kind were included among the burial equipment of several New Kingdom pharaohs. H. 21.5 cm.

Blue faience *shabti* figure from the tomb of Tuthmosis IV. The *shabtis* found in this tomb vary considerably in size and in the details of their inscriptions, wigs and other attributes. Many, like this specimen, were made of faience with a deep blue glaze. The inscription and other details are painted in black. The king wears the striped tripartite wig and holds, in his crossed hands, two hoes and bags of grain suspended on ropes – the necessary equipment for the agricultural duties which the *shabti* was to perform. Tuthmosis IV is the first king whose *shabtis* carry these items, which became a regular feature of such statuettes in later periods. The vertical inscription reads: 'The Son of Re, of his body, Tuthmosis, beloved of Osiris, the great god'. H. 18.5 cm.

Lid of a miniature coffin, in blue faience, to contain a *shabti* figure, from the tomb of Tuthmosis IV. Thirteen model mummy cases were discovered in the tomb, some of them still containing a small, crudely modelled *shabti*. The decoration of this example copies that of the full-size coffins of the period, with central inscription and lateral bands dividing the sides of the lid into rectangular compartments. H. 22.5 cm.

The tomb of Hatshepsut, 1903–4

From Carter's autobiographical sketches

... When I was able to study in detail the objects found in the Tuthmosis IV [foundation] deposits ... I noticed the following interesting fact. Some of the objects bore evidence of having palimpsest dedications: there had been an alteration in the royal names. Under the prenomen of Tuthmosis IV, the prenomen of Hat.shep.sût could be traced. In one case the original dedication of the Queen had been rubbed out and the King's dedication engraved over it ...

Carter began to suspect that Hatshepsut herself might have been buried in the Valley of the Kings – and as pharaoh. But how could he find the tomb?

From Carter's autobiographical sketches

It was Emerson, I believe, who said that it is hardly possible to state any truth strongly, without apparent injustice to some other truth. As a matter of fact, what was foremost in my mind at the moment, was to try and apply this newly discovered piece of knowledge – the existence of foundation-deposits being laid down before rock-hewn tombs – as a means of discovering the ownership of the uninscribed tombs in the Valley, which had been plundered and left open to the elements ever since dynastic times. For without some means or process of elimination of this kind, you might easily be hunting for a tomb which already lies open and staring at you ...

To test his theory, Carter turned to a tomb not far from that of Tuthmosis IV – one which had stood partially open since the time of Strabo and had been investigated in a rather superficial manner by several nineteenth-century scholars (Napoleon's expedition, Giovanni Battista Belzoni and Karl Richard Lepsius among them). Carter instructed his workmen to search in front of the tomb and soon discovered a foundation deposit whose model implements and vessels were inscribed with the name of Hatshepsut as pharaoh. The tomb had been identified with relative ease; clearing it would prove quite another matter.

From Carter's autobiographical sketches

It was one of the most irksome pieces of work I ever supervised. The tomb proved to be 700 ft. long, and had a vertical depth of 320 ft. With the exception of the first portion cleared by former explorers, almost the entire length was filled to the roof with rubble, most of which had been carried in by water from spates of past centuries. The filling was cemented into a hard mass by the action of water. To excavate it needed heavy pickaxes, and the whole of this rubble had to be carried to the mouth of the tomb by a continuous chain of men. Outside it was pitched into a small tributary valley I had just exposed. Half way down its corridor the white limestone stratum came to an end, and a stratum of brown shaly rock of uneven fragile nature commenced. It was here when our difficulties began, for the latter stratum of rocks was so bad there was a serious danger of its falling in upon us. To add to our troubles the air was also very bad; candles would not give sufficient light to enable the men to see to work. Consequently I was obliged to introduce electricity and an air-pump. Even then the workmen could only work for 3 hrs. at a time ...

When we reached the bottom part of the corridor, we began to find in the lower layer bits of broken stone jars bearing the family names, such as Aahmes-Nefe[r]t.âri, Tuthmosis I, and Hat.shep.sût. Eventually when the men succeeded in making a passage in the filling sufficiently large enough for me to enter the Sepulchral Chamber, all my expectations fell at finding that the ceiling had collapsed and the chamber [was] completely choked-up with fallen rock. We had literally to dig our way in foot by foot.

Apart from the few fragmentary remains of the Queen's funerary equipment I have referred to above, all that we discovered was her quartzite sarcophagus and that of her father, Tuthmosis I.... Both ... were beautiful specimens of workmanship and elaborately engraved ...

From the diary of Emma B. Andrews, 12 February 1904
... Carter and Newberry went into the tomb – as the Reis had reported to Carter the evening before that an unsealed doorway had been found at the end of the corridor, very much blocked with debris. Newberry did not go to the bottom, being overcome by the foul air, and emerged after a time looking very ill. Carter went on to the end, and found the room into which the door opened, choked with rubbish to within 2 feet of the ceiling. He pushed his head into the opening, but found the air so foul, that he had to retreat to one of the upper parts of the corridor and stop awhile – then he went back and made a hurried reconnoitre, which revealed a large room with what appeared to be other chambers opening from it. Theo said that when Carter emerged from the tomb, he was a horrid object – dripping and wet from the heat, with a black dust over his face and hands – he was very sick too, and had to lie down for sometime. He said the air was filled with a suffocating odour, like ammonia, and that great masses of black stuff like black stalactites were hanging from the ceiling. It is a hard business for him and the workmen ...

More recent studies have suggested that the tomb Carter cleared, KV 20, had originally been prepared for Tuthmosis I and only subsequently adapted (by the addition of a further chamber) to accommodate the burial of Hatshepsut. Tuthmosis III seems to have been responsible for transferring the body of Tuthmosis I to a new tomb, KV 38, which he had excavated for his predecessor on the opposite side of the Valley.

Debts repaid

Carter was nothing if not immensely loyal to the few close friends he had and he never forgot the debt of gratitude he owed the Amherst family; when an opportunity arose for him to oblige, he invariably did so.

Letter from Carter to Lady Amherst, 19 December 1900
... Newberry has been most fortunate in finding 3 gold and copper dishes with Hathor cows in them – they are very beautiful and unique – Shall do all I can to let him carry one away for you for I think two are ample for the Museum ...

The importance of an Aramaic archive discovered at Aswan by the locals and acquired by Lady William Cecil, Lord Amherst's daughter, and Robert Mond, the industrial chemist, was clear to Carter and he did everything in his power to see that the papyri were

Carter's telegram to Lord Cromer announcing the news of the incident at Saqqara, 8 January 1905. In autumn 1904 Carter had been appointed Chief Inspector of Antiquities for Lower Egypt, with a base in Cairo. Shortly after this move he was involved in a fracas with a group of disorderly French tourists at Saqqara, some of whom received slight injuries. Carter's stubborn refusal to apologise for his part in the incident caused embarrassment in diplomatic circles and made his position a difficult one. Further reorganisation of the Antiquities Service inspectorates enabled Maspero to move Carter again, this time to Tanta in the Delta—an archaeological and social backwater vastly different from Luxor and Cairo. Bored and frustrated in his new surroundings, suffering from poor health and smarting at this 'exile', Carter resigned from the Service des Antiquités in October 1905, intending to occupy his time with painting.

acquired for the Cairo Museum. Mond was persuaded to present his documents outright; for the daughter of Lord Amherst, an exchange for one of the statues brought to light by the Egyptologist Georges Legrain in the Karnak *cachette* in 1904 seemed a more appropriate manner of acquisition. The papyri were eventually published by A. H. Sayce and A. H. Cowley, with photographs by Carter, who was responsible for unrolling them; the cost of the publication was borne by Robert Mond.

Letter from Carter to Lady William Cecil, 11 June 1904
... Monsieur Maspero told me that he had sent you some photos of statues from the Karnak [cachette] for you to choose from in exchange for the papyri that we took from you. He shewed me the statues today and suggested that the large standing one was the best – this I certainly agree, and it is really a very good one and personally I advise taking it, but if Lord Amherst

does not think he would like it, I will do what I can [to get something else], though I cannot say that you can [do] much better ...

Transfer to the north and the Saqqara Incident, 1905

Howard Carter's achievements in the Luxor Inspectorate had proved beyond any doubt what an inspired choice he had been for the post. But change was to come. The intention had always been, from the start of his employment with Maspero, that at the beginning of 1903 Carter should be transferred to the northern Inspectorate and J. E. Quibell to the south. Because of work in progress, Carter argued for a stay of execution – and this Maspero agreed to. By the autumn of 1904, however, Carter's time as Inspector in the south had finally come to an end: with stiff upper lip, though secretly harbouring no little regret, he left Luxor for pastures new.

Letter from Carter to Lord Amherst, 2 December 1904
... I am now down in Cairo for good in possession of the Lower Egyptian inspectorate. It is a nice change though perhaps not so interesting, but after 11 years of Luxor one can get a little tired and slack ...

As things turned out, there would be little opportunity for Carter to become bored with his new fief. His tendency towards obstinacy, as we have seen, was noted by Maspero within a very short time of his appointment to the Antiquities Service; the years of authority in the service of the Egyptian Government had only hardened this aspect of his personality – with catastrophic consequences.

Telegram from Carter to the Earl of Cromer, 8 January 1905
My Lord
I am exceedingly sorry to inform you that a bad affray has occurred today here [at] Mariette's House Saqqara 5 pm with 15 French tourists who were here in a drunken state. The cause of the affray was started by their rough handling both my inspectors and gaffirs. As both sides have been cut and knocked about I feel it my duty to inform your Lordship immediately and will report the matter to you personally tomorrow morning.
Carter Services des Antiquités

Summary [by Carter] of Case against a party of visitors at Saqqara on Sunday last – Jan: 8th 1905
Director
About 3. pm. on the 8th of Jan: 1905 some 15 visitors, whom I believe to be French, arrived at the Necropolis of Saqqara in a rowdy condition, some of them going to Mrs Petrie's Camp and behaving in an offensive manner. They eventually came to the Service's Rest-house (known as Mariette Pasha's House) where they stayed for an hour or so talking in a loud manner and drinking. They afterwards stated a wish to visit the monuments. Upon this, the Ticket Inspector Es-Sayid Effendi Mohammed informed them that they must take tickets and he requested the necessary fees. It was not until after some trouble that he was able to collect the money for 11 tickets. The whole party then went to the 'Serapeum' accompanied by a gaffir, who at the entrance of the monument requested to see who had tickets and who had not, knowing that some of the party had not obtained tickets and thus had no right to enter. The party would not wait for this inspector, but rushed

at the door and forced it open breaking one of the side catches which held the padlock. Upon their finding, when they entered, themselves in darkness they returned and demanded candles from the gaffir. The gaffir explained to them that he had not any candles nor did the Service supply visitors with candles. The party then roughly handled the gaffir and demanded their money back. The gaffir called for assistance, to which the Inspector Es-Sayid Effendi Mohammed came, and he was treated in even a rougher manner; his tarboush was knocked off his head and trampled upon. Reis Khalifa was also called for and was also treated in a similar way. Reis Khalifa, on hearing from the gaffirs that one of the party had taken the padlock of the door, demanded it to be given up; this was done after some difficulty. The party still continuing to give trouble, he returned with them to the house, where they entered with Es-Sayid Effendi Mohammed and the gaffir, and came at once to fetch me.

I was at that time some distance away, near the edge of the desert, with Mr Weigall and the Misses Kingsford and Hansard; and upon hearing from Reis Khalifa of what had occurred I immediately returned with him to the house.

During the meantime the party had turned out the gaffirs from the house and barricaded the doors, and attempted to get the money from Es-Sayid Effendi Mohammed, the Ticket Inspector, by force.

I found the East door of the house to be closed, the gaffir outside, and had some difficulty in entering. Here I found the whole party in an excited state, and on finding one of them knew English I requested him to give an explanation. He and all of them spoke to me in an exceedingly rough way and I was unable to get from them a proper explanation. I then requested the above Inspector to explain what had occurred, and he told me how they had entered the 'Serapeum' by force and of their general behaviour. I then explained to them that they had no right to take such steps or touch the men and that they had no right to be in the house, it being private property, and that they must leave it at once. This they refused to do. I told them that if they did not go out steps would have to be taken to remove them and at the same [time] I requested their names. They refused to do both and became more offensive. On my again warning them, and on my telling the gaffirs that the party must be turned out, one of the party immediately without any reason struck a gaffir with his fist in the face and knocked him down in a savage manner. On my interfering the same man raised his hand and threatened to strike me. I arrested his striking arm and warned him. The number of gaffirs, then there, being inadequate to remove these people, I commanded Reis Khalifa to send for more and on their entering by the second door (South door) the whole of the party immediately attacked them with their sticks and chairs belonging to the Service. Seeing that the gaffirs were being very badly knocked about I at once gave them the order to defend themselves and drive the people out. In the affray some of the party were hit, one of them being knocked down. The party fled leaving one injured man which I attended to and during the mean time one of the party returned. From outside stones were hurled at us.

I demanded the names from these two last men – this they gave me on a visiting card. Their names given were:- Georges Fabre and Ferdinand Estienne. At their request I gave them my name and official capacity. They left the house threatening prosecution. I sent for the Ombdeh of Saqqara and requested the Ombdeh of Abou-zeer, who was there, to inform the police at once of what had happened and request them to take the necessary steps against these people. The Ombdeh of Saqqara came as soon as possible and made a small enquiry and informed the [...] of Ayat of the same.

Some of the gaffirs were badly hurt. Chairs of the Service [were] broken by thé party. Strict instructions were given to the gaffirs not to leave the house while the party was outside – which order was carried out and I wish to commend the gaffirs on their behaviour during the whole affray.

Upon the arrival of the police a complete enquiry and procès verbal was made, consisting of some 35 sheets of foolscap.

I beg to request that legal steps should be taken against these people for assaulting the gaffirs, in raising a hand with intent to attack me, and for damaging Government property.

Howard Carter

10.1.905

To the Director General
Service des Antiquités ...

Letter from Gaston Maspero to Carter, Esneh, 30 January 1905
... How is the Sakkara business progressing? The more I look at it, the less I like it, not that I think you were wrong in the mean facts but you put appearances against us by giving the order. I have been corresponding about it with Sir W. Garstin and with M. de la Boulinière ...

Carter (left) with Sir Gaston Maspero, his wife and an unidentified lady. Maspero (1846–1916), a Frenchman, was Director-General of the Egyptian Antiquities Service during much of Carter's time in Egypt. A scholar of very wide-ranging interests, he produced a vast quantity of publications on all aspects of Egyptology. He had a high opinion of Carter, treating him with sympathy and patience throughout the crisis of the 'Saqqara Incident' and its aftermath. He was also instrumental in bringing about Carter's collaboration with Lord Carnarvon. This photograph was taken in 1913 when Maspero was visiting Carter and Lord Carnarvon at their Theban excavations.

Letter from Gaston Maspero to Carter, Cairo, 3 February 1905

... I am come from Louxor to arrange the Sakkarah business and I saw Sir William Garstin at half past ten this morning. It is agreed with him, and I may say with Lord Cromer, that you are to come with me tomorrow between nine and ten and pay a call on M. de la Boulinière there to express our regrets that the order you gave brought so strong consequences. That will stop the matter which was becoming irritating ...

Letter from Theodore M. Davis to Carter, 10 February 1905

... there is only one manly, upright and gentlemanly thing to do, and that is to express your regrets etc. Pay no attention to whatever the papers or vain and silly people may say! All men whose respect is worth having will praise and approve of your action. Contemplate the harm of being dismissed from the service 'for disobedience'. It will stick to you as long as you live, and all your justification will be forgotten ...

Letter from Gaston Maspero to Carter, 17 February 1905

... A letter which I received this morning from Sir William Garstin informed me that the matter was arranged between Lord Cromer and M. de la Boulinière. The question of excuses is settled, but as you refused to do what was asked from you [offer an apology], you are to be reprimanded somewhat for it. I am asked to send you from Cairo to Tantah and this as soon as possible, telling you at the same time that this is done not on account of your action at Sakkara, but because of your subsequent conduct ...

Pray do not let yourself to be carried too far by your feeling, but remain with us: you know that I, for one, will not esteem you less nor be your friend less than I had been up to the present time ...

Letter from Carter to Gaston Maspero, 21 February 1905

... I may say that I feel the humiliation to an exceeding extent. The treatment I have received after I have carried out my duty which has always been my endeavour and after my services to the department is inconceivable ...

Carter, writing to Maspero earlier that same day, had requested three and a half months' leave from 14 March, 'owing to the strain of work during the last 17 months'. Depressed and demoralised, he took an extended leave before returning to his new post in the relative backwater of Tanta. Here he continued to demonstrate his efficiency by retrieving for the authorities a large portion of a treasure illicitly excavated at Tukh el-Qaramus ('some 117 ozs. of Greek gold jewellery and coins of Ptolemy Soter and the early part of the reign of Philadelphus; together with silver coins of the same date, two large silver incense burners, and an altar service in silver'). Increasingly disillusioned with the conditions of his new posting, however, on 21 October that same year he tendered his resignation and left the Service des Antiquités for good.

From the diary of Emma B. Andrews, 24 November 1905

... Saw much of Mr. Carter – who has at last resigned from the Service des Antiquités. I was very glad to hear it. Jean and I drove out to the country to the pretty little house he has taken, and had tea with him. He is going to devote himself to painting – a thing he should have done years ago ...

3

Digging with Lord Carnarvon
'A learned expert'

The commercial watercolourist, 1905–7

Carter, unemployed, faced an uncertain future. He had for some years been producing watercolours, mostly on Deir el-Bahri themes, for sale to passing tourists and to friends (such as Mrs Andrews). He had also undertaken occasional commissions for colleagues, such as the German Egyptologist Friedrich Wilhelm von Bissing, for whose monumental *Ein thebanischer Grabfund aus dem Anfang des Neuen Reiches* – an account of the treasure of Queen Ahhotpe – Carter had prepared several plates. Such work had then proved a useful supplement to his draughtsman's salary; now it was to provide the basis for his very survival. The going would have been harder still, had not Theodore M. Davis, in the continuation of his work in the Valley of the Kings the previous February, stumbled upon the richly stocked tomb of Amenophis III's parents-in-law, Yuya and Tjuyu (KV 46). For his publication of the new find, Davis required a series of watercolour illustrations of the more spectacular pieces; the commission went to Carter at £15 a plate. The results, however, were not entirely to Carter's liking.

Letter from Carter to Percy E. Newberry, 29 September 1907
... I received only a few days back the copy of Davis' 'Yua and Tua'. What has happened? It seems an absolute bungle and minus seemingly the most important points. My plates have been reproduced fearfully and absolutely contrary (in some cases) to my instructions. No proof was ever submitted to me. Do tell me what you think of the whole thing ... If there are any criticisms I am going [to] answer with full explanations as I do not think it fair. Davis has behaved like a bear to me of late but no matter ...

Although other work came Carter's way (including a scene from the tomb of Nebamun [TT 146] for the Marquis of Northampton's 1908 *Report on Some Excavations in the Theban Necropolis*, and other illustrations for Janet R. Buttles' *The Queens of Egypt* published that same year), commissions were few and far between, and anything but lucrative. There had to be a better way – and there was. Fate now intervened, in the form of the fifth Earl of Carnarvon. Having been trained, educated and experienced in the service of Egyptology, Carter readied himself for gentrification.

Lord Carnarvon

The fifth Earl of Carnarvon was born on 26 June 1866 at the family home, Highclere Castle in Hampshire. The only son of the fourth Earl, he succeeded to the title in 1890, shortly afterwards marrying into the Rothschild family. Enormously rich, for the first part of his adult life he was best known as a race-horse owner and as a rather reckless 'automobilist', in 1901 suffering a serious motoring accident in Germany which left him a virtual cripple. A latent interest in archaeology had always been present, but not until

Howard Carter as a tramp; a caricature drawn by Arthur Weigall about 1909. Following his resignation from the Antiquities Service Carter spent a short time in Cairo before moving to Luxor. Here he survived as best he could, acting as a guide and painting watercolours for tourists and on commission from excavators such as Theodore Davis. This collapse of the fortunes of the former Chief Inspector must have struck some of his colleagues as particularly ironic. Though Carter and Weigall were often at odds, this sketch, humorously evoking Carter's straitened circumstances, conveys a hint of sympathy on Weigall's part.

Lord Carnarvon first visited Egypt in 1903 did this predilection, ultimately to dominate his entire life, begin to assert itself.

Text of a talk by the sixth Earl of Carnarvon, undated

... Many people have asked me how it came about that [my father] should have interested himself in [Egyptology]. In the early part of this century he was advised by his medical attendants that he had a weak chest and in order to prolong his life he was told that he should spend every winter away from England in a warm climate such as Egypt. After he had spent his first winter on the banks of the Nile, he did not share in that popular conception of the slogan which says: 'Those that have drunk of the waters of the Nile shall always drink again'. Far from it. He found that there was little to do and he suffered from the ennui that any man of his active temperament would inevitably feel under such circumstances.

One day, talking to the late Lord Cromer, who was then our representative in Egypt, he confided that he found an increasing sense of boredom and wondered whether there was anything to do in Egypt to distract him. Lord Cromer told him that he thought it would be an admirable idea if he were to take up the fascinating subject of Egyptology ...

Extract from an autobiographical sketch by the fifth Earl of Carnarvon

I may say that at this period I knew nothing whatever about excavating, so I suppose with the idea of keeping me out of mischief, as well as keeping me employed, I was allotted a site at the top of Sheikh Abdel Gurna. I had scarcely been operating for 24 hours when we suddenly struck what seemed to be an untouched burial pit. This gave rise to much excitement in the Antiquities Department, which soon simmered down when the pit was found to be unfinished. There, for six weeks, enveloped in clouds of dust, I stuck to it day in and day out. Beyond finding a large mummified cat in its case, which now graces the Cairo Museum, nothing whatever rewarded my strenuous and very dusty endeavours. This utter failure, however, instead of disheartening me had the effect of making me keener than ever.

A fateful introduction, 1908

Letter from Lord Carnarvon to Arthur Weigall, Chief Inspector of Antiquities for Upper Egypt, prior to his second excavating season in March 1907.

... Maspero has advised me to apply for the ground from Sheik abdel Kurnah to the tomb of Entoof at Drah Aboul Neggah ... If I get what I want I shall bring out a learned man as I have not time to learn up all the requisite data ...

But, since no 'learned man' had at that time been forthcoming, the idea was shelved. For Carnarvon's second season, the problem was not so much a shortage of finds as an embarrassment of riches – the discovery of the tomb of Tetiky and the so-called 'Tablet Tomb' containing an enormously important hieratic text recording the war against the Hyksos by king Kamose. These were impressive finds – but finds with which Carnarvon discovered he had little idea how to deal. In desperation, he turned again to the Egyptian authorities for guidance.

The large wooden coffin containing the mummy of a cat, which was the only substantial 'find' made by Lord Carnarvon during his first season of excavation in Egypt. The coffin, now in the Cairo Museum, comprises two halves meeting along a line running down the length of the body, and secured with mortise and tenon joints. It was coated with black resin, and the details of the eyes, ears and mouth were added in yellow paint. Unlike most cat-coffins, which take the form of a tall and slender animal with feet placed close together, this specimen is distinguished by a very large head with ears reminiscent of those of some larger feline (Arthur Weigall described it as resembling 'a small tiger'), squat body and widely spaced feet.

In 1907 Lord Carnarvon obtained the concession to excavate in more promising ground at the northern end of the Theban necropolis. His permit covered part of the Asasif (the area in front of Queen Hatshepsut's Deir el-Bahri temple), and part of the region known as Dra Abu el-Naga, to the north. This latter area had been used intensively as a cemetery for both royal and private individuals during the 17th and early 18th Dynasties. Two weeks' work here in the spring of 1907 brought to light the tomb of Tetiky, Mayor of Thebes during the early years of the 18th Dynasty. On account of the enormous quantities of debris encumbering the site, and the presence of modern houses above, it was not possible to clear the tomb completely, but Carnarvon was able to reveal an open courtyard with a shaft leading to the burial apartments, and three brick-vaulted chambers, two of which contained well-preserved wall-paintings which were among the earliest examples to have survived from the beginning of the New Kingdom. The section illustrated here comes from the north wall of the main chapel and shows Tetiky and his wife Senbi seated beneath a canopy supported by columns, before which stand two of Tetiky's daughters (or grand-daughters). To the right a banquet is in progress, with female servants waiting upon a group of men, the first of whom appears to be vomiting (a realistic detail shown in several Theban tomb-chapels). Although this find was made before Carter's association with Lord Carnarvon, he was responsible for making a photographic record of the tomb and for preparing an account of it for publication.

Lady Burghclere, Lord Carnarvon's sister

The more [Carnarvon] toiled, however, the more it became clear to him that he needed expert aid; accordingly he consulted Sir Gaston Maspero, who advised him to have recourse to Mr. Howard Carter.

Sir Gaston Maspero's advice proved even more fruitful of good than Lord Carnarvon anticipated. In Mr. Howard Carter Carnarvon obtained the collaboration not only of a learned expert, an archaeologist gifted with imagination, and as Lord Carnarvon said 'a very fine artist', but that of a true friend. For the next sixteen years the two men worked together with varying fortune, yet ever united not more by their common aim than by their mutual regard and affection ...

Although the tomb of Tetiky had been plundered in antiquity, some objects from the original burial were recovered. This stone offering table is inscribed with standard offering formulae addressed to Osiris on behalf of Tetiky, and also names his parents Rahotep and Seneb. It would have been installed in the funerary chapel to receive offerings of water to sustain Tetiky's spirit, and comprises of six small troughs, each perforated to enable the liquid to drain to the spout. L. 43.5 cm.

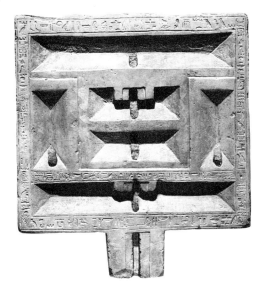

OPPOSITE The Sailmakers' Bazaar, Cairo, watercolour signed and dated 1906. This painting was probably one of many pictures Carter produced following his resignation from the Antiquities Service, for sale or as gifts (this one belonged to the Egyptologist Somers Clarke). The Cairo bazaars were an irresistible attraction for European visitors at the turn of the century. Amelia Edwards, writing in 1877, pictured the scene: 'The houses are high and narrow. The upper stories project; and from these again jut windows of delicate turned lattice-work in old brown wood ... The street is roofed in overhead with long rafters and pieces of matting, through which a dusty sunbeam straggles here and there, casting patches of light upon the moving crowd. The unpaved thoroughfare ... is lined with little wooden shop-fronts, like open cabinets full of shelves, where the merchants sit cross-legged in the midst of their goods, looking out at the passers-by and smoking in silence'.

Oval tinted photograph of Lord Carnarvon as a young man.

COFFER BEARING THE NAMES OF AMENOTHES III.

Two of the watercolours which Carter painted to illustrate Theodore Davis' publication of the tomb of Yuya and Tjuyu. This tiny sepulchre in the Valley of the Kings had escaped serious plundering and yielded one of the finest collections of funerary furniture ever discovered in Egypt. Carter's paintings of the finer pieces occupied fourteen of the plates in Davis' publication of the tomb: left, a wooden chest, possibly intended to hold jewellery, decorated with gold leaf and plaques of blue-glazed faience. The two leaves of the lid are inscribed with the names of Amenophis III supported by figures of Heh, the personification of 'millions of years', and around the sides is a repeating frieze of the hieroglyphic signs for 'dominion', 'life' and 'stability'. Chests with similar decorative elements were found in the tomb of Tutankhamun. H. 51 cm. Above, Yuya's chariot is made of wood, gilded and covered with leather decorated with spirals, rosettes and plants and animals. The chariot is much smaller and of lighter construction than those found in the tombs of Tuthmosis IV and Tutankhamun and, on account of its size and fragility, could not have been drawn by horses. It was arguably made specifically for the tomb, for Yuya's use in the afterlife. L. 245 cm.

OPPOSITE ABOVE One of the main areas investigated by Carter and Carnarvon was the 'Birabi', adjoining the lower slopes of the Dra Abu el-Naga, north-east of the mouth of the Deir el-Bahri valley. This region was rich in tombs of the Middle Kingdom (some reused in later periods) and the Ptolemaic Period. Already in 1907 Carnarvon had discovered a tomb here (numbered '9' in the excavation record) which yielded important finds – among them two writing boards, one of which (subsequently known as 'Carnarvon Tablet I') was inscribed with the important text describing king Kamose's war against the Hyksos. In another part of the tomb were three pottery canopic jars associated with remains of a wooden canopic chest inscribed for a man named Katynakht – perhaps one of the original occupants. The jars have lids representing the head of a man, a falcon and a jackal – three of the four sons of Horus; the lid of the missing fourth jar doubtless took the form of a baboon's head. The group appears to date to the early or middle 18th dynasty, and is the earliest instance known in which the lids of the jars represent the different zoomorphic heads of the Sons of Horus – in other groups from the 18th Dynasty all the heads are human. H. 28.8–30.5 cm.

OPPOSITE, BOTTOM LEFT During 1909 and 1910 Carter and Carnarvon investigated the cliffs along the northern face of the valley of Deir el-Bahri, bringing to light several tombs and other objects. Approximately half-way down the slope of the hill was a rock-cut court with tomb-chambers opening to the north and east ('site 5' in the sequence of excavations). These proved to contain the undisturbed burials of eight adults and a child in wooden coffins, dating from the Third Intermediate Period. Most of the coffins were uninscribed, but three were decorated and belonged to a man named Pedikhons, his wife Irtyru and their son Pedeamun, who had lived during the 25th Dynasty. That of Irtyru was the most elaborately decorated of the three; the paintings on the lid included the weighing of the dead lady's heart in the balance of judgement, to determine whether or not she was fit to enter the afterlife, while the interior is occupied by a large figure of the goddess Nut represented full-face with arms outspread in a symbolic embrace around the mummy. H. 190 cm.

Explorations at Thebes, 1907–14

Carnarvon's 1907–8 excavations at Dra Abu el-Naga, with their stimulating finds, proved to be only the first in a series of richly rewarding seasons of work. Under the expert supervision of Howard Carter the excavators brought to light burials of the Middle Kingdom, early New Kingdom, Third Intermediate Period and Ptolemaic Period (several of them undisturbed), a hitherto unknown temple of Queen Hatshepsut and another begun by Ramesses IV. Carter ran a tight ship, keeping a close watch on his workers and supervising the more ticklish areas of work personally, not at all afraid of getting his hands dirty. He rapidly earned the respect both of his employer and his workmen. With the publication in 1912 of *Five Years' Explorations at Thebes*, Lord Carnarvon's massive report to which Carter had contributed a very great deal, he could add to this respect the acclaim of his Egyptological colleagues.

Extract from Carnarvon's introduction to Five Years' Explorations at Thebes
… With a view to making systematic excavations in this famous necropolis I began tentative digging among the Kurneh hills and desert margin in the spring of 1907. My workmen were all from the neighbouring villages and their number has varied from seventy-five to two hundred and seventy-five men and boys … I made it a rule that when a tomb was found, as few workmen as possible should be employed; and, in order that the opportunity for stealing should be reduced to a minimum, no clearing of a chamber or pit was carried on unless Mr Carter. or I was present. That nothing should escape us, we also, in certain cases, had to sift over the rubbish from the tombs three times.

My preliminary excavations eventually resulted in my confining attention to three sites in that part of the necropolis which lies between the dromos leading to Dêr el Bahari and the great gorge giving entrance to the valley of the Tombs of the Kings. These three sites were: (1) a spot a few metres to the north of the village mosque, where, according to the natives, lay a hidden tomb; (2) the Birâbi, which is near the desert edge, between the hills of Drah abu'l Nagga and the cultivated land, and adjoins the entrance to the dromos of Hatshepsût's famous terrace temple; and (3) that part of the XIth Dynasty cemetery which lies along the hill slope, on the northern side of the Dêr el Bahari valley …

Letter from Carter to Mrs Newberry, 16 March 1910
… Yes! At last we have had better luck and found quite a nice lot of things. Under the wall, which turns out to be the unfinished position of a terrace temple of (?)Hatshepsut, we find there is a XIIth dyn. cemetery and quite a rich one too. It has been badly plundered but [there are] still good pickings left. In one tomb there was a mummy untouched and on it we found a beautiful obsidian necklace mounted in gold … Also a copper gilt mirror with ebony handle mounted and inlaid in gold. Under the coffin was, though smashed, a most beautiful ivory toilet box – inscribed and dated Amen-em-hat IV which will please your husband and prove his conjecture true. Besides these on other mummies in the tomb was a heavy gold fillet for the hair and with the ivory toilet box another small ivory box in the form of an axe on four bull's legs. This had a cornelian and gold brooch [*sic*] and 10 most beautiful hair pins – 5 with jackal heads and 5 with slughis' (hunting dogs') heads. In the rubbish was an immense amount of beautiful beads of silver, gold, cornelian, turquoise and such kinds. At Deir El Bahari

BELOW RIGHT Irtyru's mummy was unwrapped by the excavators and pronounced by Carter to be that of a woman of about 35 years of age. Four wax figures of the Sons of Horus and the *Bennu* Bird were found among the wrappings, and a fillet of leaves had been placed at the head. The outer shroud of dark reddish-brown linen had concealed inner wrappings made from discarded clothing, among which was a large portion of a garment resembling the modern 'galabieh'. Old clothes have often been found used as mummy-wrappings. The significance of this circumstance was not lost on Carter, who noted the ironic observation on death inscribed in the Theban tomb of Neferhotep: 'He who was rich in fine linen … lies now in the cast-off garments of yesterday.'

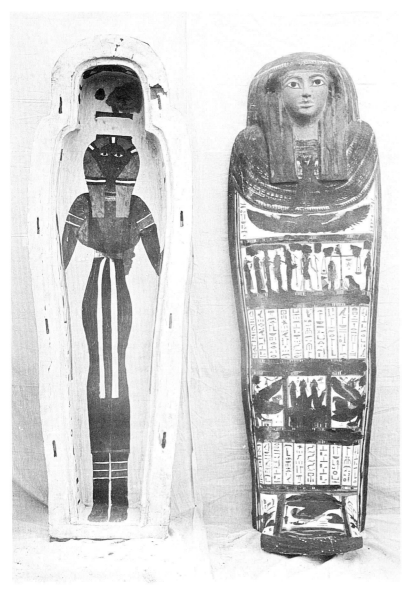

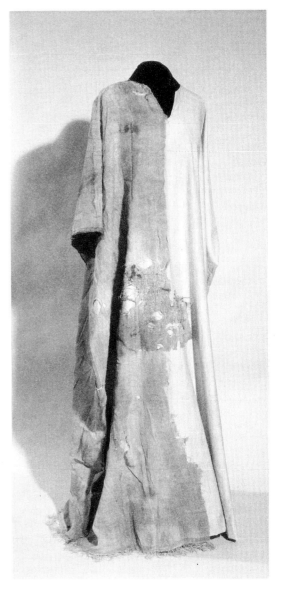

ABOVE The tomb of Tetiky yielded many crude wooden *shabtis* characteristic of the 17th and early 18th Dynasties, contained in miniature coffins and found *in situ* in four niches cut into the western wall of the courtyard. In addition to these there was a remarkable series of large *shabtis* of better quality. Eight of these were found, buried in pairs in holes cut on all four sides of the shaft in the courtyard of the tomb leading to the burial chambers. Each *shabti* was enclosed in a miniature rectangular wooden coffin decorated with blue stripes and with the owner's name roughly inscribed on the lid. The *shabtis* themselves are of painted wood with gilded faces, and have the text of Chapter 6 of the *Book of the Dead* inscribed in black ink on the body. They bear the names of eight different individuals among whom were the parents of Tetiky. The identities of the other persons—including Senbu, whose miniature coffin and *shabti* are shown here—remain unknown but they were probably close relatives. This is the only known instance of the depositing of *shabtis* around a burial shaft, and it is conjectured that they were intended to guard the cardinal points. H. of *shabti*: 25.5 cm; L. of coffin: 32.5 cm.

OPPOSITE Two well-preserved redware storage jars with conical lids, painted with black lines. They were found in tomb '9', the courtyard of which contained large quantities of pottery and plundered mummies. H. 49 cm.

OPPOSITE The Valley Temple of Hatshepsut, as first uncovered. During the clearance of tomb '9' in 1909 a well-constructed wall of limestone blocks came to light. The structure was aligned with the causeway leading to the queen's great funerary temple under the Deir el-Bahri cliffs, and the masonry discovered by Carter and Carnarvon turned out to be the enclosure wall of the temple which had formed the entrance to a complex in which part of the funeral rituals would have taken place. The Valley Temple had perhaps never been completed and had suffered from being used as a limestone quarry at a later date, but enough remained to determine that it was to have been of terraced design like the main temple, consisting of an upper and a lower court with a dividing colonnade. Close by, partly hidden by brick-vaulted tombs of Ptolemaic date, were traces of a colonnaded temple begun by Ramesses IV but never completed.

OPPOSITE Underneath the foundations of Hatshepsut's Valley Temple in the Birabi, Carter and Carnarvon discovered several rock-cut tombs originally dating to the Middle Kingdom, the clearance of which occupied much of their time in the 1910–14 seasons. Although the tombs had suffered from plundering and the destructive activity of white ants, much material of interest remained. Objects from the original burials of the 11th and 12th Dynasties were found; several of the tombs had been reused in the Second Intermediate Period and early 18th Dynasty and these burials yielded large numbers of coffins of the *Rishi* type. In this photograph Lord Carnarvon, with his dog, is seen supervising the removal of debris from one of the larger tombs.

Limestone 'name-stone' of Hatshepsut from the vicinity of her Valley Temple. Stones of this kind, made from granite, sandstone, quartzite, limestone or diorite, have been discovered in the foundations and enclosure walls of several of Queen Hatshepsut's buildings at Thebes. One surface is smoothed and incised with the queen's name in a cartouche, sometimes accompanied by a royal epithet such as 'the Good God' or 'Son of Re', and many examples also carry hieratic dedications from private individuals to various high officials who were responsible for the construction of the buildings. The example illustrated carried on one side an ink inscription (now almost faded from view) including the name of Hatshepsut's overseer of works Senenmut, and the date 'Second month of the summer season, day 9'. These texts suggest that the stones were intended as votive offerings, contributions by their dedicators to the building of the temple, in return for which they presumably expected some divine favour. Such offerings were particularly numerous at Hatshepsut's Valley Temple at Deir el-Bahri, excavated first by Carter and Carnarvon (who referred to them erroneously as 'tally-stones'). H. 28 cm.

Two blue faience bowls found in tomb '24' (in Carter's sequence), one of the largest of those excavated in the Birabi. The tomb had been plundered and reused in the early New Kingdom but these vessels belong to the original burial, and can be dated, on the grounds of their shape and decoration, to the 13th Dynasty. They are of interest as being early examples of this type of bowl decorated with lotus flowers. Such vessels were probably used for funerary libations, the blue lotus being a favourite symbol of resurrection (the opening and closing of its petals at sunrise and sunset respectively was seen as a metaphor for the continuous cycle of birth and death). One has an invocation to the goddess Hathor on behalf of the owner, the lady Ibiau. Shallow bowl, Diam. 14 cm; deep bowl, Diam. 11.2 cm.

we also found a very fine foundation deposit of model tools etc. (nearly life size). Unfortunately these are uninscribed and their true meaning not yet understood. We have also got a beautiful blue glaze Hippo: quite perfect and from 4 other mummy pits opened many small and pretty objects . . .

Letter from Lord Carnarvon to E. A. Wallis Budge, of the British Museum, 25 February 1911
. . . I am still going on finding stuff necklaces scarabs etc. yesterday a bronze snake about 5 ft long buried in a coffin. We have now come to the conclusion that the place is a cachette of bodies nearly all of which are of the Hyksos time. This is the opinion of Spiegelberg and Muller and there are a good many very ugly coffins decorated in the 'Richi' style. The Berlin people want 1 or two of them & have offered to exchange. Do you think you would like one? I think I could get one that would stand the journey. They are very ugly but possibly interesting to you at the Museum. There is I think now no doubt that this tomb was never entered into after the beginning of the 18th Dynasty . . .

The excavations in the Birabi brought to light many burials, often accompanied by objects of exceptional interest. Among the coffins found in 1911 within tomb '37' was an anthropoid case of early 18th Dynasty type bearing the name Mentuhotep. Lying on the mummy, under a shroud, was a long bronze serpent–a very rare type of object whose precise function is uncertain. The closest parallel to the tomb '37' specimen is a bronze cobra, found in 1896 in a disturbed grave of the 13th Dynasty close to the Ramesseum, the funerary temple of Ramesses II. This piece differs from the Carnarvon serpent chiefly in its smaller size (L. 16 cm) and its elaborately coiled tail. The objects found with the Ramesseum serpent indicate that it formed part of the equipment of a magician, a man whose services would have been much in demand for the performance of rituals aimed at warding off or curing the illnesses and accidents of everyday life. Although the inscriptions on Mentuhotep's coffin gave no indication that he was a magician, the evidence of the serpent points in this direction. L. 164 cm.

RIGHT Obsidian and gold necklace from an unrifled mummy of the Middle Kingdom found in Birabi tomb '25'. The wood of the coffin had been eaten by white ants and the mummy (that of a person named Renseneb) had decayed to a black powder, but the necklace survived intact, together with a fine bronze mirror with a gold-inlaid ebony handle, a blue faience hippopotamus and a gold and cornelian *shen* amulet. The tomb also contained a toilet box with the name of Amenemhat IV (of the 12th Dynasty), giving a valuable clue to the date of the burials, and the earliest date for the tombs in this area. L. 79 cm.

BELOW Tomb '37' was the largest and richest sepulchre cleared by Carter and Carnarvon in the Birabi. It dated originally to the Middle Kingdom but had been reused in the early New Kingdom as a cache for burials which had evidently been brought from elsewhere. These interments, which had survived undisturbed, dated to the Second Intermediate Period and early 18th Dynasty, and included sixty-four coffins, many of the *Rishi* type, and other early 18th Dynasty varieties, both rectangular and anthropoid. In some cases up to four mummies were discovered in a single coffin, and a number of interesting finds were made among the associated burial goods. This photograph shows the pit (at left) dug to gain access to tomb '37' and some of the coffins found inside, awaiting recording and photography.

Statuette of the boy Amenemheb from tomb '37'. This figure was found together with a larger wooden statue of his brother Huwebenef inside an anthropoid wooden coffin of early 18th Dynasty type belonging to a woman named Ahhotep Tanedjmet. The two statuettes lay to either side of the mummy's knees, underneath the shroud. That of Amenemheb shows the boy nude and holding a lotus flower in his left hand. The figure is a small masterpiece; it is solid cast in copper; details of the face carefully tooled after the metal had hardened; the lotus was added in silver. Both statuettes were mounted on wooden pedestals bearing inscriptions which give the names of the persons represented and add that the figures were made by their father Djehuty, presumably the husband of Ahhotep Tanedjmet. H. 15.5 cm.

Letter from Carter to Lord Carnarvon, 4 January 1913

... I started the excavations on the 1st and am now hard at it. I am clearing away the top layer (a very large area) so that next week I can put numbers of men on [to] trench down and find the head end of the court for eventual clearance down to oil level[?].

Have found at right angles to the Rameses IV colonnade three bases of Osirite pillars in sandstone which for the moment I am not quite clear as to what they are, but believe part of the Rameses IV construction.

A nice sandstone stela (late) has turned up and some interesting tally stones of Queen Hatshepsût, as well as the usual odd bits of blue from the Ptol. Tombs. Have 180 men and boys for the present and hope to get many more on next week ...

LEFT *Rishi* coffin from one of the intrusive burials found in tomb '41'. Carnarvon was embarrassed by the large quantity of coffins he discovered, and a number of them seems to have been sold or given away. This example is stylistically a hybrid, combining features of traditional *Rishi* coffins (the large wings painted on the lid which gave rise to the modern term, deriving from the Arabic word for 'feather') with those of the simpler type of coffin which superseded them (broad bands crossing at right angles on the lid and extending down the sides of the case; striped 'divine' wig). Quite exceptional is the decoration of the panels between the vertical bands on the case, which are filled with a motif usually used by Egyptian artists to represent sandy desert tracts. The base of the foot on the lid is decorated with a painting of Isis and Nephthys face to face with their arms raised in lamentation. The coffin was prefabricated and a blank space was left in the inscription for the insertion of the name of the eventual owner, in this instance a woman called Ta-iuwy. H. 185 cm.

ABOVE Fragment of a painted limestone stela belonging to a man named Intef. It was found in tomb '41' and perhaps formed part of the burial equipment of the original occupant. The finely carved figure of Intef is executed in raised relief, as is the text to his right. The horizontal inscription above is in sunk relief. On stylistic grounds the stela has been dated to the late 11th or early 12th Dynasty. H. 25 cm.

Ivory head and torso of a woman, from tomb '64' – a fine piece of small-scale composite sculpture, with the wig made from painted gypsum flecked with gold leaf. 13th Dynasty. H. 5.4 cm.

Female figurine of blue faience with hair, facial features and body ornaments in black, found by Carter and Carnarvon and probably dating to the 12th Dynasty. This statuette belongs to a category of figures frequently found in tombs, particularly in the Middle Kingdom, and as votive offerings to the goddess Hathor. As is often the case with statuettes of erotic significance, 'unessential' parts of the body such as the feet are not represented (an omission which, in this case, may also have been intended to deprive the figure of the power of movement), while prominence is given to the sex organs and to bodily adornments endowed with sexual significance – tattoos and girdles of beads or shells, both of which are depicted on this example. These figurines were erroneously identified by earlier scholars as depictions of dancers, prostitutes, harem women or concubines of the deceased. It is now recognised that, rather than representing particular individuals, they are embodiments of human sexual urges, buried with the dead to ensure them continued sexual activity and fertility in the afterlife. H. 8.5 cm.

Shaving set comprising a bronze mirror, razor and tweezers, and a whetstone, found in a basket in one of the chambers of tomb '37' in the Birabi. Among other items, the basket also contained a scarab with the names of Amenophis I. When found, the razor was so well preserved that the cutting edges were still sharp and the finger-prints of the last user visible on the polished surface. H. of mirror: 16.5 cm.

Carter, using his umbrella as a sunshade, supervising excavations in the Birabi area. The work of clearing the tombs was often exhausting and uncomfortable; Carter's patience and tenacity ensured that the maximum amount of archaeological information was salvaged even under difficult and dangerous conditions.

Although the principal results of Carter and Carnarvon's Theban excavations of 1907–11 were published in their *Five Years' Explorations at Thebes* (1912), work in the Asasif area continued until 1914. The discoveries of these later seasons were never fully published, although in many ways they were no less interesting than what had been found earlier. A large Middle Kingdom tomb with a pillared portico, numbered '41' by the excavators, had been disclosed in the 1911 season, but it was not until 1913 that it could be fully explored; it was found, like tomb '37', to have been reoccupied in the Second Intermediate Period and early 18th Dynasty. Adjoining this tomb to the east was another portico behind which were several further tombs. Top, workmen clear the corner of the courtyard with the façade of tomb '41' to the left and that of the eastern tombs ('64' and '63') to the right. Bottom, workmen carry a coffin out of tomb '64', followed by Carter and a colleague.

Letter from Lord Carnarvon to E. A. Wallis Budge, 14 March 1913

... I finished up at Luxor yesterday in a blaze of disaster, found really nothing and was in bed for the last week [with] a sort of influenza bronchitis, altogether a dreadful fiasco. I brought the [bronze] snake down yesterday to you. I have found about 3 good rishi (feathered) coffins one with a name on & rather curious scenes on the sides. I can sell it but I don't believe you have got one. If you want it I could I think get it for you but the trouble will be the transportation. It will all have to be waxed & I should propose taking it to pieces. The question is do you want it. I can get Carter to do it but it will be a good deal of trouble so if it comes to the B.M. a nice letter will have to be written to him ...

Castle Carter

As Chief Inspector of Antiquities for Upper Egypt, Howard Carter had occupied a house next to the temple at Medinet Habu and in a grand gesture from Maspero he was allowed to take up his residence there once again shortly after he had begun working for Lord Carnarvon. In 1910, however, with Lord Carnarvon's financial assistance and for their second joint season, he erected for himself a charming house at Elwat el-Diban (in translation the rather less appealing 'Mound of the flies') at the northern end of Dra Abu el-Naga. Lord Carnarvon had the bricks for the foundations produced at his Bretby works in England and shipped to Luxor.

Inscription impressed in bricks employed for the foundations of the house
Made at Bretby/England/for Howard Carter/A.D. Thebes 1910

Letter from Alan H. Gardiner, the philologist, to his wife Heddie, 4 October 1911
... By noon we had reached the new house that Carter had built for himself ..., and, it being very warm, we determined to call upon Carter and take drinks off him. I was glad to have an opportunity of looking over his house, which is quite delightful; simple mud walls, not rendered conspicuous by any plaster; very little furniture, but what there is artistic. In the middle is a little domed hall quite in the ancient Arabic style ...

Sakha, 1912

Despite their enormous successes, both Carnarvon and his excavator were becoming a little tired with the work at Thebes. They decided to broaden their outlook by extending their activities into the Delta from where, in recent years, increasing amounts of precious objects had been finding their way on to the antiquities market. The site Carnarvon and Carter chose was Sakha, ancient Xoïs. The season appears not to have been an altogether unqualified success, though the excavations were never published. No finds are known, but a few 'strays' seem to have found their way on to the market. The episode is notable primarily for the light a contemporary letter relating to the excavation sheds upon Lord Carnarvon's idea of 'roughing it' in the field.

By 1910 Carter's association with Carnarvon was firmly established. That winter a new excavation house was erected at the northern end of Dra Abu el-Naga, close to the site of the excavations in the Theban necropolis. This 'Castle Carter (II)' was designed by Carter himself, and some of the large bricks used in its construction were manufactured at a brickworks in England belonging to Lord Carnarvon. Perhaps inspired by the ancient Egyptian custom of stamping bricks with the name of the ruler responsible for a building, Carnarvon arranged that those made for Carter's house should bear an impressed legend. On the back of a photograph of the new house Carter's niece Phylis Walker, who visited him at Luxor in 1931, wrote a short description: '"La maison Cartaire"! showing front of house which looks toward Luxor. Left window, dining room; right, U.H.'s [Uncle Howard's] room; middle window, spare room; extreme left kitchen and servants quarters: the rest is desert!'.

Letter from Lord Carnarvon to Percy E. Newberry, 13 December 1911
... Since my wife phoned you I have had a letter from Carter. He tells me I have got the concession for Sakha ... Now I think we ought to begin ... not later than the 15th March – the climate should be all right then. When can you come out and would you start operations? ... I thought you might begin with 15 men and 15 boys picking up local boys to help carry. These men I presume you would get from Guft. I should come down then with my Gurnawis perhaps 20 of each. I personally think that the mixture of Guftis and Gurnawis would make for efficiency but I don't know what Carter would consider.

Another thing is that my wife proposes to come and camp out at Sakha. As at present constituted the camp would consist of

Lady C	1
Lord C	1
Mr Newberry	1
Mr Carter	1
Lady C's maid	1 possibly
Lord C's serv't	1 possibly
Doctor Johnson	1

7 tents besides at least 2 living tents and such things as 2 w.c.s, bath room, kitchen, &c &c, besides one or two native servants, a cook and washer up.

Should one have to buy beds &c would you go to Cook's and ask them to fit you out possibly and probably the latter plan would be the best. Money is scarce and a consideration and you must remember I pay Carter 200£ per mensem ...

Letter from Percy E. Newberry to Alan H. Gardiner, 25 December 1947
I visited [Sakha] twice in pre-war 1914–1918 days, the first time by myself and later with Carnarvon, Maxwell and Carter. If I remember rightly we estimated the mounds cover some 80 acres and in places they were 80 ft high. ... Carnarvon began digging there but we had to abandon the place on account of the numbers of cobras and cerastes [horned vipers] that infested the whole area ...

Tell el-Balamun, 1913

The disappointment of Sakha was not allowed to cloud Carnarvon and Carter's desire to establish an excavating foothold in the Delta and the following season they transferred their attention to Tell el-Balamun. Balamun, also known as Tell el-Ahmar ('The red mound') on account of the rich iron content of its soil, is an ancient settlement mound located 19 km from the Mediterranean coast and some 5 km to the west of the Damietta branch of the Nile. It is currently being excavated by the British Museum. Carter believed Balamun to be identical with the ancient Paiwenamun, capital of Smabehdet, the 17th Lower Egyptian nome. In 1913 in an attempt to prove his theory, he surveyed and superficially explored the site on behalf of Lord Carnarvon.

Letter from Carter to Mrs Newberry, 18 April 1913
... Here at Ballaman I am making an experimental dig to endeavour to find out something about [the site]. It certainly must have been an exceedingly important place – and I think there can be little doubt that it was 'Diospolis

Carter's local workforce equipped with pickaxes excavating 'Trench 7' at Tell el-Balamun in the northern Delta, 1913. In contrast to the custom in Upper Egypt peasant women regularly worked alongside men at sites in the Delta, a distinction which persists to the present day. At this part of the site, inside the massive temple enclosure, Carter found a building which he interpreted as a palace. Re-examination of the structure by a British Museum expedition in 1992 has established that it is actually a 26th Dynasty fort, similar to one found by Petrie at Naucratis and recalling Herodotus' account of the forts constructed by Psammetichus I (664–610 BC) to house his Greek mercenaries.

Parva'. The modern name suggests that it is a contraction of Bellad Amon (town of Amon) which seems in favour of the conjecture.

But up to the present I have been able to find but little, the ground being so hard and difficult to work. Still, from the fact of it being untouched, one is able to get a good idea of the plan and general formation of the ancient town and temple buildings ...

For camping it is very nice – we are in among the reeds and bullrushes [*sic*] where it swarms with warblers and other small birds. But bad for mosquitoes. It is beautifully cool even though at Cairo and still more in Upper Egypt there is great heat ...

The progress of Carter's work at the site, and the difficulties he encountered, are recorded in a letter written to Lord Carnarvon from 'Tell Ballaman – Ras El Khalig', on 17 April 1913.

My dear Lord Carnarvon

This site is certainly one of great interest and with great labour should produce rich results – but oh how laborious. Below the soft crust (about 75 c/ms) the ground is like that at Sakha, and only here and there is one able

By comparison with the rich haul of objects discovered in the Theban necropolis, finds at Tell el-Balamun were meagre. One of the few inscribed pieces to turn up was this fragment of a grey stone statuette dating to the Late Period and representing a man presenting a figure of Osiris. The inscriptions on the plinth which supported the divine figure are parts of prayers for offerings on behalf of the dedicator whose name is incompletely preserved (possibly Djehutyemsaef or Minemsaef). The sculpture is of importance on account of the references in its inscriptions to the gods Amun-Re, Lord of Smabehdet, and Osiris of Behdet foremost of 'The Porch of Lower Egypt' – significant evidence in favour of the identification of Tell el-Balamun with the ancient town of Smabehdet. H. 9.4 cm.

to detect the walls of the houses. In fact if it were not from the untouched upper surface one would not know what one was digging.

The mound is enormous – it covers over 130 acres. The enclosure or girdle wall of the temple and palace zone alone encloses over 38 acres. Outside of this enclosure seems to be the town or towns – for there are two high mounds (at the north end). One on each corner (E. and W.) ... The temple, which apparently was built of limestone, sandstone and granite, is [at] so low a level that the men, in digging, almost at once reach the shiny mud and water below, thus making it for the present impossible to investigate. It is with regret for I had hoped there to have found the name of the place by temple inscriptions, though I think there can be little doubt that it is really Diospolis Parva. The fact that this is the largest and most important mound in this neighborhood (sic) is certainly one point in its favour. And, that the modern name Ballaman could easily mean or be a contraction of Balled Amon (the town of Amon) is probably another reason in its favour. But I only hope that we get something more conclusive. The excavations have produced but little as yet.

In one place we found some Greco-Roman burials in the low lying ground

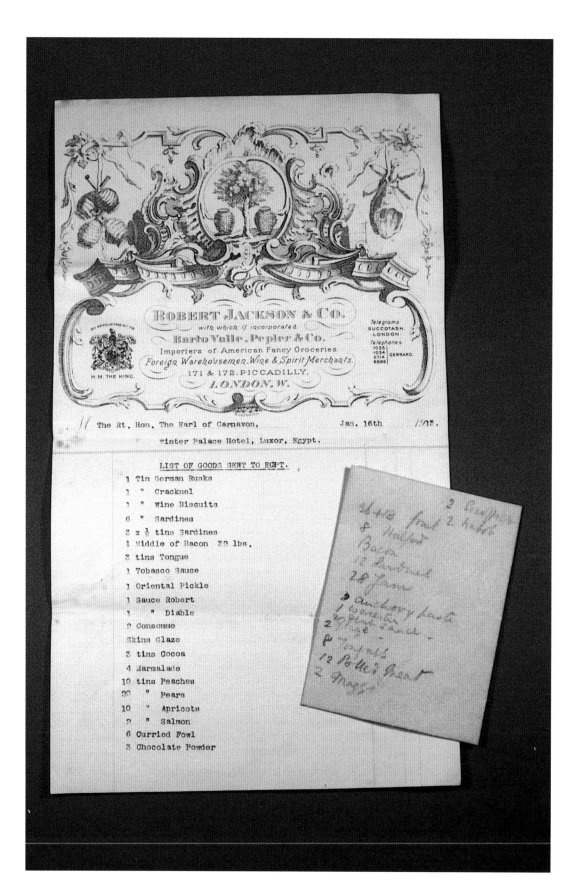

List of provisions ordered for Lord Carnarvon and his team of excavators at Tell el-Balamun, 1913. In place of the meagre rations he had been allotted at Amarna, Carter could now look forward to bacon, tongue, curried fowl and a selection of sauces and condiments.

RIGHT Two 'mosaic glass' rods, dating to the Ptolemaic or Roman Period, found at Tell el-Balamun. Rods such as these were built up from thin strands of differently coloured glass arranged so as to form a pattern or motif running through the section from end to end. Thin slices cut from the finished rod were used as inlays. The examples illustrated show a uraeus and a palace façade design. Max. H. 2.4 cm.

BELOW Two bracelets, decorated with uraeus serpents, which formed part of a hoard of base silver jewellery found in a pottery jar at Tell el-Balamun. Carter dated the group to the late Ptolemaic Period (305–30 BC), though it may be as late as Roman. It appears that the hoard had been hidden for safety and never subsequently recovered by its owner. Other pieces from the find are in Cairo and the Metropolitan Museum of Art; the two illustrated here were brought to light at Highclere Castle, where the residue of Lord Carnarvon's collection had remained after the sale of the principal pieces in 1926. Diam. 7.5 cm.

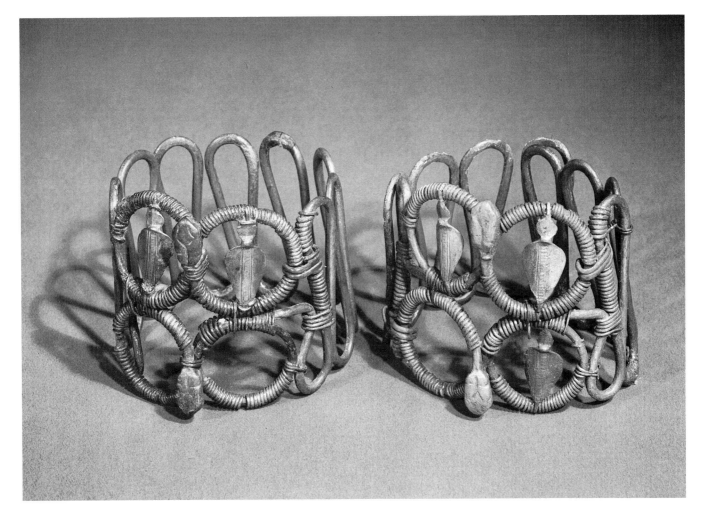

with pots similarly placed as at Birabi, one of which is quite nice in form (late Greek) and decorated.

In another spot (what I believe to be a detached house), in the centre of the temple enclosure, we found some fragments of sculpture (Ptolemaic) and some coins (Ptol: and Roman).

Another spot has produced two scarabs, some plaques, and amulets of the 26th Dyn. to Ptolemaic Period.

But as yet we have found nothing of real interest or value. Still it is hardly time yet to judge, and like all these Delta sites one may at any moment have a wonderful find. Still from [the] actual excavating point of view the periods between finds are exceedingly dull.

As regards labour, there is plenty here but the very worst. The people are *superficially* ignorant, know absolutely nothing of antiquities and their value or meaning, and are exceedingly lazy.

Maspero has behaved like a dog, and to start with stopped the work. It began thus:- Before leaving Cairo I asked him to inform the authorities here of your permit to dig. This he promised but did not do. Then when I telegraphed him on two occasions for the same, he calmly replied both to the authorities (police) and me that the tell Ballaman was not within the concession. And it was not until I sent Mansur to Cairo with a curt and 'direct to the point' letter [that] he gave me the necessary and proper orders and instructions to the officials here, making feeble and incorrect excuses to cover himself so apparent that even the natives were able to see through him. For the moment I appeared to be an imposter but now Maspero has become one and our position here elevated. I cannot make out Maspero now. He must be either mad or really dishonest. Even the dates on his letters are incorrect . . .

April 19th 1913. I kept the letter open in case there was any further news but I am sorry to say none . . .

I will continue another week and see if further chances may turn up. . . .

Collecting

Extract from an autobiographical sketch by Lord Carnarvon
. . . My chief aim was then, and is now, not merely to buy because a thing is rare, but rather to consider the beauty of an object than its pure historic value. Of course when the two, beauty and historic interest, are blended in a single object the interest and delight of possession are more than doubled . . .

Lord Carnarvon's excavations in Egypt were carried out with great professionalism, thanks to Carter's supervision, and the results of their collaboration represented an important addition to the body of exisiting knowledge about ancient Egypt. But Carnarvon was also a keen collector of antiquities and it is hardly surprising that several of the finer objects which were ceded to him as his 'share' in the official division of finds were welcomed as additions to his personal collection. Many of his finest pieces, however, were acquired through purchase. The buying and selling of antiquities, now forbidden by law within Egypt, was a commonplace and acceptable practice in the early years of the century. Antiquities dealers offered genuine pieces for sale and competition among prospective purchasers was often fierce. Here, too, Carter proved his skill, scouting the

Miniature vase of porphyritic diorite with two tubular handles, each of which is covered with a rectangular plate of gold foil decorated with an openwork cross. The vase dates probably to the 1st or 2nd Dynasty and is one of a small group of miniature vessels of similar type. Some of these are made of materials rarely used at so early a date, such as amethyst and obsidian, and most have ornamentation of sheet gold covering on the handles and sometimes the mouth. Three examples come from Abydos, but the majority, including this specimen from Lord Carnarvon's collection, have no recorded provenance. H. 5.9 cm.

Three jerboa mice, or desert rats, in white faience, represented with their tails curled over their backs and with paws raised to their mouths as if feeding. The details are in brown. These mice formed part of a large group of objects said to have been found in a vaulted brick tomb at el-Matariya, near Heliopolis, which was discovered by bedouin in about 1913. The objects (perhaps representing the equipment of several burials) passed into the hands of the Cairo antiquities dealer Maurice Nahman and many were bought by private individuals. Among the group were figurines of 'magical' significance: hippopotami, a frog and a female figurine similar to the one found by Carter and Carnarvon at Thebes (page 101). A dating to the 12th or 13th Dynasty seems likely. The function of the mice is not clearly understood but they may have served as symbols of the desert environment, the home of various creatures regarded by the ancient Egyptians as having magical properties which could be beneficial to both living and dead. H. 4 cm.

Gold statuette of the god Amun-Re, formerly in the Carnarvon collection and now in the Metropolitan Museum of Art, New York. This statuette may have served as the cult image in a temple or shrine, or as an offering of unusual richness. The god originally wore his distinctive cap-like headdress surmounted by tall plumes (now lost). He holds an *ankh* in his left hand, while his right, flexed across the breast, grasps a sickle-sword. The figure is one of the masterpieces of ancient Egyptian metalwork. The facial features were thought to resemble those of statues of king Tuthmosis III and, mainly on the strength of this, the figure was for many years assigned to the 18th Dynasty. The inclusion of a sickle-sword, however, points to a later – Third Intermediate Period – date, and the modelling of the body, kilt, divine beard and other features have clear parallels in the gold figures of Osiris and Horus which, with Isis, form part of a miniature triad dated to the reign of king Osorkon II of the 22nd Dynasty, now in the Louvre. The provenance of the Carnarvon figure is unknown, but there is a strong possibility that it originated in the temple of Amun at Karnak. H. 17.5 cm.

OPPOSITE Wooden figure of a man of high rank wearing a kilt with a triangular apron. The eyes are inlaid, and the kilt gilded over a layer of plaster. The figure originally wore a gilded collar which has all but disappeared. The legs are restored. It has been assigned to the 6th Dynasty, but a later dating is possible. H. (without legs) 21.5 cm.

Painted limestone head and shoulders from the statuette of a woman. With its vivid colours and attractive face this piece recalls the finest female statuary dating from the height of the Old Kingdom. In an account of the figure, published in 1917, Alan Gardiner ventured to describe it as 'assuredly one of the greatest achievements of Egyptian sculpture', and drew attention to the similarities the piece shared with sculptures such as the seated statue of Nofret from Meidum and the figure of Mycerinus' queen in the Museum of Fine Arts, Boston – although the Carnarvon piece is much smaller in size than both. In spite of the enthusiastic assessment of Gardiner and other scholars, doubts have been cast on the authenticity of the sculpture. As long ago as the 1920s H. E. Winlock asserted that the piece showed similarities to the work of Oxan Aslanian, the 'Berlin forger' and maker of some of the most convincing forgeries of Egyptian sculpture, while recent analyses of the colouring matter on the figure have revealed that all the pigments used (with the exception of the white) contain chemical elements not found in ancient paints. H. 24 cm.

OPPOSITE Page from the sumptuous manuscript catalogue of Lord Carnarvon's collection of Egyptian antiquities, written in Carter's hand and illustrated with his typically small and precise drawings.

antiquities markets and judiciously purchasing items which Carnarvon wanted. Carter was unique among Egyptologists of his day in being able to appreciate fully an object on two separate and quite distinct levels: as contexted artefact and as uncontexted work of art. For him there was no conflict between archaeology and connoisseurship and, from 1908 on, he bought and sold for Carnarvon as happily as he excavated for him, with great imagination and extraordinary results.

Extract from the text of a talk by the sixth Earl of Carnarvon, undated
... Carter suggested ... that some of the expenses of the work might well be defrayed by buying antiques in the bazaar in Cairo or elsewhere to sell them to collectors at a handsome profit! Carter proved very apt at this business and I have heard [my father and he] talk of many good deals that they brought off in this fashion ...

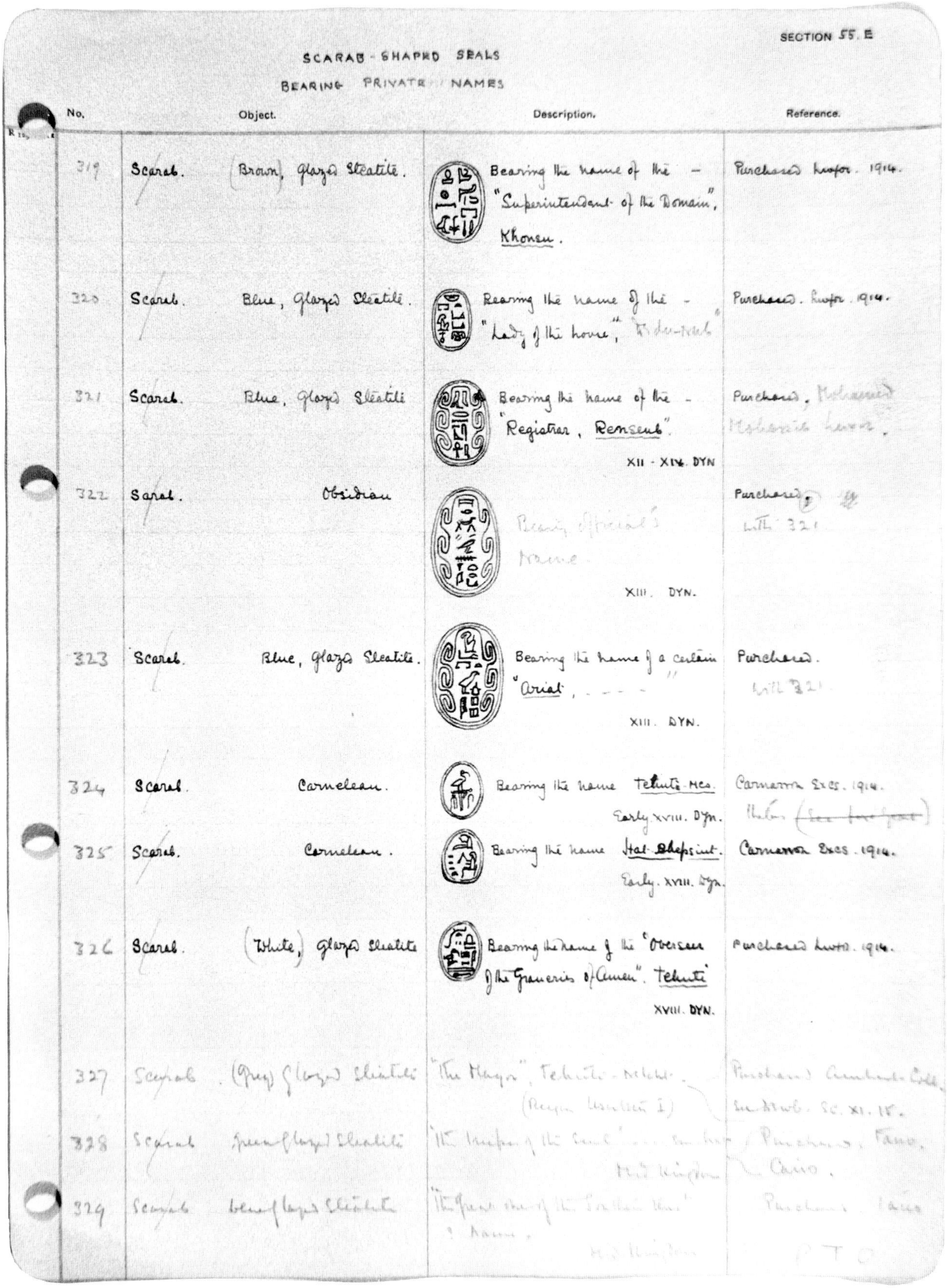

SCARAB - SHAPED SEALS

BEARING PRIVATE NAMES

No.	Object.	Description.	Reference.
319	Scarab. (Brown), glazed Steatite.	Bearing the name of the — "Superintendent of the Domain", Khonsu.	Purchased Luxor. 1914.
320	Scarab. Blue, glazed Steatite.	Bearing the name of the — "Lady of the house," ⟨name⟩	Purchased. Luxor. 1914.
321	Scarab. Blue, glazed Steatite	Bearing the name of the — "Registrar, Renseneb". XII - XIV. DYN	Purchased, Mohammed Mohassib Luxor.
322	Scarab. Obsidian	Bearing Official's name. XIII. DYN.	Purchased ⟨...⟩ with 321
323	Scarab. Blue, glazed Steatite.	Bearing the name of a certain "Ariat, ____ " XIII. DYN.	Purchased. with 321
324	Scarab. Carnelean.	Bearing the name Tehuti Mes. Early XVIII. Dyn.	Carnarvon Excs. 1914. Thebes ⟨...⟩
325	Scarab. Carnelean.	Bearing the name Hat Shepsut. Early XVIII. Dyn.	Carnarvon Excs. 1914.
326	Scarab. (White) glazed Steatite	Bearing the name of the "Overseer of the Graneries of Amen". Tehuti XVIII. DYN.	Purchased Luxor 1914.
327	Scarab. (Grey) glazed Steatite	"The Mayor", Tehuti-nekht. (Reign ⟨...⟩ I)	Purchased ⟨...⟩ Coll. Sn Nrwb. Sc. XI. 18.
328	Scarab	green glazed Steatite	"The ⟨...⟩ the ⟨...⟩" ⟨...⟩ Mid Kingdom	Purchased. Fano, ⟨...⟩ Cairo.
329	Scarab	⟨...⟩ glazed Steatite	"The ⟨...⟩ of the ⟨...⟩" ⟨...⟩ Amen. ⟨...⟩ Kingdom	Purchased. Cairo P T O

Faience chalice in the form of a blue lotus flower, decorated with scenes in relief, showing men and birds, cattle and ibexes and, below, scenes of boating in the papyrus marshes in which human figures are again juxtaposed with birds, cattle and an ibex. Below this latter scene the Nile is represented by a band of fish and a rippled motif denoting water. Chalices in the form of the blue lotus are attested from the beginning of the 18th Dynasty, but the variety with relief decoration dates to the 22nd Dynasty. This specimen, purchased by Carter for Carnarvon's collection, is one of the finest known. It is said to be from Tuna el-Gebel, the source of a number of similar examples. H. 14.5 cm.

OPPOSITE Ribbed cup of turquoise-blue glass, reputed to have come from Qurna, in the Theban necropolis. It was one of the treasures of Carnarvon's collection and is scarcely to be paralleled for the richness of its colouring. On stylistic grounds it has been attributed to the reign of Amenophis III. Diam. 11.5 cm.

Coloured glass inlay in the form of a falcon. This fine piece forms part of a group of inlays from Ashmunein (Hermopolis Magna) which seems originally to have been attached to a wooden shrine. The others include figures of deities in both human and bird forms, some of which probably formed an elaborate hieroglyphic writing of the names and titles of a king, perhaps Nakhthorheb (Nectanebo II of the 30th Dynasty). All are distinguished by extremely fine craftsmanship and detailed surface modelling. L. 30 cm.

Letter from Carter to the fifth Earl of Carnarvon, 21 October 1912

My dear Lord Carnarvon

From my wire of this morning you must be anxiously waiting for news. Well I think I may safely say that I have got for you three unique pieces, one of which is really superb. They are two carnelian and one agate Egyptian cameos of Amenhetep III. I should say without doubt from his tomb in the second Valley of the Kings (which as you know has never been properly cleared neither inside or out) and from what must have been a magnificent piece of jewelry ...

... also there is a kohl pot of Hatshepsût, which I had thrown in, of white arragonite (almost marble) and bearing her name and titles. It is about 3 inches high of seven cylinder form ... It is quite a good piece but not of great worth.

ABOVE Calcite kohl pot bought by Carter in Luxor together with the bracelet plaques. It comprises seven cylindrical cavities designed to hold a variety of different cosmetics and is inscribed with the name of Hatshepsut, preceded by the sacerdotal title 'God's Wife'. H. 6.5 cm.

RIGHT Carter's sketch of the bracelet plaques which he purchased for Lord Carnarvon's collection, as referred to in his letter of 21 October 1912. They are made from cornelian and sard (called 'agate' by Carter) and represent, from the top: a winged female sphinx supporting the cartouche of Amenophis III; the king enthroned under the dual canopy associated with the *Sed*-festival (a ritual renewal of kingship); and Amenophis with Queen Tiye, receiving the adoration of two princesses who shake *sistra* and proffer notched palm-ribs symbolising countless years. The plaques doubtless came from the trappings of a royal burial and Carter and Carnarvon believed they originated in the tomb of Amenophis III, where a fragment of a fourth (faience) plaque was recovered in February 1915.

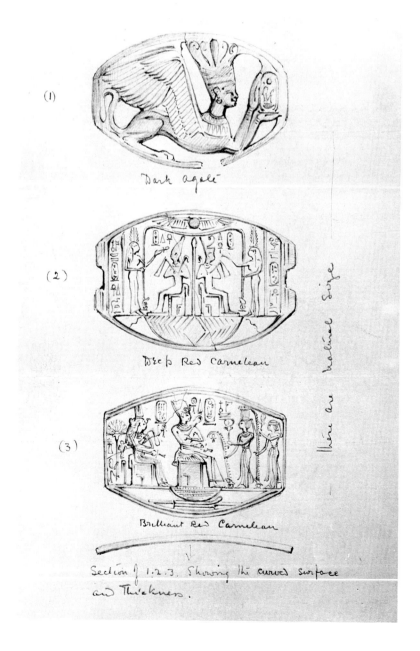

ABOVE Gold earring bearing the cartouche of Queen Tawosret of the 19th Dynasty, from tomb 56 in the Valley of the Kings. This small tomb was excavated by Edward Ayrton for Theodore Davis in 1908, and contained the remains of a burial much decomposed by water. The body, perhaps that of a child belonging to the family of Sety II, had been richly adorned with jewellery. This ring, probably pilfered by one of Davis' workmen, found its way into the possession of the Luxor antiquities dealer Mohammed Mohassib, who showed it to Carter (see Carter's letter to Carnarvon, 20 Nov. 1912, there called a hair-ring). Carnarvon did not purchase it and it was eventually bought by the British Museum. External diam. 2.4 cm.

Letter from Carter to Lord Carnarvon, 20 November 1912

My dear Lord Carnarvon

I had another look round the antiqua shops in Luxor yesterday – and there are certainly things of interest, though not exactly the kind of stuff you want ...

I find that Mohamed Mohassib has still that lion – the said sale was blarny – I told him to keep it until you came as I cannot make up my mind to buy it. I believe he will take 60–70£. He has a hair-ring (gold) from Davis' find. Good but nothing extraordinary. He declares that he is keeping it for you – I am going to have another good look and if second examination strikes well I shall take no risks and buy it. ...

Have been painting hard but without result. Messed the whole of my work and am no nearer than the day I came, which is very depressing. I fear the result of trying a new field of work.

My very best wishes to her Ladyship and yourself

Yours most sincerely

Howard Carter

Blanchard [a Cairo dealer] is in Luxor! I wonder what he is up to? ...

Letter from Carter to Lord Carnarvon, 29 November 1912

My dear Lord Carnarvon

I purchased for you yesterday a charming little head in dark green (?)basalt of either Amenhetep II or Thothmes IV. The enclosed photo is slightly smaller and really does not do it credit. Some say that it is of Thothmes III or Amenhetep III but I think that after comparing it with the known portraits of the above kings you will agree with me. ... It is I think the very thing you wanted and I do hope you will like it. ... I was so pleased to get Lady Carnarvon's wire – which means I conclude that you have received the cameos. I am in terrible agony here in the hands of a dentist. Have had but little sleep for a week ...

I gave Kyticas your present. He is quite pleased and wishes me to carry to you his gratitude and thanks. He has a shawabti figure in brown stone of what appears to [be the] age of the Khuenaten [Akhenaten] period – it is fine but not good enough for you. He asks 115£ and is keen that you should have it.

I shall buy nothing unless it is *very* fine but please tell me if I am over spending. Everybody (the dealers) are sick with me over the cameos and say that I paid far too much etc. etc. Nahman has some ivories which I am to see on Monday ...

With every good wish,

Yours very sincerely

Howard Carter

Head from a statuette of a king in basalt, purchased by Carter for Carnarvon's collection in November 1912. On stylistic grounds the piece can be dated with certainty to the 18th Dynasty, but there is no consensus among scholars as to which king it represents. Carter initially thought that it came from a figure of Amenophis II or Tuthmosis IV, but he subsequently asserted that it represented Amenophis I, claiming that it belonged to the same statue as fragments of a headdress found 'by Lord Carnarvon' in the tomb at Dra Abu el-Naga which Carter believed to be the sepulchre of that king. The evidence of the headdress fragments was later refuted and other royal candidates were proposed by experts such as Cyril Aldred, H.W. Müller and Jacques Vandier. H. 5 cm.

The antiquities Carter obtained for Carnarvon were added to the rapidly accumulating collection at Highclere Castle where they were catalogued and arranged by Carter during the summer months. Carter took his role as curator of Carnarvon's collection seriously and the catalogue volumes he produced in his neat and meticulous handwriting were embellished with attractive and detailed sketches of the objects and copies of their inscriptions. The prices paid by Lord Carnarvon for pieces he needed were, for the time, very high; because of an understandable wish for discretion, where quoted in the Carnarvon manuscript catalogue these prices were coded. The key to their code was the word REPUBLICAN, where R = 1, E = 2, P = 3, and so on. The £151 paid by Carter for the green stone head mentioned in the above letter, for example, was coded as RBR in Carter's catalogue entry for the piece.

Personalities

Carter's close and successful relationship with Lord Carnarvon merely highlights the difficulties he experienced with other workers in what was and still is a very small field. The following two extracts will illustrate Carter's propensity for taking against people for reasons real or imagined. Arthur Weigall, Carter's eventual successor as Chief Inspector of Antiquities of Upper Egypt, was a constant nuisance; the grudges held by the two went back to the Saqqara incident and before and would surface intermittently over the course of the next few years. The eminent English philologist Alan Gardiner was another with whom Carter was never able to feel fully at ease. Because of Gardiner's close friendship with Carnarvon, however, and his high academic standing – and influence – Carter could at this stage do little but put up with him. Indeed, Carter and Gardiner would work increasingly closely on the Tutankhamun discovery until a final rift in the 1930s.

Letter from Carter to Percy E. Newberry, 2 October 1909
... Weigall has behaved stupidly. My existence I fear will always be an irritation to him. Why I do not know for my intentions towards him have, I may say, always been to his welfare than otherwise ...

... I had [him] over to lunch with Gardiner (who by the by I am as a man much disappointed with). I gave Weigall a good quiet talking to in regard to his insinuations and accusations and I think his private feelings were somewhat uncomfortable ...

Letter from Carter to Percy E. Newberry, 27 October 1911
... Citoyen Gardiner is still here – the more I see of him the less I like him, and am even more sure that as far as any real friendship goes he is not to be trusted. Certainly, living alone as I do often is inducive to one letting the milk curdle, but to real friends I have never had that occur. Even forgive me if I warn you against him – I have already nearly punched his head for nasty insinuations against my friends ...

The tomb of Amenophis I and Ahmose-Nefertari, 1914

The burial place of Amenophis I, second king of the 18th Dynasty, had long been famous to Egyptologists from a passage in Papyrus Abbott, one of the most extraordinary of the so-called 'tomb-robbery papyri'. It records an official inspection of the royal tomb in Year 16 of Ramesses IX. The mummy of the king had been brought to light in 1881 in the well-known Deir el-Bahri cache, having been restored, recoffined and reburied during

Section of the Abbott Papyrus, in the British Museum, which contains an account of an official inspection of royal tombs in the Theban necropolis in the 16th regnal year of Ramesses IX. Among those investigated was that of Amenophis I, the location of which was described in some detail, partly by reference to a structure called the 'house of Amenophis of the Garden'. Arthur Weigall argued, somewhat unconvincingly, that the sepulchre should be identified with tomb KV39, south of the Valley of the Kings, but this explanation did not find universal support; Carter, for one, was convinced that the tomb lay elsewhere and over a period of several years he patiently gathered clues to its location.

the Third Intermediate Period. The precise location of the king's original tomb, however, had proved elusive, despite the testimony of Papyrus Abbott. It was the kind of loose end that Carter delighted in seeking to tie; but by 1914 he had been wrestling with the problem for several years, to little avail.

Letter from Carnarvon to E. A. Wallis Budge, 11 March 1914

I believe I really have found the tomb of Amenhotep I, at all events a great deal of inscribed stone and as to its being a Royal Tomb there is no possible doubt. Could you get one of your underlings to copy the passage in the Abbott Papyrus (about A[menhotep] 1st) in the hieroglyph & if you could just add the translation ...

From Carter's autobiographical sketches

About 1907, M. Seymour de Ricci obtained a part of the 'Book of the Dead' bearing the name of Amenophis I, which purported to have come from the King's tomb. Shortly afterwards I acquired from an antiquity dealer in Luxor two fragments of alabaster (calcite) vases with the names and titles of Amenophis I and Queen Ahmes.Nefert.âri engraved upon them. Despite the fact that they were but small fragments, they were to me of great interest. For, judging from similar specimens that I found in the tombs of Hat.shep.sût and Tuthmosis IV, they were obviously fragments of vases of a kind usual among the furnishings of the earlier Eighteenth Dynasty Royal Tombs. ...

Following a clue provided by an overseer who had formerly worked for the Antiquities Service, Carter instituted a search of the outlying valleys of Deir el-Bahri, though without success. The search waned until one balmy evening in the late spring of 1912, when Carter's interests were rekindled by the visit to his house of a local worker, Gad Hassan.

In 1912 a native of Luxor showed Carter fragments of calcite funerary vessels bearing the names of Amenophis I and his mother queen Ahmose-Nefertari. These came from a tomb at Dra Abu el-Naga; a preliminary investigation suggested that this might be the 'missing' tomb of Amenophis I and in 1914 Carter cleared it completely on behalf of Lord Carnarvon (to whom he tactfully gave the credit for the discovery). It had been plundered, but among the debris Carter found fragments of statuettes and of many more stone vessels similar to those which had led him to the spot. The photograph shows a modern reconstruction of one of the vessels, incorporating a fragment inscribed with the cartouche of Ahmose-Nefertari. H. 25 cm.

From Carter's autobiographical sketches

He professed to have some 'antiquas' to sell, and enquired whether I would like to see them. [Since] it was but a week since I had closed down Lord Carnarvon's excavations, the season's work being finished, ... I thought for the moment I had had enough of antiquities. Upon second thoughts, however, as I recognized the man, ... I replied '*Fadle* – Make yourself welcome – and show me what you have got!'

... He ... slowly opened his basket and displayed its contents: a number of splinters from funerary alabaster jars. The moment I saw them my curiosity was aroused. One by one he handed them to me, and ... I was able to see that many of them were engraved with the designations of Amenophis I and the Queen Mother Ahmes.Nefert.âri. They were almost replicas of the two pieces I had acquired formerly ... I thought to myself, 'Then it must be true! The local tomb-plunderers have found the King's tomb!'

I reflected, however, for a moment, then, after a little preliminary conversation, I ventured to ask him whence they came.

Carter's own photograph showing the location of the tomb he identified as that of Amenophis I and now listed as 'AN B'. The inscriptions on the jar fragments, and the fact that the tomb had apparently been enlarged to receive another body after the original burial suggest that Amenophis I and Ahmose-Nefertari were both buried there. The 'house of Amenophis of the Garden', mentioned in Papyrus Abbott can be plausibly equated with the *Meniset*, the funerary temple at the edge of the cultivation, which served the cult of both Amenophis I and his mother.

'Mîn el-gebel! – From the mountain!' . . .

'Most antiquities,' I remarked with a smile, 'come from the hills!'

'True,' he said, 'but these are unusual, they come from a large tomb! Ishtaree! – Buy them! . . . They truly come from a very large tomb in the hill!'

'In the hill!' I replied, – 'What hill?'

'El-Dirâ!' he remarked, while pointing over his shoulder towards the hill of Dirâ Abou'l-Neggâ. And then I found it very difficult to suppress my excitement.

Carter continued his questioning of the local digger and by degrees he learned that the tomb from which the fragments came stood quite alone, and that its entrance was hidden under a rock. More significantly, it had a well – the vertical shaft which was characteristic of royal tombs of the earlier New Kingdom. Carter offered Gad Hassan money if he would reveal the whereabouts of the tomb, and the opportunity of overseeing the work should he, Carter, decide to clear it on Lord Carnarvon's behalf. Carter was shown the prize.

Two faience mummy-amulets representing the goddess Sekhmet, found among the debris in tomb 'AN B'. In the period after the New Kingdom the tomb had been used for the burials of several non-royal individuals. These had subsequently been burnt and only small traces of coffins, *shabtis* and amulets such as these remained, dated by a small lapis-lazuli inlay bearing the cartouche of one of the Osorkon kings of the 22nd or 23rd Dynasty, which had probably been attached to an item of jewellery placed on one of the intrusive burials. Each, H. 4 cm.

From Carter's autobiographical sketches

I procured a few men, some rope and tackle, and in the afternoon set forth and descended that yawning shaft, which proved to be some twenty-five feet deep. At the bottom there were decided traces of recent digging. An immense boulder that had fallen from above blocked the greater part of the doorway opening into the first corridor, leaving but a small space at the side to squeeze through. Our candles but dimly lighting the way, we passed through into a narrow corridor partially filled with rubble, and half-way along it were two small chambers, one on each side, also filled with rubble. At the end of the corridor, about forty feet in length, we reached the brink of a great protective-well ... some twelve or more feet square, choked almost to the brim with desert-silt that had accumulated by the slow process of water pouring in from spates of centuries past. In the centre of the silt filling a deep hole bore evidence of the activities of my friend Gad Hassân and his accomplices, and from that excavation came the odour of soil thousands of years old. The atmosphere of the tomb was quietly full of the silent flittering of bats, which, though near at hand, were nowhere visible. An unpleasant sensation, since one felt every moment they would flutter into one's face ...

Opposite, on the further side from where we stood, the gleam from our candles was sufficient to disclose an opening to another corridor. We cautiously crossed the filling that choked the protective-well. The dried water-deposited silt crunched under our feet, and I was in fear lest the crumbling sides of the hole in the centre might give way and let us down into the yawning gap. Upon entering this second corridor I noticed that it deviated to the left and that its ceiling was low. And then, suddenly, something moved. I perceived two eyes like balls of fire, [and] a terrific screech broke the silence. We had disturbed an eagle-owl, and at our approach it made one dash for liberty, knocking out our candle as it passed ... We were in darkness save for a beam of daylight in the far distance that glimmered down the entrance-shaft.

While Gad Hassân cursed the forebears of the owl, I recovered my wits, struck a match and re-lit our candles. We moved along the corridor for about twenty-five feet, where it emerged into a low spacious pillared hall, some forty feet in length and twenty-odd feet wide. It was bare and empty save for broken and shrivelled members of mummies partially buried in the rubbish strewn over the floor. ...

Carter's clearance of the tomb, on behalf of Lord Carnarvon, took place the following winter, 1914.

From Carter's autobiographical sketches

... The clearance was systematic: beginning from outside the entrance-shaft and ending in the innermost chamber. Each basket of rubbish as it came up was sifted for what it might contain.

... Although there were no inscriptions upon its walls to verify it as being the sepulchre of Amenophis I, it may be affirmed that it was the tomb for which we had been in search. All that was left of its original equipment were debris of stone-vessels and statuettes wrought in alabaster (calcite), green felspar, white and yellow limestone, a red conglomerate, serpentine and basalt. These fragments were scattered in the rubbish outside its adit, in the lowest part of the entrance-shaft, on the floors of the interior, and at

Faces broken from wooden *shabtis* of Amenophis III, found during Carter's excavations at the king's tomb. Numerous *shabti* fragments came to light, in a variety of materials (wood, stone and faience) and representing the king wearing different headdresses and equipped with various royal attributes.

Calcite foot of a *shabti* of queen Tiye, wife of Amenophis III, an object found during Carter's clearance of the king's tomb. This was one of the pieces which led Carter to conclude – mistakenly it now seems – that the queen had been buried in the tomb together with her husband. H. 4.7 cm.

the bottom of the protective-well. Among fifty-four individual stone-vessels that could be partially reconstructed or recognized from the various fragments, nine were inscribed with the prenomen and nomen of Amenophis I; eight of them bore the name and titles of the Queen Mother, Ahmes. Nefert.âri; three bore the name of King Ahmes (Amasis I), the father of Amenophis I; and one was inscribed with the cartouches of the Hyksos King Apepi, together with the cartouche of his daughter, Herath, hitherto unknown. There is little doubt as to whom the tomb belonged. Its position coincides with the one mentioned in the Papyrus Abbott. The names of those patron saints, Ahmes.Nefert.âri and Amenophis, coincide with what one would expect to find from the evidence manifested by the mortuary temple discovered on the fertile plain. The plan of the tomb agrees with the plan of the early Eighteenth Dynasty hypogeum....

Carter's identification of the tomb has not been accepted in all quarters and in some details of his reconciliation of the Papyrus Abbott description and the topographical situation of the tomb, his elaborate published analysis is undoubtedly open to question. In his overall conclusions, however, the likelihood must be that he was correct: that this, the extended and adapted tomb of Queen Ahmose-Nefertari, was the burial place of Amenophis I and was the tomb examined by the burial commission during the reign of Ramesses IX.

Digging at the tomb of Amenophis III, 1915, and war-work

Shortly before his death, Davis, the aged American amateur whom Carter had so enthusiastically encouraged while Chief Inspector at Luxor, gave up his concession to excavate in the Valley of the Kings. The way was open at last to Lord Carnarvon, whose long-standing enthusiasm for royal tombs had been newly whetted by Carter's recent clearance of the tomb of Amenophis I and Ahmose-Nefertari at Dra Abu el-Naga. But the timing could have been better: the world was at war and the opportunities for

Objects from the foundation deposits discovered by Carter in 1915 at the entrance to the tomb of Amenophis III in the West Valley of the Kings. They include miniature tools and pottery vessels and small blue faience plaques. The latter bore the names of Tuthmosis IV, father of Amenophis III, and indicate that the construction of the tomb had begun in the reign of the elder king. For reasons now unknown, Tuthmosis was ultimately buried in the main Valley, in the tomb which Carter had cleared in 1903, while the sepulchre in the West Valley was taken over by Amenophis III.

archaeological work were restricted. The best that Carter could manage, in between war-work in Cairo, was a month's clearance at the tomb of Amenophis III in the West Valley of the Kings – a tomb high on the Carnarvon list of priorities ever since Carter's purchase of the three exquisite bracelet plaques of the king in October 1912.

Carter in The Tomb of Tut.ankh.Amen, I

... War-work claimed most of my time for the next few years, but there were occasional intervals in which I was able to carry out small pieces of excavation. In February, 1915, ... I made a complete clearance of the interior of the tomb of Amen.hetep III, partially excavated in 1799 by M. Devilliers, one of the members of Napoleon's 'Commission d'Égypte', and re-excavated later by Mr. Theodore Davis. In the course of this work we made the interesting discovery, from the evidence of intact foundation-deposits outside the entrance, and from other material found within the tomb, that it had been originally designed for Thothmes IV, and that Queen Tyi had actually been buried there ...

Shortly after his work at the tomb of Amenophis III came to a close, Carter was drawn into the general mobilisation for the war against Germany and her allies. His position, which carried no military rank, was with the British Intelligence Department in Cairo.

During the years of the First World War Carter still found time to engage in copying work. In 1916 he agreed to supply for Alan Gardiner pencil copies of the reliefs and inscriptions in the temple of Luxor showing the procession at the Opet festival, in which the cult images of Amun, Mut and Khonsu travelled in their divine barques from their shrines at Karnak to the temple of Luxor. The reliefs, full of interesting detail, are located on the walls of the colonnade south of the first court of the temple. The carving of them was apparently begun under Amenophis III, but was not completed until the reign of Tutankhamun, and the work was subsequently usurped by Horemheb. The copies show that Carter's skills as a draughtsman were still as sharp as they had been during his work at Deir el-Bahri twenty years before. This section shows a detail of the elaborate escort of the barques, including soldiers carrying military standards, and musicians playing lutes and clappers. By spring 1917 Carter had produced copies sufficient to occupy fifteen plates of the lavish publication which Gardiner had in mind and the philologist, delighted with the results, began to suggest other tasks with which Carter could occupy his time. But, although Carter was paid for the work, he was ever mindful that Lord Carnarvon was his true employer. Perhaps unsettled by Gardiner's increasingly importunate suggestions, he abandoned the copying of the Opet scenes and the projected publication never appeared.

Letter from Carter to Albert M. Lythgoe, curator of Egyptian Art at the Metropolitan Museum of Art, 4 June 1915
... I am a fixture here [in the Intelligence Department] for the summer and possibly longer – we must all do the best in the terrible struggle – to win we shall even if the last drop of blood is necessary ... [I]t is up to us all to do something ...

Carter's 'something' may have included a little selective demolition work, carried out with explosive (a substance with which he had gained a useful acquaintance while working for Naville at Deir el-Bahri). Carter, at least, was for many years the prime suspect for the following 'action' recorded by Somers Clarke, British architect and archaeologist.

Letter from Somers Clarke to E. A. Wallis Budge, 4 November 1915
... In these doleful days there is not often to be told news even of a slightly satisfactory nature but I have learnt one little bit that may please you. Possibly you may know it already. You remember that ugly ridiculous red abomination [the German dig-house] emblematical of German pushful vulgarity which stands – stood – behind the Ramesseum at Thebes. It stands no more. I arrived at Luxor last week and stayed there a day or two whilst the house at El Kab was being dusted. Then I heard that the thing had vanished ...

As it progressed the war seems to have disrupted Carter's life much less than others, leaving him with abundant free time to pursue his pottering for Lord Carnarvon and, in the drawing work alluded to in the following extract, to Alan Gardiner's commissioned copies of the Opet scenes of Amenophis III, Tutankhamun and Horemheb in the temple of Luxor. The pre- and post-Amarna pharaohs were again rearing their heads to tempt him for the future.

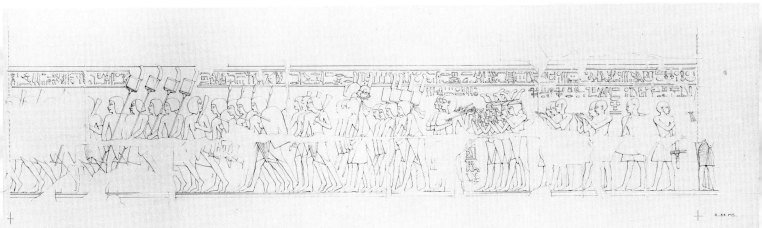

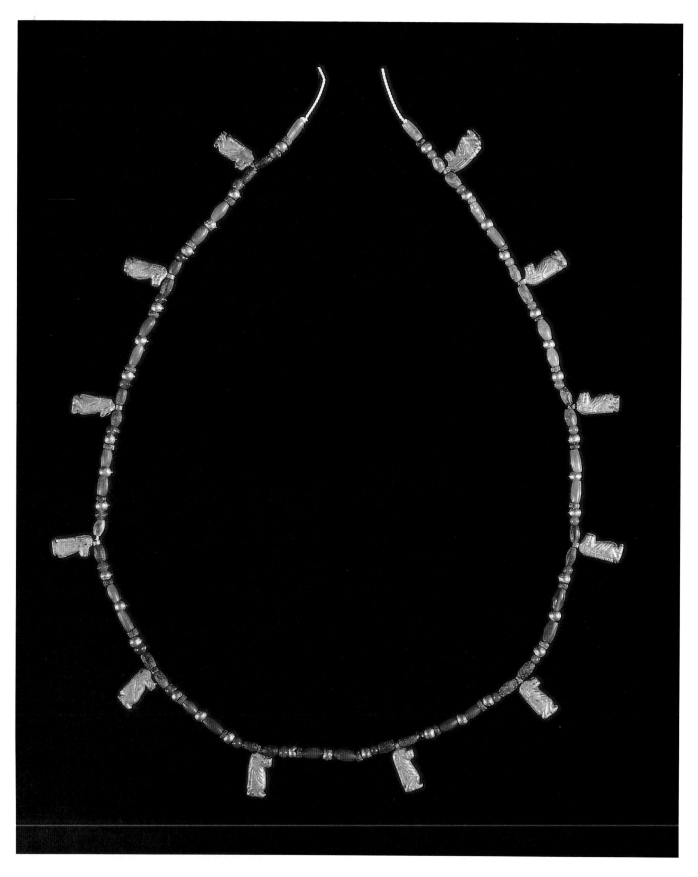

In 1916 an important royal tomb was discovered by natives of Luxor. It was the burial place of three minor wives of Tuthmosis III and, by a fortunate chance, it had been overlooked by ancient plunderers. Though the burials had been badly damaged by water, a rich haul of funerary trappings was recovered and soon appeared on the antiquities market. Through Carter's efforts to obtain the remnants, most of this 'Treasure of the Three Princesses' (as it is popularly known) eventually entered museums, while a few pieces surfaced in private collections. The necklace opposite, probably from this tomb, is composed of beads of gold, cornelian and lapis lazuli interspersed with sheet-gold pendants in the form of the hippopotamus goddess Taweret. Amulets representing this goddess, whose role involved the protection of women in childbirth, occur frequently from the New Kingdom onwards and gold figures similar to those illustrated formed part of other items, of jewellery from the 'Princesses'' tomb. The group of beads and pendants from the tomb, including gold *nefer* signs and an inlaid gold drop-shaped pendant, have been restrung as a necklace in recent years (right). The beads are made from gold, cornelian, jasper, lapis lazuli, blue glass and green feldspar; most are spherical or barrel-shaped, while others represent nasturtium seeds. L. (opposite) 52.5 cm; L. (right) 65.5 cm.

Letter from Carter to Mrs Newberry, 20 October 1917
... at present I am nearly dotty. They don't or won't give me any more war work in Cairo. So here I am [in Luxor]. Glad to say well occupied with drawing and painting ...

The cliff-tomb of Hatshepsut and other discoveries, 1916–22

Over the years, Carter had taken every opportunity to explore the remoter wadis of western Thebes in search of evidence of human activity, revelling in their solitude and natural beauty. He poked and pried where few had gone before, noting graffiti and possible hidden tombs. These forays sometimes led to confrontations with inhabitants of the west bank whose motives for investigating the ancient necropoleis were of a more mercenary nature. Carter's fearless personality has already been noted in connection with the investigations into the robbery in the tomb of Amenophis II. His bravery finds further testimony in this account of his 'reclamation' from robbers of the cliff-tomb prepared for Queen Hatshepsut.

Carter in The Tomb of Tut.ankh.Amen, I
... The absence of officials owing to the war, to say nothing of the general demoralization caused by the war itself, had naturally created a great revival of activity on the part of the local native tomb-robbers, and prospecting parties were out in all directions. News came into the village one afternoon

The tomb in the Theban necropolis prepared for Queen Hatshepsut as wife of Tuthmosis II. This remote and inaccessible sepulchre was cut 70 m high, in a narrow cleft in the vertical cliff-face (visible as a dark shadow in the centre of the picture) in the Wadi Sikket Taqet Zaid. In 1916 Carter was informed that local villagers had discovered the tomb; alone and unarmed, he climbed down the cliff by means of a rope, confronted the eight robbers in the tomb and persuaded them to leave. A formal clearance of the tomb followed, but it proved to contain only an unfinished sarcophagus. After her elevation to the status of king, Hatshepsut had abandoned the cleft-tomb and apparently planned to be buried in the sepulchre of her father, Tuthmosis I, where a new sarcophagus was installed to receive her mummy.

that a find had been made in a lonely and unfrequented region on the western side of the mountain above The Valley of the Kings. Immediately a rival party of diggers armed themselves and made their way to the spot, and in the lively engagement that ensued the original party were beaten and driven off, vowing vengeance.

To avert further trouble the notables of the village came to me and asked me to take action. It was already late in the afternoon, so I hastily collected the few of my workmen who had escaped the Army Labour Levies, and with the necessary materials set out for the scene of action, an expedition involving a climb of more than 1,800 feet over the Kurna hills by moonlight. It was midnight when we arrived on the scene, and the guide pointed out to me the end of a rope which dangled sheer down the face of a cliff. Listening, we could hear the robbers actually at work, so I first severed their rope, thereby cutting off their means of escape, and then, making secure a good stout rope of my own, I lowered myself down the cliff. Shinning down a rope at midnight, into a nestful of industrious tomb-robbers, is a pastime which at least does not lack excitement. There were eight at work, and when I reached the bottom there was an awkward moment or two. I gave them the alternative of clearing out by means of my rope, or else of staying where they were without a rope at all, and eventually they saw reason and departed. The rest of the night I spent on the spot, and, as soon as it was light enough, climbed down into the tomb again to make a thorough examination.

The tomb was in a most remarkable situation. Its entrance was contrived in the bottom of a natural water-worn cleft, 130 feet from the top of the cliff, and 220 feet above the valley bed, and so cunningly concealed that neither from the top nor the bottom could the slightest trace of it be seen. From the entrance a lateral passage ran straight into the face of the cliff, a distance of some 55 feet, after which it turned at right angles, and a short passage, cut on a sharp slope, led down into a chamber about 18 feet square. The whole place was full of rubbish from top to bottom, and through this rubbish the robbers had burrowed a tunnel over 90 feet long, just big enough for a man to crawl through . . .

Carter and his men spent an exhausting twenty days clearing the tomb, hoisting themselves up to the entrance on ropes. 'It was not a very comfortable operation even then', Carter recalled, 'and I personally always made the descent in a net'.

Carter in The Tomb of Tut.ankh.Amen, I

Excitement among the workmen ruled high as the work progressed, for surely a place so well concealed must contain a wonderful treasure, and great was their disappointment when it proved that the tomb had neither been finished nor occupied. The only thing of value it contained was a large sarcophagus of crystalline sandstone, like the tomb, unfinished, with inscriptions which showed it to have been intended for Queen Hat.shep.sût. Presumably this masterful lady had had the tomb constructed for herself as wife of King Thothmes II. Later, when she seized the throne and ruled actually as a king, it was clearly necessary for her to have her tomb in The Valley like all the other kings . . . and the present tomb was abandoned . . .

Towards the end of October 1918, Carter got wind of a second tomb deep in the

Theban cliffs, brought to light quite by chance by Emile Baraize of the Cairo Museum. Carter vents his fury in a letter to Lord Carnarvon shortly after hearing of the find.

Letter from Carter to Lord Carnarvon, 25 October 1918

My dear Lord Carnarvon

... A new tomb has been discovered ... in the new site behind and west of the mountain. Actually, quite close to Hatshespuit's tomb in Wady E'Taqa E'Zeide, between Nos. 25 & 28 marked on our survey ...; to which hangs an extraordinary piece of luck. Though I hadn't actually got windward of it, I think that in two more days I would have, for I was beginning to get on the track; but that is neither here nor there; it is the following which is the knockout:- Baraize, who is working in Nubia on some reparation work, came down for a day, to see – for the first time, not even knowing the locality nor the site at all – what would be required for the eventual removal of Hatshepsuit's sarcophagus. He, guided by the Service's ghaffirs, when approaching Hatshepsuit's tomb, or rather the cliff in which it is hidden, came suddenly upon a suspicious group (eight in number) of natives resting in an alcove in the cliff – they apparently just as surprised as he. He questioned them as to what their business was there, and not getting satisfactory answers, followed up their tracks to a crag above, where he found traces of digging and a newly discovered tomb that they had been endeavouring to open. Over the tomb he very rightly placed his ghaffirs, took the names of the arabs, and having seen the whereabouts and conditions of Hatshepsuit's tomb, left, to return to Nubia – he reporting to the police, who since have arrested the men – those foolish diggers! And to think of it – never there before in his life – only there for a space of twenty minutes, and to walk into a thing like that – what extraordinary luck!

Though I have not seen the tomb, and for reasons kept away from it, from various reports it appears to be of pit-tomb type, hidden in a crag, heavily caked up with water deposit, and towards the bottom of the shaft (as far as the men had got) carefully blocked with heavy stones. Now that it is too late, they ... come and appeal to me, but little can I do, beyond, what I should like to do, give them a thrashing until they howled – the devils!! ...

What appears to have been a third tomb discovered and exploited by the locals around the same time was the 'Tomb of the Three Princesses'. This new sepulchre had been the burial place of three royal women – Menhet, Merti and Menwi – of the court of Tuthmosis III of the 18th Dynasty. They had been interred with a rich panoply of funerary equipment: gold headdresses, collars, gold-mounted heart-scarabs, finger rings and other jewellery, gold sandals, calcite canopic jars and a whole range of vessels in hard and soft stones and in glass. Carter, appreciating the importance of the find, did what he could to track down on the Luxor antiquities market as much as possible of the plundered burial equipment, which is now housed in the Metropolitan Museum of Art, New York, the Musée du Louvre in Paris, the British Museum in London and elsewhere. Though the robbery of such a splendid tomb is to be deplored, it is thanks to Carter's diligence that so much of the archaeological integrity of the find could be salvaged.

4

The Search for Tutankhamun
'Something good'

The search begins

There were by the start of Carnarvon's excavations in 1915 few gaps in the list of pharaohs thought to have been buried in the Valley of the Kings: the missing included the enigmatic Smenkhkare; his successor, the equally obscure Tutankhamun; and Ramesses VIII. Only for Tutankhamun had any indications of a burial in the Valley come to light.

Carter in The Tomb of Tut.ankh.Amen, I
Ever since my first visit to Egypt in 1890 [*sic*] it had been my ambition to dig in The Valley, and when, at the invitation of Sir William Garstin and Sir Gaston Maspero, I began to excavate for Lord Carnarvon in 1907 [*sic*], it was our joint hope that eventually we might be able to get a concession there ...

Mr. Theodore Davis, who still held the concession, had already published the fact that he considered The Valley exhausted, and that there were no more tombs to be found, a statement corroborated by the fact that in his last two seasons he did very little work in The Valley proper ... We remembered, however, that nearly a hundred years earlier Belzoni had made a similar claim, and refused to be convinced. We had made a thorough investigation of the site, and were quite sure that there were areas, covered by the dumps of previous excavators, which had never been properly examined ... At the risk of being accused of *post actum* prescience, I will state that we had definite hopes of finding the tomb of one particular king, and that king Tut.ankh.Amen.

To explain the reasons for this belief of ours we must turn to the published pages of Mr. Davis's excavations. Towards the end of his work in The Valley he had found, hidden under a rock, a faience cup which bore the name of Tut.ankh.Amen. In the same region he came upon a small pit-tomb, in which were found an unnamed alabaster statuette, possibly of Ay, and a broken wooden box, in which were fragments of gold foil, bearing the figures and names of Tut.ankh.Amen and his queen. On the basis of these fragments of gold he claimed that he had actually found the burial place of Tut.ankh.Amen. The theory was quite untenable ... Obviously, the royal material found in it had been placed there at some later period, and had nothing to do with the tomb itself.

Some little distance eastward from this tomb, he had also found in one of his earlier years of work (1907–8), buried in an irregular hole cut in the side of the rock, a cache of large pottery jars, with sealed mouths, and hieratic inscriptions upon their shoulders.... Mr. Davis refused to be interested in them, and they were laid aside and stacked away in the storeroom of his Valley house. There ... Mr. Winlock noticed them, and immediately recognized their importance. ... There were clay seals, some bearing the name of

Tut.ankh.Amen and others the impression of the royal necropolis seal, fragments of magnificent painted pottery vases, linen head-shawls – one inscribed with the latest known date of Tut.ankh.Amen's reign – floral collars, . . . and a mass of other miscellaneous objects; the whole representing, apparently, the material which had been used during the funerary ceremonies of Tut.ankh.Amen, and afterwards gathered together and stacked away with the jars.

We had thus three distinct pieces of evidence . . . which seemed definitely to connect Tut.ankh.Amen with this particular part of The Valley. To these must be added a fourth. It was in the near vicinity of these other finds that Mr. Davis had discovered the famous Akh.en.Aten cache [tomb KV 55] . . .

By 1915 Lord Carnarvon had obtained the concession to excavate in the Valley of the Kings, retaining the services of Howard Carter as supervisor of the excavations. Theodore Davis had declared that nothing further was to be found in the Valley, but Carter, undeterred, worked for season after season, systematically digging down to bedrock in areas he thought likely to contain a tomb. From the beginning he was convinced that the tomb of Tutankhamun lay hidden somewhere in the Valley; one of the main pieces of evidence in favour of this view was a cache of pottery vessels – one of which is illustrated – found by Davis in 1907, in a small tomb now numbered KV 54. The American Egyptologist Herbert Winlock recognised that among this material were items left over after the embalming and funeral ceremonies of Tutankhamun – a certain indication that he was buried nearby. It now appears that the materials found in tomb 54 had originally been placed in the entrance passage to Tutankhamun's tomb and had been removed and buried in the pit following the first ancient robbery of the king's sepulchre. H. 25.9 cm.

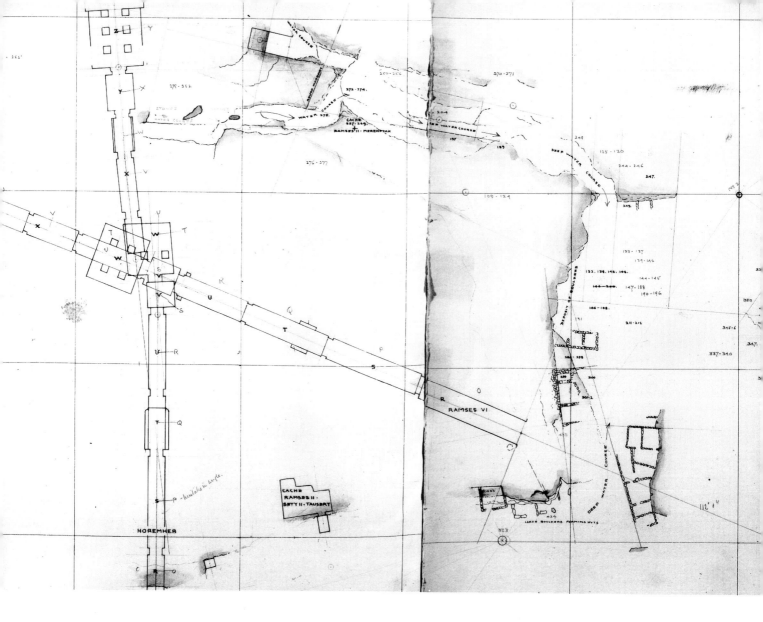

Valley of the Kings, 1917–22

Apart from vague plans to extend their work to Middle Egypt (notably Amarna) and a brief trial season at Meir in 1918/19, Carter's efforts for Carnarvon would be concentrated for the next years on the royal Valley. The search for Tutankhamun was on. The work was to be carried out systematically, clearing away the massive mounds of chippings produced during the ancient quarrying of the tombs, to reveal bedrock below. Carnarvon and Carter left nothing to chance: they were determined that if there was anything at all to be found it would not escape them.

Letter from Pierre Lacau, Director-General of the Antiquities Service, to Carter, 8 April 1918
... I entirely approve your plan for work in the Valley of the Kings. By laying bare the rock in large areas no tomb entrance can escape you ... Your project for a complete plan is naturally essential, and will be an important part of your work ...

Carter in The Tomb of Tut.ankh.Amen, I
... In the autumn of 1917 our real campaign in The Valley opened. The difficulty was to know where to begin, for mountains of rubbish thrown out by previous excavators encumbered the ground in all directions, and no sort of record had ever been kept as to which areas had been properly excavated and which had not. Clearly the only satisfactory thing to do was to dig

In 1917, after delays and interruptions caused by the First World War, Carter was able to commence work in the main Valley of the Kings. In order to make a systematic search he drew up a detailed map, on which he marked every area investigated and the exact find-spot of each object excavated. Ironically, for the first seasons this painstaking approach was rewarded by very few finds. The section of the map illustrated here shows, on the extreme right, the 'Amarna Cache' (KV 55) and, in the centre, the tomb of Ramesses VI, below the entrance to which lay that of Tutankhamun.

RIGHT Limestone ostracon with a sketch showing a king spearing a lion. This was one of the few objects of interest discovered by Carter in the Valley of the Kings before the tomb of Tutankhamun was located in 1922. The king, wearing the Red Crown of Lower Egypt, dressed in a tunic and kilt and accompanied by a dog, delivers the *coup de grâce* to a lion already wounded with arrows. The drawing is executed in red and black ink and can be dated on stylistic grounds to the 19th or 20th Dynasty. Hieratic inscriptions on the front and back of the piece contain extravagant praise of the king who, however, is not identified. H. 12.5 cm.

Ostracon showing a cockerel (Red Jungle Fowl). This sketch on a fragment of limestone, found in the Valley of the Kings during Carter and Carnarvon's 1920–21 season, shows a bird which must have been a great rarity in ancient Thebes; the cockerel's natural habitat was India and Malaya, and it was not introduced into Egypt until a relatively late date. A reference in the Karnak 'Annals' of Tuthmosis III, however, mentions that 'four birds which give birth (i.e. lay eggs) every day' were presented to the king as tribute from an unidentified region of Syria-Palestine, and from this it may be supposed that small numbers of cocks and hens were kept as curiosities; the sketch, drawn by one of the workmen employed on the construction of the royal tombs of the New Kingdom, was probably done from life, and is perhaps the earliest surviving depiction of a cockerel from ancient Egypt. H. 15.7 cm.

systematically right down to bed-rock, and I suggested to Lord Carnarvon that we take as a starting-point the triangle of ground defined by the tombs of Rameses II, Mer.en.Ptah, and Rameses VI, the area in which we hoped the tomb of Tut.ankh.Amen might be situated.

It was rather a desperate undertaking, the site being piled high with enormous heaps of thrown-out rubbish, but I had reason to believe that the ground beneath had never been touched, and a strong conviction that we should find a tomb there. In the course of the season's work we cleared a considerable part of the upper layers of this area, and advanced our excavations right up to the foot of the tomb of Rameses VI. Here we came on a series of workmen's huts, built over masses of flint boulders, the latter usually indicating the near proximity of a tomb. Our natural impulse was to enlarge our clearing in this direction, but by doing this we should have to cut off all access to the tomb of Rameses above, to visitors one of the most popular tombs in the whole Valley. We determined to await a more convenient opportunity. So far the only results from our work were some ostraca, interesting but not exciting.

We resumed our work in this region in the season of 1919–20. Our first need was to break fresh ground for a dump, and in the course of this preliminary work we lighted on some small deposits of Rameses IV, near the entrance to his tomb. The idea this year was to clear the whole of the remaining part of the triangle already mentioned, so we started in with a

Discovery of a cache of thirteen calcite jars at the entrance to the tomb of Merenptah in the Valley of the Kings. This find, made on 26 February 1920, so inspired Lady Carnarvon (not noted for her interest in Egyptology) that she insisted on digging the jars out of the ground herself. Some of the vessels bore hieratic texts indicating that they had held oils used at the funeral of Merenptah.

fairly large gang of workmen. By the time Lord and Lady Carnarvon arrived in March the whole of the top debris had been removed, and we were ready to clear down into what we believed to be virgin ground below. We soon had proof that we were right, for we presently came upon a small cache containing thirteen alabaster jars, bearing the names of Ramesses II and Mer.en.Ptah, probably from the tomb of the latter. As this was the nearest approach to a real find that we had yet made in The Valley, we were naturally somewhat excited, and Lady Carnarvon, I remember, insisted on digging out these jars – beautiful specimens they were – with her own hands.

With the exception of the ground covered by the workmen's huts, we had now exhausted the whole of our triangular area, and had found no tomb. I was still hopeful, but we decided to leave this particular section until, by making a very early start in the autumn, we could accomplish it without causing inconvenience to visitors ...

We had now dug in The Valley for several seasons with extremely scanty

One of the calcite jars from the cache found outside the tomb of Merenptah. The handles are in the form of ibex-heads. It was originally decorated and bore two hieratic dockets, one of them the king's name. H. 34.5 cm.

results, and it became a much debated question whether we should continue the work or try for a more profitable site elsewhere. After these barren years were we justified in going on with it?...

But the excavations continued, Carter directing the work and reporting regularly to Lord Carnarvon, back in England, by letter.

Letter from Carter to Lord Carnarvon, 27 December 1920
... The small lateral valley is now finished – results nil I regret to say, and I am now continuing southwards – actually at this moment round the tomb (No. 9) of Ramses VI.

I have had two terrible disappointments. At the end of the lateral valley I thought we found a tomb which proved to be a natural cutting. And, just below Ramses VI – very fine stone masonry carefully plastered, like the superstructure of another tomb. This last proves, though not yet fully

Work in progress in the Valley of the Kings, 24 January 1920. The tomb entrance in the centre of the photograph is that of Ramesses IX; to the right lies 'KV 55', the cache in which Theodore Davis' team found the body of a member of the Amarna royal family, believed by many Egyptologists to be that of Akhenaten himself. The tomb of Tutankhamun lies in the area in shadow at the lower right; although Carter was working within a few metres of the tomb, another two and a half years were to elapse before it was discovered.

uncovered, to be an elaborate dwelling place for some chief-of-the-workmen. At any rate that it is a tomb now seems improbable – another day will tell me.

We are working in untouched stuff so one never knows what may come – I hope a hundred times something good ...

As things were to turn out, there was 'something good' within a matter of feet, but Carter's decision temporarily to abandon his work at that spot meant that the Valley would hold on to its secret for another two years.

The final season

As time drifted past, Carter settled into the old, pre-war routine: winters spent digging in Egypt, summers in England with a good deal of the time at Highclere, happily mixing business with pleasure.

Letter from Carter to Percy E. Newberry, September 1921
... Have been here [at Highclere Castle] practically the whole time – shooting and arranging antiqs. Today we shot again and Friday and Saturday racing at Newbury ...

But the axe was about to fall: all this digging and expense and without anything substantial to show for it. It was a situation that could not be allowed to continue indefinitely.

From Charles Breasted, Pioneer to the Past

None of the three books Howard Carter published on his discovery of Tutenkhamon's tomb made any mention of an incident which was virtually the determining factor in bringing about his superlative find. He personally described it to me, and when I asked him why he had omitted it, merely shrugged his shoulders.

In the summer of 1922, he said, soon after he had returned to England from still another unsuccessful season of excavation for Lord Carnarvon in the Valley of the Kings' Tombs at Luxor, his patron summoned him to Highclere Castle to discuss the question of whether they should continue this expensive and thus far fruitless task. Carnarvon rather dreaded the interview which as it then seemed to him could end only in a decision even more saddening for Carter, if possible, than for himself. ...

Carter also anticipated their interview with anxiety, for he better than anyone knew that thus far the record warranted no other conclusion. His one hope resided in a simple plan which he proposed to lay before Carnarvon.

When they finally met at Highclere, Carnarvon reviewed the history of their work, expressed again his appreciation of the years of effort Carter had given to it; and with genuine regret, stated that in view of the post-war economic stringency, he would find it impossible to support further this obviously barren undertaking.

In reply Carter said that their consistent failure to find anything had not in the slightest weakened the conviction he had held for years, that The Valley contained at least one more royal tomb, probably that of Tut-enkhamon, the existence of which was strongly indicated by circumstantial evidence. He granted again that perhaps even this problematical tomb might have been robbed in antiquity – but there was always the possibility that it had not!

Carter now laid before him the familiar map which showed, season by season, the record of their probing and excavation. At first glance, not a square metre of Valley floor and slopes appeared unchecked, but Carter reminded him that just below the entrance to the tomb of Ramses VI there remained a small triangular area, clearance of which they had postponed for some later, off-season time because it would temporarily prevent visitors from entering the foregoing tomb. In this area he had noted the foundation remains of a row of crude stone huts, evidently built by ancient tomb workmen, which he would have to remove in order to probe the terrain beneath them.

Now, said Carter, only when this triangle had been cleared would he feel that their work in The Valley had been absolutely completed. He therefore wished to propose that Carnarvon grant him permission to undertake one more season's work at his – Carter's – own expense, using Carnarvon's concession, and the same workmen and equipment he had employed for years; and if at the end of this final season he found nothing, he would of course, and with a good conscience, agree that they should abandon The Valley. But if on the other hand he should make a discovery, it should belong to Carnarvon exactly as under their long-standing arrangement.

Carnarvon was by nature a sportsman, and Carter's proposal appealed to

View of the entrance to Tutankhamun's tomb (centre of picture) with the expedition tents pitched nearby. The entrances to other tombs appear along the path in the background and, just visible in the projecting spur at the right, that of Ramesses VI.

him as eminently fair – in fact, as too generous. He would agree, he said, to another and final season of excavation; but it would be at his own, not Carter's expense. . . .

'Would he find the missing tomb of Tutenkhamon?' my father [the historian James Henry Breasted] later wrote of this extraordinary quest. '. . . If the missing tomb existed at all and had escaped the post-Empire robbers, perhaps it might contain some of the artistic splendour of this remarkable period. Who could say?'

Tutankhamun, 1922 – discovery!

After the years of hope and anticipation, the discovery on 4 November 1922 of the first step beneath the ancient workmen's huts came as a complete surprise. By the following day the plastered blocking to the entrance corridor was reached. And then Carter, mustering all his will-power and restraint, recovered the tomb, wired Lord Carnarvon and settled down to await his associate's arrival from England, three nail-biting weeks later.

Typescript description by Lord Carnarvon of the discovery and entry into the tomb of Tutankhamun, dated 10 December 1922
. . . On my arrival at Thebes we at once set to work to clear away the rubbish

and, as we did so, we came across various broken objects such as broken pottery, flowers and some skins which had been used to carry water. The doorway now being completely free we again examined the sealings and discovered that in the right hand corner an entrance had been effected by a thief and had afterwards been re-closed and sealed by the inspectors ..., for on the undamaged portion the cartouche of Tutankhamen was apparent, although very much worn, and on the small portion of the plaster, broken into by the robber, the seal of the '9 captives' could be seen. All these seals were very indistinct and most of them have been preserved for future examination.

A whole day was then spent in fixing a kind of wooden grill with 4 padlocks, – as a protection against robbery. I may state that by now the tomb was guarded by soldiers, police, Sudanese Camel Coast-Guard men, and my own reises or headmen. Mr. Carter and Mr. Callender, his assistant, used now and then to sleep at the tomb. The weather was luckily very still and very hot.

The next day we began clearing the passage which proved to be about 8 metres in length. Objects mostly broken kept on turning up, amongst others a broken box with various cartouches upon the top-rib, which later on may help us considerably to reconsider the duration of the two anterior reigns.

At last this passage was cleared and we again reached a sealed door or wall, bearing the same seals as on the former one. We wondered if we should find another staircase, probably blocked, behind this wall or whether we should get into a chamber.

I asked Mr. Carter to take out a few stones and have a look in. After a few minutes this was done and he pushed his head partly into the aperture.

With the help of a candle he could dimly discern what was inside. A long silence followed until I said, I fear in somewhat trembling tones, 'well, what is it?' 'There are some marvellous objects here' was the welcome reply!

Having given up his place my daughter and myself went to the hole and I could with difficulty restrain my excitement. At first sight with the very inadequate light all one could see was what appeared to be gold bars. On getting a little more accustomed to the light it became apparent that these were colossal gilt couches with extraordinary heads, boxes here and boxes there. We enlarged the hole and Mr Carter managed to scramble in – the chamber is sunk 2 feet below the bottom of the passage – and then, as he moved around with the candle, we knew that we had found something absolutely unique and unprecedented. ...

The excitement felt by the archaeologists at this marvellous discovery is clear from a letter written by Lord Carnarvon to Alan Gardiner within hours of their first entry.

Letter from Lord Carnarvon to Alan H. Gardiner, 28 November 1922
My dear Gardiner
... The find is extraordinary. It is a cache and has been plundered to a certain extent but even the ancients could not completely destroy it. After some slight plundering the inspectors shut it again. So far it is Tutankamon [*sic*] – beds, boxes and every conceivable thing. There is a box with a few papyri in – the throne of the King the most marvellous inlaid chair you ever saw – 2 life size figures of the King bitumenised – all sorts of religious signs hardly known up to date – the King's clothing, rotten but gorgeous.

ABOVE and OPPOSITE The antechamber of Tutankhamun's tomb: the view which met the eyes of Carter, Carnarvon, Lady Evelyn Herbert and Arthur Callender on 26 November 1922, for Carter, 'the day of days, the most wonderful that I have ever lived through, and certainly one whose like I can never hope to see again.' After clearing the entrance passage and noting with misgivings the evidence that robbers had entered the tomb, Carter broke through the sealed door and revealed the first of four small chambers crammed with the funerary equipment of the young king: gilded couches, chairs, chariots, boxes, clothes, statuettes. The small size and irregular plan of the tomb indicated that it was of non-royal type and had been hastily adapted for Tutankhamun, without regard for the careful arrangement of objects in specially designed chambers usual in a full-scale royal burial at this period.

Everything is in a very ticklish state owing to constant handlings and openings in ancient times (I reckon on having to spend 2000£ on preserving and packing). [There is] the most wonderful ushabti in wood of the King, wood portrait head ditto, endless staves etc. some with most wonderful work, 4 chariots, the most miraculous alabaster vases ever seen, 3 colossal beds of honour with extraordinary animals. There is a further room so packed one can't see really what is there – some of the boxes are marvellous, chairs innumerable, a wonderful stool ... [of] ebony and ivory.

Then there is a bricked up room which we have not yet opened ...

There is enough stuff to fill the whole Egyptian section upstairs of the B[ritish] M[useum].

I imagine it is the greatest find ever made.

Tomorrow the official opening and before I leave we peep into the walled chamber ...

Carter has weeks of work ahead of him ...

A few days later, evidently after 'peeping into' the Burial Chamber, Carnarvon wrote again.

Letter from Lord Carnarvon to Alan H. Gardiner, 1 December 1922
My dear Gardiner
... what I have so far found I believe to be little to what will eventually turn up and I have scarcely broken into a box. This discovery transcends anything that has ever occurred I believe anywhere. I have got Tutankamen [sic] (that is certain) and I believe ... intact ...

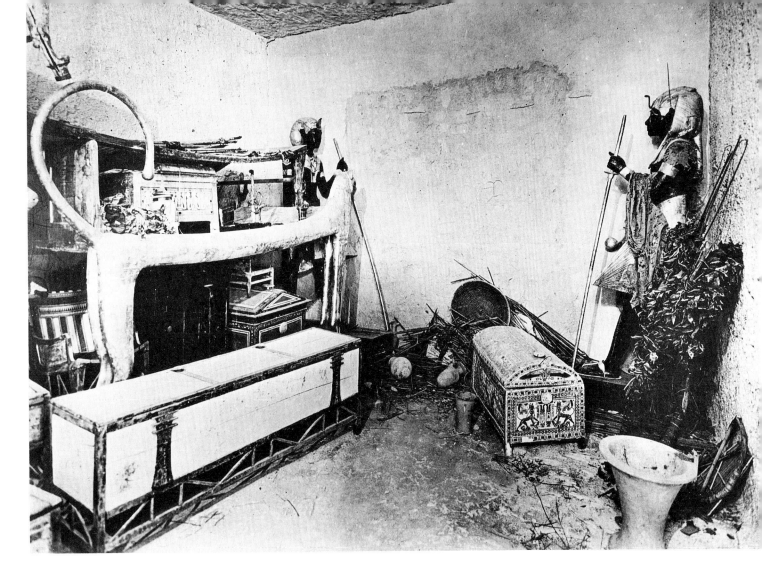

Carnarvon and Carter had decided, quite prudently in the light of Carter's embarrassing 'official' opening of the empty Bab el-Hosan tomb in the presence of Lord Cromer twenty-one years before, to establish as soon as possible and to their own satisfaction what precisely they had found. Their preliminary exploration enabled them to say with confidence that, despite its size, this modest four-chambered sepulchre was a royal tomb. The occupant was, quite clearly, the king for whom they had been searching – the little-known Tutankhamun. But it would do no harm to keep the world guessing a bit longer, to maintain the suspense and maximise the lucrative press potential. The archaeologists therefore concealed their route into the Burial Chamber behind a basket lid and kept quiet.

From the diary of Mervyn Herbert, Carnarvon's half-brother, 29 November 1922
... Porch [Carnarvon] whispered something to Evelyn and told her to tell me. This she did, under the strictest promise of secrecy. Here is the secret. They both had already been into the second chamber! After the discovery they had not been able to resist it – they had made a small hole in the wall (which afterwards they filled up again [with the lid of a basket]) and climbed through. The only others who know anything about it are the workmen.

Practicalities

Clearance of the tomb of Tutankhamun was in prospect an archaeological and financial nightmare. The four small chambers were found to contain an astonishing store of thousands of unique and precious objects of immense scientific and intrinsic value, all threatening to fall apart as soon as looked upon. Thanks to the *Times* agreement and

ABOVE Detail of the gessoed and painted wooden box found in the 'antechamber', with a double scene of Tutankhamun as a sphinx trampling on fallen and defeated enemies. The cartouches in the centre contain the king's *prenomen* (Nebkheperure) and *nomen* (Tutankhamun, Ruler of Southern Heliopolis–i.e. Thebes). H. 44.5 cm.

LEFT Gilded wooden figure of Selket, one of the four statues of protective goddesses placed around the gilded shrine which housed the king's canopic chest. The goddess wears a pleated robe secured at the waist with ribbons; on her head is her emblem (a scorpion), and her arms are outstretched in a gesture of protection. The slight turn of the head and the naturalistic treatment of the whole figure are exceptional and are clearly influenced by the artistic trends of the Amarna Period. H. (without emblem) 76.8 cm.

OPPOSITE The funerary mask which covered the head of Tutankhamun's mummy. It is made of beaten gold, comprising two sheets joined together by hammering, chased, burnished and inlaid with cornelian, lapis lazuli, faience and coloured glass. The lifelike eyes are made from quartz and obsidian. The vulture and uraeus representing the goddesses Nekhbet and Wadjit rest on the king's brow, and the curled and plaited false beard, worn by gods and deceased persons, is attached to the chin. Carter described it as 'a beautiful and unique specimen of ancient portraiture'. H. 54 cm.

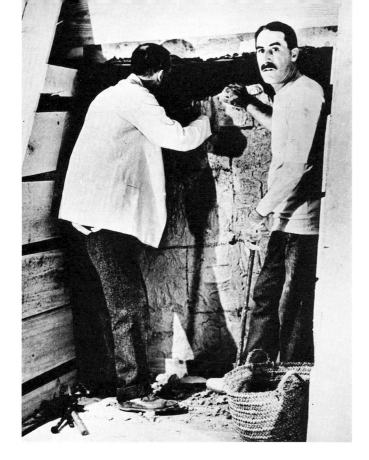

LEFT Carter and Carnarvon dismantling the sealed doorway leading to the burial chamber on 16 February 1923. The 'antechamber' had been cleared of its contents and a wooden platform had been constructed in front of the doorway, protecting the two 'guardian' statues from damage. The platform also concealed the existence of a small hole at the base of the door, through which the excavators had crawled to make a hasty inspection of the burial chamber on the night following their first entry into the tomb. Carter wrote of the occasion: 'There before us lay the sealed door, and with its opening we were to blot out the centuries and stand in the presence of a king who reigned three thousand years ago. My own feelings as I mounted the platform were a strange mixture, and it was with a trembling hand that I struck the first blow'. Alan Gardiner, who was present, later recalled: 'First Carter got up and said a few words; he was terribly excited and there was a quiver in his voice. "Perhaps", he said, "in a few minutes we are going to find Tutankhamun buried in all his glory." … It was quite half an hour, full of tense excitement, before a hole large enough was made to reveal anything of the content of the chamber. Then Carter took an electric torch and threw in a ray of light. "I see a great golden shrine", he said …'.

RIGHT One of Carter's Egyptian workmen carries the mannequin of Tutankhamun out of the tomb, closely followed by Arthur Weigall in a new role as one of the many newspaper correspondents refused entry to the tomb in consequence of the *Times'* monopoly on reporting the clearance. Carter, while adamant that the safety of the objects should not be jeapordised by being exposed unnecessarily to strong sunlight or human contact, was sensitive to the eagerness of the spectators to see the discoveries and whenever possible items were brought out uncovered.

OPPOSITE BOTTOM The sealed entrance to the burial chamber partly dismantled, revealing the outermost of Tutankhamun's four gilded wooden shrines, decorated with alternating pairs of *djed* and *tyet* amulets. The two 'guardian' figures of the king which flanked the doorway were left *in situ* throughout the operation.

BELOW As the contents of the tomb were removed they were taken a short distance to the tomb of Sety II, which had been allocated to the excavators as a store and fitted with the equipment necessary for the objects' conservation – work which was carried out chiefly by the chemist Alfred Lucas and Arthur Mace of the Metropolitan Museum. Here the finds were conserved, photographed and packed into specially-made wooden crates for transportation to the Cairo Museum. In this photograph Carter watches as one of the king's beds is prepared for packing.

Lord Carnarvon's personal wealth, money was not an insurmountable problem. But where to find expert assistance? This was clearly too enormous a find for one man to deal with on his own.

Letter from Lord Carnarvon to Alan H. Gardiner, 1 December 1922
... I fancy that for the transportation, putting together etc. of all this stuff and getting to Cairo it will cost anything from 3 to 8000£. The Government have already through their adviser told me that I shall get a fair share but what I now want are 2 practical restorers – people who can treat wood, gilt work, gesso and are able to restore linen, leather, etc. ...

The most immediate necessity was for an experienced photographer to record the

positions of objects, before anything could be moved. Carter sought the assistance of Harry Burton, photographer to the Metropolitan Museum's Egyptian expedition, working in the Deir el-Bahri area on the other side of the Theban cliffs.

Telegram from Carter to Albert M. Lythgoe of the Metropolitan Museum, 7 December 1922
Thanks message [of congratulations]. Discovery colossal and need every assistance. Could you consider loan of Burton in recording in time being? Costs to us. Immediate reply would oblige. Every regards, Carter, Continental Cairo.

Telegram from Albert M. Lythgoe to Carter, 7 December 1922
Only too delighted to assist in any possible way. Please call on Burton and any other members of our staff. Am cabling Burton to that effect. Lythgoe.

Burton was to be one of the most valuable of Carter's assistants, making hundreds of superb photographs which record every stage in the tomb's clearance and in the treatment and conservation of the objects. In addition, Carter procured the assistance of three other members of the Metropolitan Museum's team: the draughtsmen Lindsley F. Hall and Walter Hauser, who were to draw a detailed plan of the contents of the Antechamber, and Arthur Mace, whose chief contributions were the conserving of the objects, and the composition, from Carter's notes, of the text of the first volume of the 'popular' account of the find: *The Tomb of Tut.ankh.Amen*. In the treatment of fragile objects, Carter also counted himself fortunate in securing the aid of the chemist Alfred Lucas, a former employee of the Egyptian Government. Inscriptional material was entrusted to Alan Gardiner, while James Henry Breasted offered help in the interpretation of the seal-impressions found on the doors of the tomb. Thus, together with the help of his friends Arthur Callender and Percy Newberry, Carter had a veritable 'army of generals' under his control.

Letter from Albert M. Lythgoe to Edward Robinson, Metropolitan Director, 23 December 1922
... through the organization which is now assembled and carrying out the work for [Carnarvon] and Carter, they have got a perfect working-machine and they will be credited with having taken the fullest advantage of this greatest of opportunities and with having furnished a record of the evidence on every side, uniquely complete in every detail ...

The archaeologist at work

Carter was a methodical, even pedantic man who approached the recording of the contents of Tutankhamun's tomb in an extraordinarily thorough and systematic manner. Every object or group of objects in the tomb was assigned a number from 1 to 620; subdivisions for objects within a numbered group were noted by single or multiple letters – a, b, c; aa, bb, cc; aaa bbb, ccc, etc. Additional subdivisions were marked by bracketed arabic numerals. Each numbered object or group was located within the tomb on a master plan or by means of Harry Burton's exhaustive photographic record and full descriptions were made on a card, supplemented by sketches and details of conservation where appropriate. No previous excavation in the Valley of the Kings, and very few anywhere in Egypt, had attempted such an exhaustive record of an archaeological find – and achieved their aim with such stunning success. One example of a Carter object card – chosen at random from several thousand prepared during the course of the

Removing the body of one of Tutankhamun's chariots from the tomb. The preservation and transportation of all the contents of the tomb to Cairo was carried out with the utmost care by Carter and his colleagues, over a period of ten years, often under difficult and trying conditions. The tomb was emptied methodically, chamber by chamber, and notes, drawings and photographs were taken to ensure that the position, appearance and condition of every object was recorded.

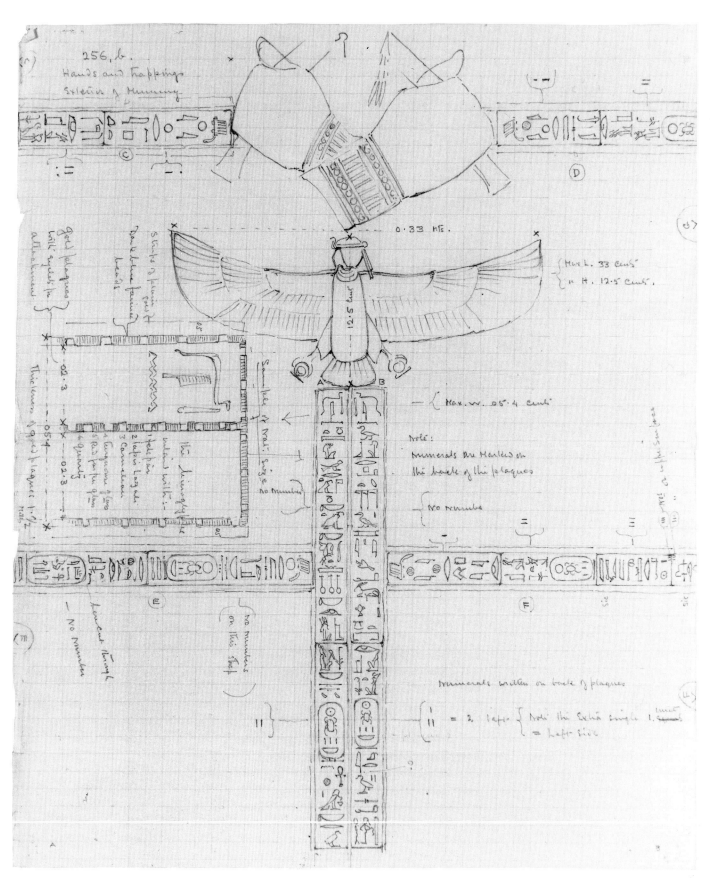

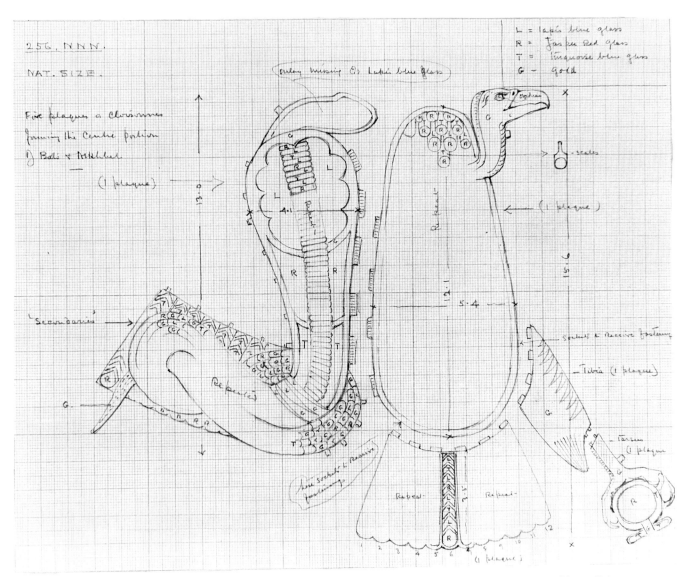

Carter's scale drawings of objects found on the mummy of Tutankhamun, with detailed notes on dimensions, materials and construction: (opposite) the crossed hands, *Ba* bird and upper section of the inscribed bands placed on the outermost wrappings; (above) part of a collar of gold and coloured glass in the form of a vulture and uraeus. The precise shape, material and colouring of even the smallest inlays are faithfully recorded.

clearance – will illustrate the scale of the task with which he and his collaborators were faced.

Tutankhamun record card for Carter Object no. 256qq
256, QQ Bracelet (see 256 YY)
POSITION:
Right forearm; fourth from elbow (of group: X, OO, PP, QQ, RR, SS and SS bis)
DIMENSIONS:
L. 17.8; W. 6.0 cents.
DESCRIPTION:
An elaborate open-work bracelet of three scarabs, four uraei and two cartouches, divided up into *nine sections* which are hinged together and bordered with small gold, lapis lazuli, carnelian, and green felspar beads.
Front central scarab section: scarab of hard pale green stone of the nature of (?)quartz, the scarab of beautiful carved open work upon gold basis support[ed with] its forelegs and solar disk (carnelian).
Either side of central scarab just described
Two uraei, inlaid with lapis blue glass, carnelian and green felspar: they support upon their heads solar-discs of gold, upon their tails [ḥ]-signs of green felspar – the combination of the central disc upon scarab making the word [ḥḥ], as a central device with scarab. The uraei rest upon nb-signs of green felspar.

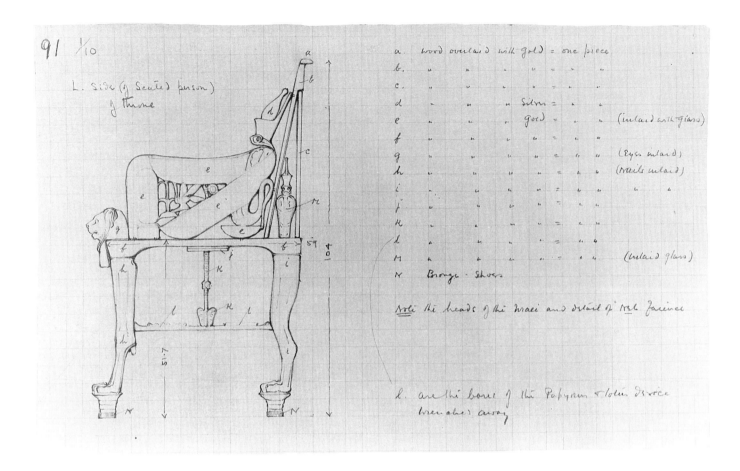

One of Carter's record cards showing a sketch of the king's gilded and inlaid wooden throne. The legs are leonine and the arms take the form of winged uraeus serpents.

Two scarabs, of lapis lazuli, exactly similar in design to the central scarab.

Two uraei; exactly similar to the above described, save they do not support [ḥ]-signs upon their tails but act as pendant supports to:-

Back central two cartouches: the prenomen and nomen of the king inlaid with carnelian, lapis lazuli, green felspar, and lapis coloured glass. The cartouches are surmounted with ... feathers inlaid with carnelian, green felspar and lapis lazuli – these last two (back) sections act as fastenings (by means of large gold pin).

Between the two cartouches, upon a broad bar which forms the actual pin and hinge fastening, the following inscription engraved:-

['The Horus, strong bull, fitting of created forms, the vital god, lord of the two lands, son of Re, lord of diadems, beloved of Weret-heqau, lady of heaven'].

The under surface of the bracelet is of plain gold with engraved details similar to the upper surface.

REMARKS:

the inlay of scarabs and details much disintegrated.

A man under pressure

The team of experts Carter had gathered together certainly looked like the perfect working machine; but characteristically Carter did not delegate easily, particularly under strain.

OPPOSITE Carter's plan of the burial chamber with the outer coffin nested inside the four gilded wooden shrines. A similar plan for the antechamber was drawn by Lindsley Hall and Walter Hauser; no plans showing the contents of the annexe and the 'treasury' were ever made.

From the diary of Lindsley F. Hall, a draughtsman with the Metropolitan expedition, 20 January 1923

... I worked in the Valley this A.M. Carter took measurements for me until his extraordinary notions about projections caused such a violent disagreement between us that he refused (fortunately) to continue his 'assistance' ...

From the diary of Lindsley F. Hall, 7 February 1923

... Walter [Hauser] rowed with Carter and ended his work with him ...

William C. Hayes of the Metropolitan Museum recalling to Cyril Aldred a comment by Harry Burton

That man Carter is quite impossible! But I must admit he showed me how to take a photograph I thought impossible ...

Carter's relations with his Egyptian staff were generally more relaxed, though he could on occasion lash out at their shortcomings too.

From Carter's diary, 15 November 1928

Having a lot of trouble from stupidity on the part of the Raises and men. It seems that they get more stupid as they get older and slacker having been perhaps too long with me.

The men, however, were well used to Carter's moods and, ignoring his waspishness, continued to serve their employer loyally to the very end.

Letter from Ahmed Kirkar to Carter, 12 May 1930. The spelling and punctuation have been left unaltered

Gentleman Kartar

I hope that you are well as much as I am.

Sir the warehouse No. 15, Tombs Tout Ankh Amon, The darkroom for the drawing, the warehouse No. 4, Autumubeel Room & Your home all are too exactly.

Remember me to The Lord's Family & your Friends.

Abd El All and his companyes are remember you.

Your obediant

El Rais Ahmad Kirkar ...

Letter from Salahedeen Lautfie (sic) to Carter, 16 May 1930. The spelling and punctuation have been left unaltered

Dear Sir.

I hope that you are enjoiong good health and happy days. Remembering the good treatment that you deal me with it, I write this letter to let you know some of the best wishes that I carry it to you in my heart. My best Salam to you and your realatives and Lord Carnarvon's family.

Always your obedient serveant.

Salahedeen Lautfie

Letter from Somers Clarke to H. R. H. Hall of the British Museum, 30 August 1925

... Poor old Carter. I fear for him. He has a liver of the first magnitude ...

Hysteria

Egyptology in the years immediately following the First World War had been at an extremely low ebb, fighting for its very survival – as the Egypt Exploration Society (as the 'Fund' was now known) warned its membership in 1921

From the Annual Report of the EES, 1921
... [The Society] has been existing very much from hand to mouth for some years past, and it seems to be becoming more and more difficult, in fact almost impossible, to excite in the general public that interest in archaeology, and in Egyptian archaeology in particular, which we feel our country should take ...

With the discovery of the tomb of Tutankhamun in 1922, all that changed for good.

From The Times, 30 November 1922
This afternoon Lord Carnarvon and Mr. Howard Carter revealed to a large company what promises to be the most sensational Egyptological discovery of the century.

The find consists of, among other objects, the general paraphernalia of the Egyptian King Tutankhamen, one of the famous heretic kings of the Eighteenth Dynasty ...

No-one could have anticipated the madness which would sweep the world during the course of the next months – or the vast numbers of tourists who would descend on the then sleepy village of Luxor in the hope of catching a glimpse of 'the find'.

From the Yorkshire Post, 12 January 1923
According to rumours here this morning the Valley of the Kings is to be closed to the public ...

It would arouse the bitterest hostility against the Egyptian Antiquities Department if the latter were to sanction this arrangement, as there are more than 10,000 tourists coming to Egypt on big cruises during February and March, all of whom are applying for accommodation at Luxor in order to visit the neighborhood of Tutankhamen's tomb ...

They would get short shrift from the increasingly harrassed excavator.

From Henry Field, The Track of Man. Adventures of an Anthropologist
... Buxton and I waited on dust-covered boulders near the entrance, trying to appear nonchalant. Howard Carter ... had the reputation of tearing into shreds the cards of would-be visitors ...

The curse of the Pharaohs

Letter from Margit Labouchere to Carter, 21 January 1925
... Nobody is allowed to open the coffin.
Listen to your inward voice.
M. Labouchere

Lord Carnarvon's first visit to Egypt had been prompted by his frail health following the motoring accident in Germany in 1903, a crash which had left him with a weak chest

'The Thrilling Moment – Lord Carnarvon leads the way' read the caption to this photograph, which appeared on the front page of *The Times Weekly Edition* for 1 March 1923. Following Carnarvon into the tomb is the select party of guests, including Sir William Garstin, James Henry Breasted and Alan Gardiner. The occasion was the removal of the sealed doorway to the burial chamber which preceded its formal opening.

and prone to infections. The excitement surrounding the discovery was becoming a strain on everyone, not least the semi-invalid aristocrat, and he decided to spend a few days in Aswan in the company of Arthur Mace, Carter's right-hand man, gathering his strength for the next round. While in Aswan, Carnarvon was bitten on the cheek by a mosquito; the miniscule wound was inadvertently reopened while shaving and erysipelas set in. Within a very short time, Lord Carnarvon was dead – and the curse of the pharaohs was born.

Letter from Lady Evelyn Herbert, Carnarvon's daughter, to Carter, 18 March 1923
... Pups [Carnarvon] asked me to write you to say that Lacau is laid up with influenza so is hors de combat and what is much more important is the old Man is very *very* seedy himself and incapable of doing anything. You know that mosquito bite on his cheek that was worrying him at Luxor, well yesterday quite suddenly all the glands in his neck started swelling and last night he had a high temperature and still has today. He feels just *too* rotten for words. I have got Fletcher Barrett looking after him and I think he is competent, but oh! the worry of it all and I just can't bear seeing him really

seedy. However there it is. I've made a point of making rather light of it to most people as I don't want an exaggerated account in the papers. Of course they may never get hold of it at all but since you've all become celebrities I feel there is nothing one does or thinks that they don't know! But I like *you* knowing exactly what's happening to us. We miss you and I wish Dear you were here.

I will let you know how he goes on
with our fond love, Eve

From Carter's diary, 5 April 1923
Poor Ld. C. died during the early hours of the morning.

Following in the wake of Lord Carnarvon's declining health and subsequent death, there was a spate of newspaper reports to the effect that the possible consequences of disturbing pharaoh's eternal rest should have been anticipated. There were two levels of concern: the supernatural ...

From Arthur Weigall, Tutankhamen and Other Essays
... There was something very solemn, and even tragic, in this awakening of the once great king now when his empire was long fallen to pieces and his glory departed; and as I took my place at the mouth of the tomb I felt, if I may say so without affectation, a sense of deep sadness weighing upon me.

The wind suddenly got up as the party went down the steps, and it blew the hot, white dust about, sending it up into the air in angry little scurries. One might almost have thought it to be connected in some way with the spirit of the dead Pharaoh, petulant and alarmed at being disturbed, or perhaps annoyed at the jokes and laughter of some of the resurrection men, who had abandoned their silence and had become jocular as they went into the sepulchre. A number of cane chairs had been taken down into the bare first room, so that the party could watch while the sealed wall was broken down; and Lord Carnarvon, perhaps somewhat overwrought by the excitement of the moment, made the jesting remark that they were going to give a concert down there in the sepulchre. His words, though of little moment, distressed me, for I was absorbed, as it were, in my own thoughts, which were anything but jocular; and I turned to the man next to me, and said: 'If he goes down in that spirit, I give him six weeks to live'. I do not know why I said it: it was one of those curious prophetic utterances which seem to issue, without definite intention, from the sub-conscious brain; but in six weeks' time, when Lord Carnarvon was on his deathbed, the man to whom I had addressed the words reminded me of them ...

... and the physical ...

Marie Corelli in the Daily News, 5 April 1923
... I cannot but think some risks are run by breaking into the last rest of a King of Egypt whose tomb is specially and solemnly guarded, and robbing him of his possessions.

According to a rare book I possess entitled 'The Egyptian History of the Pyramids', translated out of the original Arabic by Vattier who worked for Louis XVI of France ..., the most dire punishment follows any rash intruder into a sealed tomb. This book gives long and elaborate lists of the 'treasures'

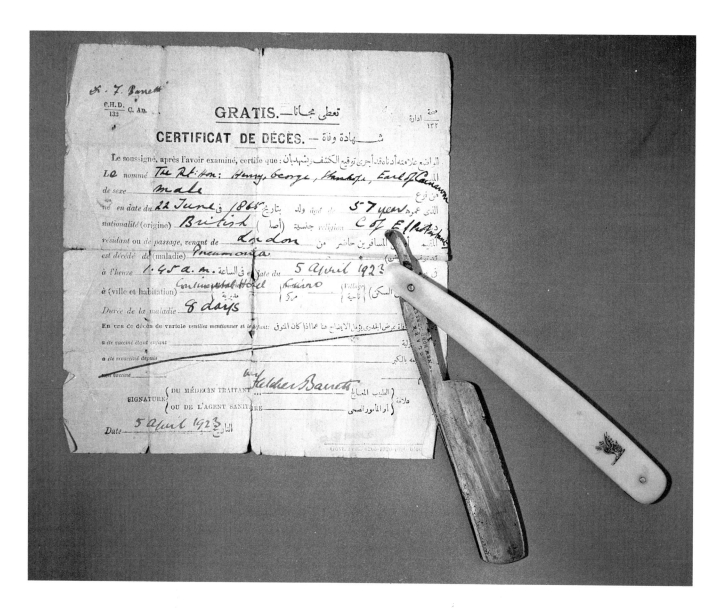

Lord Carnarvon's death certificate and the razor with which he infected a mosquito-bite on his cheek. Blood-poisoning was followed by pneumonia which, to a man of Carnarvon's weakened constitution, proved fatal. Carnarvon's illness, coming so soon after his crowning discovery, had shocked and saddened his friends. On 4 April 1923, Alan Gardiner wrote: 'I have had a few ghastly days, worried to death with old Carnarvon's illness ... Yesterday he was given up for hopeless, at least by one of the nurses, but Evelyn and Lady Carnarvon insisted that he would pull through. I have been convinced that he would from the start ... This morning he took a turn for the better; became quite conscious and absolutely insisted on being shaved ...'. This optimistic impression was misleading, however, and Carnarvon died in the early hours of 5 April.

buried with several of the kings, and among these are named 'divers secret poisons enclosed in boxes such wise that they that touch them shall not know how they came to suffer'.

That is why I ask, was it a mosquito bite that has so seriously affected Lord Carnarvon?

Carter, characteristically, subscribed to neither school of thought and went to great pains to dismiss the ridiculous notion that anything untoward could possibly result from archaeological exploration of this sort.

Carter in The Tomb of Tut.ankh.Amen, II
... It has been stated in various quarters that there are actual physical dangers hidden in Tut.ankh.Amen's tomb – mysterious forces, called into being by some malefic power, to take vengeance on whomsoever should dare to pass its portals. There was perhaps no place in the world freer from risks than the tomb. When it was opened, scientific research proved it to be

sterile. Whatever foreign germs there may be within it to-day have been introduced from without, yet mischievous people have attributed many deaths, illnesses, and disasters to alleged mysterious and noxious influences. Unpardonable and mendacious statements of this nature have been published and repeated in various quarters with a sort of malicious satisfaction. It is indeed difficult to speak of this form of 'ghostly' calumny with calm. If it be not actually libellous it points in that spiteful direction, and all sane people should dismiss such inventions with contempt ...

Politics, 1922–5

'The curse' was and remained negligible compared with the political consequences of the discovery. The seeds of man-made conflict had been sown with an exclusivity deal Lord Carnarvon had struck with *The Times* for coverage of the discovery and the tomb clearance. Like so many ideas, it seemed a good one at the time, enabling Lord Carnarvon to recoup some of his excavation costs and avoiding a great deal of time-wasting and disruption by enabling him to channel the rest of the international news corps through the one agent. But the arrangement was to prove an unmitigated disaster. The Egyptian press were up in arms – how dare these foreigners withhold from the Egyptian people information on an Egyptian discovery! The foreign press were equally incensed and mischievously supported the complaints of the Egyptian nationalists.

Letter from Lord Carnarvon to Carter, 24 December 1922
... Neither of us having much experience of Press sharks one is rather at a loss how to act for the best ... I think the Daily Mail would give more, but the Times is after all the first Newspaper in the world ...

Letter from Arthur Mace of the Metropolitan Museum of Art, to his wife Winifred, 26 January 1923
Things have got rather lively the last few days owing to Lord Carnarvon's agreement with The Times, which is much more drastic now we have seen it, than we ever imagined. It has caused a perfect storm among the other newspapers and made complications of various sorts ...

From the Yorkshire Post, 29 January 1923
... Among the Arabs there is a growing aversion to, and resentment at, what they describe as the 'sacrilegious vandalism' of foreign archaeologists in uprooting the bones of their sacred dead for 'the amusement of museum visitors and tourists, or for the gratification of scientists'. 'What would you say,' remarked a prominent Egyptian official, 'if we sunk a shaft in your Kensal Green in London a few centuries from now for the discovery of the remains of your dead, so that we could exhibit them to gaping visitors in the museums, or sell them as curios to foreigners? If one's dead are not to be held inviolate, then truly our morals are deplorably lax.' ...

Letter from Alan H. Gardiner to his wife, Heddie, 9 February 1923
... Carnarvon has been down in Cairo for a day or two. He wishes he had never found the tomb, so troublesome are the journalists proving. I think the papers have behaved scandalously ... I sincerely hope he will defeat the Daily Mail, Daily Express and the whole crowd of them. I could tell you a pretty story of their doings ...

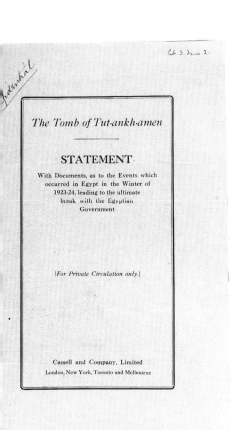

The Tomb of Tut·ankh·amen

STATEMENT·

With Documents, as to the Events which occurred in Egypt in the Winter of 1923-24, leading to the ultimate break with the Egyptian Government

[For Private Circulation only.]

Cassell and Company, Limited
London, New York, Toronto and Melbourne

At the height of the political troubles which descended upon the discoverers of Tutankhamun's tomb, Carter drew up a pamphlet outlining in punctilious detail every stage of the excavators' dealings with the Egyptian government during the crisis of 1923–4. The composition of such documents seems to have been a labour of love; he had produced something very similar, for his personal use, in connection with the Saqqara Incident of 1905. Unwisely, he arranged for the Tutankhamun *Statement* to be printed, causing acute embarrassment to his American colleagues such as Herbert Winlock of the Metropolitan Museum, New York, whose private and confidential letters were reproduced without his permission.

Letter from Alan H. Gardiner to his daughter Margaret, 16 February 1923
… the unfortunate mistake – it was no crime, but it was a mistake – which C[arnarvon] made in giving the sole rights to THE TIMES has led to dire results, and all the workers connected with the tomb are strung up to the last degree, and one feels on the verge of a volcano the whole time …

Added to the press uproar, an increasing uncertainty concerning the fate of the objects, of which Carnarvon at least felt he was entitled to a generous share (see below), proved for Carter the last straw. This is the version of events recorded by Charles Breasted, son of the famous American Egyptologist James Henry Breasted.

From Charles Breasted, Pioneer to the Past
… Just as Carter had flatly disagreed with [Carnarvon] over his arrangement with the London *Times*, so he now disagreed with him over this knotty question of a division of a portion of the tomb's contents to which, he contended, Carnarvon should unreservedly renounce any rights or claims whatsoever.

'This painful situation,' my father [James Henry Breasted] wrote on March 12, 1923, 'resulted in such strained relations between Carter and Carnarvon that a complete break seemed inevitable. Alan Gardiner and I succeeded in pouring oil on the waters, but in so doing we both fell from Carter's good graces. The man is by no means wholly to blame – what he has gone through has broken him down.'

Unbelievably, Carnarvon was barred from Carter's house. His lordship's response was touching and showed the depth of his friendship.

Letter from Lord Carnarvon to Carter, 23 February 1923
… I have been feeling very unhappy today, and I did not know what to think or do, and then I saw Eve and she told me everything. I have no doubt that I have done many foolish things and I am very sorry. I suppose the fuss and worry have affected me but there is only one thing I want to say to you which I hope you will always remember – whatever your feelings are or will be for me in the future my affection for you will never change.

I'm a man with few friends and whatever happens nothing will ever alter my feelings for you. There is always so much noise and lack of quiet and privacy in the Valley that I felt I should never see you alone altho' I should like to very much and have a good talk. Because of that I could not rest until I had written to you …

A short time later Carnarvon was dead. He had provided a crucial buffer between Carter's irascible personality and the outside world. Now this buffer was removed, and Carter was unleashed on an unsuspecting public as Lady Carnarvon's Egyptological representative. Relations with the Egyptian Government and the Antiquities Service went from bad to worse, with slights and insults on both sides, culminating in a badly judged withdrawal of labour – the first strike in archaeological history – by Carter and his team following the raising of the sarcophagus lid.

From the Daily News, 14 February 1924
LUXOR, Wednesday.
There was a regrettable development this morning in connection with the

tomb of Tutankhamen, as a result of which the following notice was posted up in the hotels here:

Owing to impossible restrictions and discourtesies on the part of the Public Works Department and its antiquity service, all my collaborators, in protest, have refused to work any further upon the scientific investigations of the discovery of the tomb of Tutankhamen.

I, therefore, am obliged to make known to the public that immediately after the Press view of the tomb this morning, between 10 a.m. and noon, the tomb will be closed, and no further work will be carried out.

(Signed) HOWARD CARTER

As a result of Carter's precipitate action, Lady Carnarvon's concession was cancelled and Carter and his co-workers were locked out of the tomb. The whole world took sides – most of the Egyptological community, seeing its interests threatened by the Egyptians' aggressive stance on the division issue, sympathising with Carter. One notable exception was the American Egyptologist George A. Reisner, director of the Giza pyramid-cemeteries excavations.

Letter from George A. Reisner to Mr Hawes of the Boston Museum of Fine Arts, 9 October 1924
Very private and confidential for yourself and Dr. Fairbanks
... The Nationalist Party, the party of Saad Pasha Zaghlûl, has had its interest excited in the Department of Antiquities by the silly estimates of three to eight million pounds put on the Tutankhamon objects by Mr. Carter. The foolish conduct of Mr. Carter during the last year, the very reprehensible contract made with the 'Times', and the manner in which Breasted, Lythgoe, Gardiner, and Newberry identified themselves with Carter and his acts, – all this has aroused a bitter feeling against archaeologists in Egypt ...

We have kept ourselves absolutely clear of all connection with Carnarvon, Carter and the Tomb. I have never accepted Mr. Carter or Carnarvon as a scientific colleague nor admitted that either of them came within the categories of persons worthy of receiving excavation permits from the Egypt. Government ...

In due course, however, the Nationalist Government, which had had a vested interest in subverting the foreigners, fell. Lady Carnarvon's licence was renewed and Carter returned to work – but on the Egyptians' terms, and with the Antiquities Service more firmly in the driving seat than ever.

From the Daily News, 15 January 1925
Mr. Howard Carter has finally come to terms with the Egyptian Government regarding the reopening of Tutankhamen's tomb, which he hopes to do within a fortnight. He is leaving for Luxor on Thursday to commence work.

The conditions under which the licence has been granted to Mr. Carter (representing Almina, Countess of Carnarvon) are practically those made by the Government last June. The Countess and the late Lord Carnarvon's executors undertake to renounce all claims on the tomb and the objects found, and agree not to take legal action against the Egyptian Government for the cancellation of the previous licence and the Government's subsequent action.

While not admitting any liability to do so the Government is prepared to allow the Countess the choice of duplicates of objects found in the tomb, provided such action does not affect the scientific value of the discoveries.

If it is decided to bring the King's mummy to Cairo the Antiquities Department will undertake the transport and assume responsibility therefor in order to avoid disagreeable criticism of Mr. Carter ...

Pharaoh revealed, 1925

As the work progressed and it became clear that what they had found was an intact burial, Carter's thoughts must have returned to the Egyptian collection at Didlington Hall and the famous Amherst Papyrus with its unique description of a Seventeenth Dynasty royal mummy 'equipped with a sword, a large number of amulets and jewels of gold ... upon his neck, and his headpiece of gold ... upon him'. How would Tutankhamun measure up? Would he, indeed, compare at all?

James Henry Breasted quoted in Charles Breasted, Pioneer to the Past
'... The sarcophagus lid trembled, began to rise. Slowly, and swaying uncertainly, it swung clear.

'At first we saw only a long, narrow, black void. Then across the middle of this blackness we gradually discerned fragments of granite which had fallen out of the fracture in the lid. They were lying scattered upon a dark shroud through which we seemed to see emerging an indistinct form.

'The ropes at the end of the cradle were stretching, and when the hoists had been drawn up as far as the low ceiling of the burial chamber permitted, the granite lid was swinging not more than twenty-two inches above the sarcophagus. Carter turned a flashlight into the interior and announced that the burial was supported upon a golden bier in lion's form.

'... There followed a complete silence which had in it something of the oppressiveness of intervals of sudden stillness at funerals of our own day. In the midst of this, and reminding one for all the world of the routine efficiency of modern undertaker's assistants, Carter and Mace stepped quietly forward to the head of the sleeping figure and loosening the shroud on either side, slowly and carefully rolled it back off the head towards the feet.

'... We suddenly saw the gleaming gold of the vulture's head and the up-reared cobra on the King's forehead. We saw his eyes, which seemed to look out upon us as in life; and soon the King's whole figure was revealed to us in all the splendour of shining gold ...'

Within was a second coffin, of gilded wood like the first; and within this coffin was yet a third.

Letter from James Henry Breasted of the Oriental Institute, Chicago, to his wife, 27 November 1925
... Carter and Lacau seem to be on better terms. They have shut the newspapers out and issue brief bulletins at long intervals. Some of these bulletins contain arrant nonsense like the statement that the innermost coffin is of 'solid gold' in a bulletin signed by both Carter and Lacau. Of course we are both familiar with the fact that Carter does not know the meaning of the English language. There can be no doubt that the coffin is wood overlaid with gold. This probably heavy sheet gold and by itself it is

solid, but this is far from justifying the statement that *the coffin* is of 'solid gold' ...

In fact, the innermost coffin *was* of solid gold, about 3mm thick and weighing 110.4 kg. Within lay the mummified body of the king himself, fitted with a gorgeous portrait mask of beaten gold, with associated cross-bands of inlaid gold. The mummy itself was adorned with over 150 separate pieces of precious jewellery. It was the most magnificent archaeological discovery ever made.

The solid gold inner coffin of Tutankhamun, representing the young king wearing the *nemes* headdress and grasping the royal 'crook and flail' sceptres. The body is adorned with a version of the *Rishi*, or 'feathered', motif – standard decoration for royal coffins of the 18th Dynasty – and over the torso and legs the goddesses Nekhbet and Wadjit (in the form of vultures) and Isis and Nephthys spread their wings in gestures of protection. H. 1.88 m.

A settling of accounts

Much of the responsibility for winding-up Lord Carnarvon's Egyptological estate following his untimely death was left to Carter who, despite the involvement of Lady Carnarvon, endeavoured to see that his late associate's wishes were carried out – primarily, the disposal of his superb art collection to the Metropolitan Museum of Art in New York, which had provided, and would continue to provide, such sterling assistance in the Tutankhamun clearance.

From The Times, 18 May 1923
The Right Hon. George Edward Stanhope Molyneux [Herbert], fifth Earl of Carnarvon, of Highclere Castle, near Newbury, Hants, of Bretby Park, Burton-upon-Trent, and of 1, Seamore-place, W., who died at Cairo on April 5, aged 56, left property in his own disposition of the gross value of £398,925, with net personalty [*sic*] £274,376. . . .

His Egyptian collection is dealt with in the first codicil, made on the same day as his will [29 October 1919], but written in his own hand. He leaves this collection to his wife, adding:-

I would like her to give one object to the British Museum, one object to the Ashmolean, and a fragment cup of blue glass (Thothmes III.) to the Metropolitan Museum, New York. The first two bequests need not be capital objects.

Should she find it necessary to sell the collection, I suggest that the nation – i.e., the British Museum – be given the first refusal at £20,000, far below its value, such sum, however, to be absolutely hers, free of all duties. Otherwise I would suggest that the collection be offered to the Metropolitan, New York, Mr. Carter to have charge of the negotiations and to fix the price . . .

It was typical of Carter that he should prepare, 'for the record', his version of any event in which his own role might be open to misconstruction or criticism. The Saqqara affair was one of the incidents he had recorded in this way; the dispute with the Egyptian Government over the Tutankhamun concession had been another; and the disposal of the Carnarvon collection was to be a third.

Note [by Carter] on the Carnarvon collection of Egyptian antiquities
1924
Contrary to my advice, and I believe the wish of the present Lord Carnarvon, the collection was removed (packed by me, in accordance with instructions from Almina, Countess of Carnarvon) from Highclere Castle where it was housed in its glass cases.

Special cases were designed and made at large expense behind the oak panelling at 1, Seamore Place, to receive the collection.

When the collection was transported by motor from Highclere to London, it was placed in the Bank of England (Burlington Gardens), instead of in the glass cases prepared for it at Seamore Place.
1925
When I returned from Egypt (Spring 1925), I found that it had been arranged to sell the collection at Sotheby's, and that dates had been allotted for that season for its sale.

I took immediate steps to prevent this sale, and with Almina, Countess of Carnarvon's sanction I instructed Sotheby's representatives to cancel any arrangements made in this connection.
1926
Notwithstanding my advice, and my earnest appeal, soon after my return from Egypt (May 1926), I was requested by Almina, Countess of Carnarvon,

and by her lawyers, to sell the collection to Sir Joseph Duveen; failing this I was instructed to place the collection for sale at Sotheby's as early as possible in July (1926). I was also told that if I did not act, Almina would do so herself.

With regard to sale at Sotheby's, I represented that to put a collection of that kind up to auction at so short a notice would be out of the question. With reference to its sale to Sir Joseph Duveen, though I opened negotiations with Sir Joseph I was careful that those negotiations failed. And as all my representations to Almina, Countess of Carnarvon were of no avail, she not allowing me to offer the collection to the British Museum, I urged her to allow me to offer it in its entirety to the Metropolitan Museum of Art, New York – to this Almina acquiesced.

H.C. August 1926

Whatever difficulties Lady Carnarvon might have placed in Carter's way regarding the disposal of the Carnarvon collection, she generously continued to support the work of clearance in the tomb. No division of objects from the tomb was ever made; as compensation, however, the Egyptian Government agreed to reimburse the costs incurred by the Carnarvon family in connection with the discovery – £35,867-13s-8d. Lady Carnarvon did not forget her late husband's loyal associate.

Letter from Lady Carnarvon's solicitor to Carter, 22 September 1930

Dear Mr. Howard Carter,

On Lady Carnarvon's instructions I am sending you herewith my cheque for £8,012.0.0.

As you know her Ladyship has recently received a sum of money from the Egyptian Government and she wishes to give to you one quarter of the net amount which will remain to her thereout after discharging the various expenses in connection therewith.

Lady Carnarvon, as I think you know, greatly appreciates the distinguished service you have rendered in the cause of scientific research and has many gratifying memories of your association with her late husband ...

I am,

Yours very truly,

Alfred W. Fryzer

Rewards for endeavour

During the years of clearance Carter guided around the tomb several members of international royalty, including the Queen of the Belgians, the Crown Prince of Sweden, the Crown Prince of Italy and numerous VIPs. Outside the United Kingdom, the discoverer of Tutankhamun had become an international celebrity, wined, dined and celebrated almost everywhere, and was a popular figure on the international lecture circuit. Abroad, he reaped his just rewards.

Letter from the Belgian Ambassador to Carter, 24 June 1932

Dear Mr Carter

I beg to inform you that His Majesty, King Albert, in accordance with the proposal of the Secretary of State for Foreign Affairs in Brussels, has bestowed upon you, by Royal Decree of the 6th of May, the decoration of Commander de l'Ordre de Léopold II.

The Insignia and Warrant of this distinction have been received at this Embassy.

I should very much like to hand these to you personally and take the opportunity of offering you my sincere congratulations. I should be glad, therefore, if you would kindly communicate with the Secretary of this Embassy (Sloane 9271) with a view to arranging an appointment in the early part of next week.

Believe me, dear Mr Carter
Sincerely yours
E. de Cartier
Belgian Ambassador

However, owing to his behaviour during the political crisis which followed in the wake of the Tutankhamun discovery, Carter was treated with distinct coolness by the British establishment, which chose to ignore all calls to honour the man or at the same time acknowledge in any real way his immense achievement. Friends and associates did try – but with Carnarvon dead and buried, Carter discovered that he had little pull in the right circles.

Letter from 'A. H. L. H [...]', Buckingham Palace, to Sir John Maxwell, 8 May 1925
Dear Sir John Maxwell,

In Wigram's absence I have spoken to the King on the subject mentioned in your letter of May 6th.

Just at present His Majesty's time is so fully occupied with interviews and other engagements that there is little chance of the King being able to receive Mr. Howard Carter.

His Majesty would certainly be interested to see his photographs, and, should time be available later on, we will communicate with him at the address which you were good enough to give us.

Yours very truly,
A. H. L. H[...]

In fact, apart from a brief introduction to King George V at a Buckingham Palace garden party, Carter never would have an opportunity to present an account of his discovery to the British royal family.

The reluctant scholar

From the speech by Provost Graves, Yale University, 16 July 1925
... In recognition of your preeminent achievements as a scientist and explorer, and more particularly of your work in Egypt that after long years of patient and courageous effort has revealed to the world the accurate story of an ancient civilization, we confer upon you the degree of Doctor of Science and admit you to all its rights and privileges ...

The Yale doctorate would be Carter's only academic distinction, but one of which he was immensely proud and determined to make the very most.

Letter from Carter to his brother Sam, undated [1930]
... Bye the bye – should you wish to address me as doctor – please don't add Esq. ...

The enormous interest generated by the discovery brought a demand for an authoritative account from the discoverer. Carter intended ultimately to publish a full and detailed 'scientific' report on the tomb and its contents – a task which would have required years of dedicated effort even from the most energetic of scholars. Something more immediate was needed; the result was the three-volume *The Tomb of Tut. ankh. Amen*, which appeared at intervals between 1923 and 1933. Though written in the first person, the bulk of the text was actually composed from Carter's notes by Arthur Mace (volume I) and Carter's friend Percy White (volume II). White, a novelist and Professor of English Literature, was rapturous in his enthusiasm for the task.

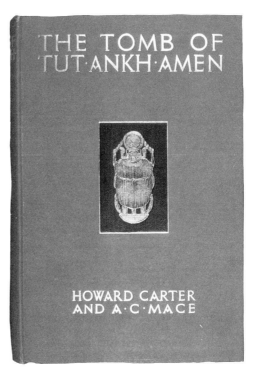

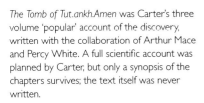

The Tomb of Tut.ankh.Amen was Carter's three volume 'popular' account of the discovery, written with the collaboration of Arthur Mace and Percy White. A full scientific account was planned by Carter, but only a synopsis of the chapters survives; the text itself was never written.

Letter from Percy White to Carter, 25 November 1925
My dear Carter,

Yours of the 17th this moment received. Magnificent! My *hottest* congratulations. But the work before you will be enormous. By all the ancient gods! – what treasures are unfolding – not only of art but perhaps of history ...

I've received *all* your diaries to date and have recast them into narrative form. They will need, of course, scissors[?]. Don't worry about writing. Rough notes will suffice. The nature and magnitude of your adventure grows[?] on my mind – as to the press – I understand. With love,

Ever yours,
Percy White

With or without his Yale doctorate, Carter was no scholar – at least of the desk-bound variety that a full scientific treatment of the tomb demanded. His projected six-volume final publication of the discovery, *A Report Upon the Tomb of Tut 'ankh Amun*, would never advance beyond the barest skeleton-outline. The real victim of 'pharaoh's curse' was to be Carter himself, shackled to a find with which, at the end, he had become hopelessly overwhelmed.

Fans and cranks

Letter from Mrs Samuel Leeper to Carter, 8 November 1925

Mr. Howard Carter –

Somewhere in Europe, presumably.

Dear Mr Carter, –

Tonight – for the third time, I have closed the book, 'The Tomb of Tut. ankh.Amen' by Howard Carter and A. C. Mace, after reading it through from 'kiver to kiver'. Thrice, then, have I been conducted page by page through one of the most compelling adventures possible only to find myself left stranded before the ultimate episode, which remains all veiled in mystery and cloaked in concealment. Do you realize, Mr. Carter, how many of us there must be awaiting with what resignation we can muster further divulgement of your research and the final explanation of it all?

... you, favoured of the gods! it is up to you and your brotherhood to tell the starving stay-at-homes the news. The thing most desired is your next book – should you be again engaged in the fairy tale business of assorting, assembling, and saving the funerary treasure of a king. Will you not say when it is to be, and what you are up to NOW? Remember – here we are! eyes bulging and mouth open – high and dry. Thrice have I cantered up to this portcullis, thus far impregnable. This beautiful red and gold book [American edition] with its adorable scarab – it is my favorite fairy story, but it does not tell what favor Prince Carter, after incredible feats, received from the hand of the ruler.

Suspended-ly yours

Jeannette Leeper

Letter from M. Hirose to Carter, 28 July 1931

Dear Sir,

I take the liberty of addressing you though I have not the honour of your acquaintance. I am a Japanese student of Egyptology.

No greater honour conferred upon me, if I could have the pleasure of seeing you.

Can you make few minutes from your precious time for me, and please let me know your most convenient time. But I am very sorry to say I am going abroad next Saturday. I will interview any place in accordance with your direction, at Wednesday, Thursday, or Friday.

I shall be greatly obliged to you, if you will grant my selfish request. I respectfully await your order.

I am sir,

your most obedient servant,

M. Hirose

Letter from Mrs Marie Coleman to Carter, 8 June 1924

Dear Sir:-

Pardon me for writing you, the case is urgent, if I had been able to get a message to your mate I could have saved his life.

I am a Divine Prophetess, and Messenger of God. Spirits pray to God to deliver some one, and I am sent with the message.

Being a Supernormalist, I'm able to get in touch with disembodied spirits of from a few moments to thousands of years duration, distance, nor time makes no difference.

King Tut, told me he was going to control this insect and make it sting the Earl, and why.

He warned me of Pres. Harding, and Wilson's, death, now I've a warning for you. If this is it prevent your and other excavator's death, if not –

If you will give me one hundred dollars I will give you this message from him. Lord Carnarvon beseech[es] you to get this for your safety, this message is a poem of 13 verses, he gave me five other messages.

Yours respectfully,

[. . . .]

Assessment

The tomb of Tutankhamun had revealed the full beauty and sophistication of Egyptian civilisation at its zenith. The image of the gold mask, with its magnificent portrait of the boy-king, had impressed itself upon the collective psyche of the world. Thanks to the efforts of one man, pharaoh – and indeed Egyptology itself – had been reborn.

Alan H. Gardiner quoted in Leonard Cottrell, The Lost Pharaohs
. . . . as a revelation of the artistic achievement of the period, the discovery was quite unparalleled. Nothing like it had been discovered before, and, in my opinion, it is extremely doubtful if any comparable discovery will be made in the future. . . .

The value of the discovery to archaeology lies not only in the wealth of objects it revealed, but in the fact that these lovely things were recorded and preserved with such consummate skill [by Carter and his team].

This, the greatest discovery in the history of Egyptology, was made by an Englishman. Yet the sad fact is that the results have never been properly published in the scientific sense; that is, with a detailed description of every object found, illustrated by coloured plates. In 1926 Carter told me he estimated that such a publication would cost £30,000. To-day [1950] it would cost little short of £100,000. All Carter's notes exist together with his photographs and drawings. But who will finance such a publication today?

The situation in 1992 is much as it was when Gardiner wrote. The definitive publication of the tomb of Tutankhamun is only now slowly beginning to appear in fascicle form.

5

After Tutankhamun

'Excellence of judgement and [a] sense of the beautiful'

Scout

Since the First World War, Carter had been acting for and on behalf of a number of American museums and several private individuals (including J. J. Acworth, George Eumorfopoulos and the great Armenian oil-magnate, Calouste Gulbenkian) in the purchase of ancient works of art for their collections. His taste and judgement were well-respected ... and the rate for his 'consultancy' work far from excessive – generally a commission of around 15%.

Letter from Henry Kent, Metropolitan Museum, to F. A. Whiting, Cleveland Museum, 2 December 1920
... [Carter] is probably the most desirable ally you can have in Egypt. He is acknowledged to be the most skilful trader with the natives, he is a gentleman, and I doubt very much whether he would be found lacking in courtesy or fairness to men of his own class. ...

Letter from Albert M. Lythgoe, Metropolitan Museum, to William Valentiner of the Detroit Institute of Arts
... There is no one more familar with the Egyptian market [than Carter,] or more closely in touch with all its best possibilities ... I need only point to our own 'Carnarvon Collection', which [Carter] formed for Carnarvon over a long period of years, to illustrate his excellence of judgement and sense of the beautiful ...

Carter's 'excellence of judgement' is well illustrated by an entry in his 'rough diary' for 6 April 1922 describing a heavily encrusted, rather lumpy grey metal figure he had seen at the shop of the Cairo antiquities dealer Nicolas Tano earlier that day.

Solid silver seated figure of Horus 40 cms high = 16 inches. Sheathed with gold – some of which is missing. ?Cleaning. Left hand and leg at knee broken off. Headdress inlaid lapis and gold – eyes crystal. Condition of silver where exposed good condition.

Despite its poor appearance, Carter clearly recognised the potential of the piece which, after having been refused by at least one institutional buyer, eventually passed into private hands at a relatively modest price. Carter's suspicion that the piece would clean, and clean well, was demonstrated in the late 1970s: Tano's silver falcon-headed god, weighing 16.5 kg, today represents one of the most impressive and important cult images to have survived from the ancient world.

Forgeries then, as now, were a perpetual menace. Carter's technique (not infallible, as we can see from a number of dubious pieces which found their way into his life over the years) is described by the late Cyril Aldred.

Letter from Cyril Aldred to Nicholas Reeves, 28 January 1989

... Howard Carter once told me that his way of dealing with a dubious piece was to put it in a prominent position and look at it frequently every day. If it were right it looked better every time he glanced at it, whereas if it were wrong it would look worse the more he studied it ...

Connoisseur

Though Egyptian art may have been Carter's forte, it was but one of a number of areas in which he had a deep and abiding interest – including oriental carpets and ceramics.

Letter from C. R. Paravicini to Carter, 11 May 1932

Dear Mr. Carter,

My brother writes to me from Paris that you will be good enough to inspect his carpets which are at present stored in the safe of the Swiss Bank Corporation, Regent Street Branch, 11, Regent Street, Waterloo Place, S.W.1.

The Manager, Mr. Huber, has got the keys for the boxes and has been informed of your impending visit ...

If you will let me know what day and time you might find it convenient to call there, I shall make arrangements, if possible, to be there myself in order to take this welcome opportunity to have the pleasure of meeting you.

Believe me, dear Mr. Carter,

Yours very truly

C. R. Paravicini

Letter from Spink and Son Limited to Carter, 21 May 1930

Dear Mr. Carter,

... I have pleasure in sending round the KHANG H'SI yellow porcelain vase and cover which we have had repaired and the two KHANG H'SI porcelain yellow bowls, also the 'gadget' for the pillow.

I have made a careful note of your enquiry for a very fine dish decorated with flowers and without any green in it, also an emerald green jade saucer and, as soon as I come across anything of this description, I will at once let you know.

Thanking you again for all your kindness and hoping for better luck next time,

I remain, with kind regards,

Yours sincerely,

[...] Spink

... P.S. Since writing the above, I have just received confirmation from the owner of the very fine Yung Chêng eggshell porcelain cup and saucer that she is willing to accept £15 for it which, you will remember, you told me you would be willing to give for it. I therefore have pleasure in sending it to you herewith, together with stand.

Benefactor

Carter's increased financial security during and after the Tutankhamun discovery was to benefit a number of the major national collections – including the British Museum, the Victoria and Albert Museum and the Science Museum.

Statue of a falcon-headed god. This large and exceptionally heavy figure – weighing 16.5 kg – is one of the few examples of a cult-image to have survived from ancient Egypt. It appeared on the art market in Egypt in the 1920s and Howard Carter was among the first to recognise its importance, despite its encrusted condition at the time. The figure is made from solid silver, originally overlaid with thin sheet gold; the eyes were made from rock-crystal, and the stripes of the wig of lapis lazuli. Such a combination of precious materials occurs more than once in ancient descriptions of divine beings: as early as the New Kingdom, the *Book of the Divine Cow* describes the aged sun-god Re as follows: 'his bones being of silver, his flesh gold, and his hair true lapis lazuli' – and this figurative description of the god's old age was reflected in the composition of the divine image housed in the temple. This particular image is uninscribed and the identity of the god represented is uncertain: the cylindrical mounting on the wig seems more suited to support a royal crown than a solar disc, and hence the figure probably represents Horus (the Elder – Haroeris) rather than Re or one of several other deities who were usually represented as falcon-headed. The seated pose may indicate that it was installed in a divine barque. Stylistically, the figure may be assigned to the Third Intermediate Period or Late Period; a more precise dating cannot at present be ventured. H. 42 cm.

OPPOSITE Portrait in oils of Howard Carter by his elder brother William, 1924. This painting, perhaps the most familiar image of Howard Carter, represents him at the highest point of his career. It remained in his possession until his death, and is recorded as having hung in the dining room-study of his London home. Like other members of the family, William Carter's (1863–1939) skill as an artist became apparent at an early age. His father obtained the recommendation of Sir John Everett Millais to gain him entrance to the Royal Academy Schools in 1874, and he went on to acquire a considerable reputation as a painter of stylish portraits of wealthy and distinguished clients.

Letter from Frederick G. Kenyon, British Museum, to Carter, 15 October 1925

My dear Carter,

I am instructed by the Trustees of the British Museum to convey to you their special thanks for your gift to them of some interesting and beautiful examples of Egyptian faience of the early Ptolemaic period, formerly in the Macgregor collection. This particular form of technique has not hitherto been well represented in the Museum, and these are fine examples of it, besides being attractive in colour.

The Trustees appreciate the value of the gift, and your kindness in presenting it.

Let me take this opportunity of wishing you the fullest success in the great enterprise which you are resuming [at the tomb of Tutankhamun] this autumn.

Believe me

Yours very sincerely

Frederick G. Kenyon

Sandstone stela given by Carter to the British Museum in 1926. It was commissioned by a Slaughterer (of sacrificial animals) of Amun called Tjaenamun, who is shown kneeling in the lower register with his arms raised in adoration. The objects of his worship, the deified king Amenophis I and his mother queen Ahmose-Nefertari (whose probable tomb Carter had found in 1914), appear above, sitting in the shade of a palm tree. The affectionate grouping of the royal pair, with the queen's arm draped around the king's shoulders, is a legacy of the artistic innovations of the Amarna Period. The original intention of the sculptor seems to have been to depict only the king (he alone is addressed in the hymn of praise inscribed in front of the dedicator), but the figure of his mother has been squeezed in as an afterthought and her name added below those of Amenophis. Ramesside Period. H. 51 cm.

Bronze astronomical instrument, inlaid with electrum (an alloy of gold and silver), dating to the Late Period. Probably a model of the full-scale object, the instrument comprises a bar, rectangular in section, with a perforated block at one end and a falcon-headed aegis at the other. A hieroglyphic inscription incised on each side names the owner as one Bes, son of Khonsirdis, and this is probably the man whose figure appears on one of the long sides and on the end. The instrument belongs to a group of measuring devices, the ancient name for which is *merkhet* or 'indicator' (literally 'instrument of knowing'). More than one type of *merkhet* is known; the term could be used to designate a shadow-clock or water-clock, but the type exemplified here was used in making astronomical observations to determine the correct orientation for important religious buildings such as temples. In this operation it was used together with another instrument, the *bay en imy wenut* ('palm-rib of the observer of hours'). One observer would take a sighting on a star through the *bay* (a palm-rib with a V-shaped notch cut into one end), while another aligned it with a plumb-line suspended through the perforation at one end of the *merkhet*, using the line as a guide to make a permanent record of the position. By means of a series of such observations the position of true north could be discovered. L. 8 cm.

BELOW Among the American institutions which employed Carter's services as a dealer was the Detroit Institute of Arts, on behalf of which he purchased several fine antiquities, including this painted limestone relief from an Old Kingdom tomb of the 5th or 6th Dynasty at Saqqara. It shows, on the left, herdsmen driving cattle, one of them carrying a calf on his shoulder; on the right are fishermen hauling in a catch. The quality of the relief carving is particularly fine, and the introduction of appealing details such as the calf turning apprehensively to receive a reassuring lick from its mother betray the hand of a master artist. L. 150 cm.

Dealer

By the 1930s, Carter's activities in the art world were becoming increasingly commercial.

Letter from R. Forrer, Spink and Son, to Carter, 13 May 1931
… We beg to confirm the arrangement made by our Mr Forrer that we hold the small Egyptian stone head of the Ramesside period on sale or return at the net price to you of £35.0.0. (Thirty-five pounds) …

Letter from Carter to Eustache de Lorey, Carter's associate in Paris, 15 September 1935
… I do not, I must confess, like parting with my little Saite schist head, which I believe, as a matter of fact from the shape of the cranium, is really of the Ethiopian twenty-fifth Egyptian Dynasty (700 to 650 BC). With regard to the head of the Princess of Akhenaton I mentioned I will give you more precise details and the possibilities when in Cairo. It is in a dealer's hands and it is difficult to now say what can be done. Possibly he would allow of a photo being taken. …

Shawabtis I have none available, nor do I know of any good ones on the market at present.

But you will be interested to know (between ourselves) that I have just received, on approval, two magnificent statues. A IVth Dyn. coloured limestone group of man, wife and daughter, about 60 cent[imetres] in height, and a standing black granite … Mid-Empire figure of Amen-em-hat III which I should like … you to see one day …

LEFT Polychrome linen cloth presented by Howard Carter to the Victoria and Albert Museum, London, in 1921. This elaborate textile is said to have been found in an 18th Dynasty tomb at Qurna; unfortunately, no more precise identification of the findspot is available. The original proportions of the piece are unknown, as a section of uncertain length has been torn away, but what remains is in good condition. The cloth is decorated with a repeating rhomboidal pattern woven from threads of red, blue and uncoloured linen. Small feathers, now barely visible, were originally woven into the cloth as well. From representations found at Amarna it is known that cushions were decorated with this type of pattern; Akhenaten and Nefertiti are shown resting on one while rewarding the official Parennefer at the 'Window of Appearance' (tomb of Parennefer), and the two young daughters of Akhenaten are shown sitting on such cushions in the well-known painting now in the Ashmolean Museum. The presence of the fringe on the textile illustrated here, however, argues against its use as a cushion-cover, and it is perhaps more likely that it acted as a wall- or door-hanging. L. 104 cm.

ABOVE One of several pieces which Carter bought for the Cleveland Museum of Art was this section of inlay representing the so-called 'vulture-headdress' worn by queens and goddesses. Dating probably to the 4th century BC, it is made of gold, the upper surface of which contains over one hundred cloisons inlaid with coloured glass. The inlays themselves are remarkable, for those occupying the area of small feathers at the front of the headdress are made from mosaic glass. This miniature masterpiece was said by the Cairo dealer Ralph Blanchard to have come from the 'Treasure of Dendera', a series of discoveries of temple equipment made by local villagers during the First World War and the years following. H. 3.1 cm.

RIGHT Carter had received an advance of $30,000 to purchase ancient Egyptian works of art for Detroit. At his death in 1939 part of this amount still remained unspent; instead of returning the unused money, Carter's executor, the photographer Harry Burton, arranged to send three objects which were in Carter's possession: a faience cinerary urn (p. 185) and two fine statue-heads dating from the late first millennium BC (below and right). This head in diorite dates to the 3rd or 2nd century BC. It is a non-idealistic image and, as such, appears to belong to one of several specific types of sculpture which developed during the 4th to 1st centuries BC. Despite their apparent realism, it has been argued that such heads are not real portraits but merely variations on a generic type, of which the present example, with its plastically modelled folds of flesh, represents an early stage of development. H. 20 cm.

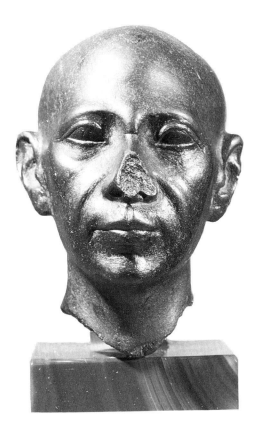

ABOVE Ptolemaic basalt statue head, now in the Detroit Institute of Arts, obtained from Carter's estate. The handling of the hard stone indicates that this is the work of an accomplished sculptor – the skin of the face follows the shape of the skull and has a plastic quality which lends the head an air of realism, despite the somewhat academic treatment of the eyes. Several peculiarities of the subject's features – the protruding ridge of the eyebrows, the oblique angle of the ears, and the sharp depression at the top of the nose – have suggested to some scholars that the head is a true portrait, but the recurrence of these features on other heads depicting different individuals may indicate that they are merely the hallmarks of a distinct sculptural type. 3rd to 2nd century BC. H. 8.89 cm.

6

The Last Years
'Sunk in gloom and talking to no one'

Howard Carter's early life had been filled with action, adventure and achievement; his last years, in contrast, were blighted by continual illness and a gnawing awareness that he had not, and would not, fulfil his obligation to archaeology by the exhaustive publication of the tomb of Tutankhamun which his colleagues expected of him. There was also an ever-present feeling of emptiness and futility: after the boy-king and his treasures, whatever else the future held in store could only be anticlimax.

A last sighting, 1936, and the fantasy of Alexander's tomb
In the years following the Tutankhamun discovery and clearance, Carter maintained his home on the Theban west bank, spending much of his time 'sitting in the foyer' of the

RIGHT Portrait photograph of Howard Carter taken during the 1930s. While he maintained the lifestyle of a gentleman of means and seems to have had a wide circle of acquaintances, Carter made very few close friends. He never married and his last years were apparently spent in loneliness and inactivity, partly in consequence of his failing health (left).

Winter Palace, 'sunk in gloom and talking to no one'; he had become as much a sight for tourists and visitors as the tomb he had discovered in 1922. Occasionally he undertook to show visiting dignitaries around the scene of his archaeological triumph, the last recorded occasion being in 1936 for the future King Farouk. Among Farouk's entourage was Prince Adel Sabit, who recorded his impressions of the elderly Carter.

From Adel Sabit, A King Betrayed
... Howard Carter is a forceful and vital personality, but grumpy and rather dour with people, tourists being his pet aversion. Carter can nevertheless be a charming and interesting man when he is not thundering imprecations

Interior of Carter's home at Prince's Gate Court, London. In his later years Carter continued to winter in Egypt and spent several weeks of the summer at St Moritz in Switzerland. During the rest of the year he lived mainly in London. The flats he occupied – 19B Collingham Gardens and 2 Prince's Gate Court – were stylishly furnished; he had travelled a long way from the relatively humble surroundings of Rich Terrace and Swaffham. The probate inventory drawn up shortly after his death shows that his last address, 49 Albert Court, close to the Albert Hall, was richly equipped with walnut and mahogany furniture, an 18th-century satinwood bracket clock, Wedgwood dinner and tea services and Oriental works of art. The walls were hung with paintings and drawings, some by Carter himself, others by or attributed to such masters as Sir Peter Lely and John Opie.

on the Egyptian government's Antiquities Department, with whom he has a long-standing feud ...

Carter concluded his tour by a reference to the tomb of Alexander the Great, for which scholars had long been searching. Carter maintained that he knew its whereabouts; 'but I shall not tell anyone about it, least of all the Antiquities Department. The secret will die with me'. And it did.

Dubious legacy

Howard Carter died at his London home, 49 Albert Court, on 2 March 1939, aged 65, a victim of Hodgkin's Disease. He was attended at the end by Phylis, the daughter of his sister Amy, who had been his secretary and staunch companion during the last years of his life.

Letter from Salah Eldeen Loutfi (sic), Qurna, 6 March 1939. The spelling and punctuation have been left as in the original.

Sir,

Having heard the death of doctor Howard Carter I became verrey sad for him and request from your kindness to forward my deep sorry to the kindreds of the great explorer.

Your obedient serveant

Salah Eldeen Loutfi

Letter from Carter's servants to Phylis Walker, 19 March 1939. The spelling and punctuation have been left as in the original.

Sir Miss Phyllis Walker Nutfield House Nutfield Place Marble Arch London

Respectifully we have heard with illness by the death of our Head Dr. H. Carter we & our famillies & all the native of our country & Egypt ill. I have sarved Dr. H. Carter 42 years pass well. This notice ill us much spacially about us & our most obbedient servants. Sir Mr Bartin gave us this notice we are ill & uncontent we are write this letter hoping that you Miss shall be well & in a good health & you shall be in the service of the Dr H. Carter. We hope that you shall be well & good health. We are waiting your notice & about health and all.

We remain

your most obbedient servants

Abd-El-Aal Ahmad Sayed & Hosein Ibraheem Sayed El-Karna Luxor Upper Egypt Egypt ...

It is perhaps significant that no letters of regret from Carter's Egyptological colleagues seem to have survived.

Howard Carter's last will and testament, 14 July 1931

I Howard Carter of Luxor Upper Egypt Africa and 2 Prince's Gate Court Kensington in the County of London Artist and Archaeologist hereby revoke all prior Wills Codicils and Testamentary dispositions of all kinds whatsoever made by me and declare this to be my last Will and Testament. I appoint Henry Burton of 21 Via dei Bardi Florence Italy and of the Metropolitan Museum of Art New York United States of America and Captain Bruce Ingram the Editor of the Illustrated London News (hereinafter called 'my Trustees') the Executors and Trustees of this my Will and I bequeath a legacy of Two hundred and fifty pounds (free of Legacy Duty) to each of them if he proves this my Will and acts as Trustee thereof. I declare that all moneys held by me or standing to my credit at any bank on behalf of or in trust for other parties companies corporations associations institutes or other like bodies are to be paid over or transferred by my Trustees to the rightful owners thereof as soon as possible after my decease. I give and devise all rights I may possess in the land and building at Goorna [...?] of Luxor known as Eluat-El-Diban at the time of my decease with all rights of preemption attached thereto and contents thereof to the said Metropolitan Museum of Art New York. I give and bequeath to Abd-el-Asl Ahmed Saide of Goorna if still in my service at my death in appreciation of his many years service the sum of One hundred and fifty Egyptian pounds to be paid to him by my Executors out of my estate. And subject to the payment by my Executors of all my just debts (other than those already referred to) and my funeral and testamentary expenses I give devise and bequeath all other property both real and personal whatsoever and wheresoever to which I may be entitled or which I may have power to dispose of at my death including any property held by the National Bank of Egypt or any branch thereof unto my niece Phylis Walker (daughter of my sister Amy Joyce Walker) and I strongly recommend to her that she consult my Executors as to the advisability of selling any Egyptian or other antiquities included in this bequest. In witness whereof I the said Howard Carter the Testator have hereunto set my hand this fourteenth day of July One thousand nine hundred and thirty one ...

The fine Egyptian antiquities which passed through Carter's hands during his lifetime must number in the high hundreds. Sadly, Carter himself kept no records of such pieces, though an interesting 'snapshot' of his personal collection at the time of his death is provided by a probate listing prepared by the firm of dealers with which he worked most closely in the post-Tutankhamun days—Spink and Son.

Probate valuation, by Spink and Son Limited, of Howard Carter's Egyptian collection, 1 June 1939

Stater of Philip II of Macedon	£2.10.0
Bronze figure of a Sphinx, Ptolemaic, 9" long	30.0.0
Bright blue faience Unguent vessel and lid, New Kingdom, 4½" high	50.0.0
Lapis-lazuli scarab, gold mounted, New Kingdom, 1" long	10.0.0
Blue faience Sphinx inscribed, New Kingdom, 9½" long	500.0.0
Blue faience Hes vase and lid, 8" high	80.0.0
Necklace of Tell-el-Amarna coloured faience beads and plaques	10.0.0
Pectoral in lapis-coloured faience beads	15.0.0
Ivory figure of a dog (ear chipped) no tail, 6" long	40.0.0
Circular pectoral of faience plaques, petals etc. in yellow, blue, red and green, 7" high	15.0.0
Lapis coloured faience thistle shaped vase, foot modern (broken), 3½" high	5.0.0
Small red jasper inlay, profile head to right, mounted as pendant	10.0.0
Minute bronze Ape; minute bronze Offerer	3.0.0
Carnelian small hand; small basalt dog; faience bull	3.0.0
Blue glass armilla (incomplete); fragment of Cameo	1.0.0
Blue scarab in faience; yellow glass minute vase; yellow glass hair-ring	2.0.0
Black basalt portrait Head of an Official, Saite, 3½" high	15.0.0
Large blue faience Romano-Egyptian two-handled vase, 9½" high	15.0.0
Blue faience Scarab as paper-weight, 1¾" high	1.0.0
Small lapis-lazuli Sphinx (one foreleg missing), 1¾" long; small faience cat; small yellow and green bull; small blue faience seated figure	8.0.0
Egyptian flint knife – surmounted in part with gold, 6¾" long	6.0.0
Small gold plaque of Psemthek, 1⅜" × ¾" long	6.0.0
Blue faience relief amulet of Maat, 1⅜" high	1.0.0
Graeco-Egyptian bronze head of a woman	1.0.0
Small gold scent bottle with filigree work, 2" high	8.0.0
29 blue and green faience finger rings	10.0.0
Bronze figure of a cat, 2⅜" long	5.0.0

Part of green faicnce Sistrum Hathor Head and twin Bes figures, $2\frac{1}{2}$" high	4.0.0
Graeco-Egyptian faience Diogenes Head – mounted as trinket box, $2\frac{1}{4}$" long	2.0.0
Aragonite pointed Vase, $5\frac{3}{4}$" high	3.0.0
Black granite head of a man, Ptolemaic period, $7\frac{3}{4}$" high	15.0.0
Portrait head, painted in oils, of a man. Egyptian Hellenistic period. 14" high	20.0.0
Two flint arrow heads – small fragment of flint; two green faience large tubular beads; amethyst Scarab & small piece of gold	2.0.0
Five Utchat eyes in green faience	2.0.0
Quantity of loose beads and minute amulets; a box of coloured pendants and beads from Tell-el-Amarna	3.0.0
Bronze part of a fitment inscribed, $9\frac{1}{4}$" × $2\frac{1}{2}$"	1.0.0
Two lapis coloured Ushabti figures in faience, New Kingdom, $6\frac{1}{2}$" high	6.0.0
Eight gold headed nails	2.0.0
Bright blue foundation deposit inscribed, 2" high	16.0.0
Two ivory toilet boxes and lids in the form of geese trussed for sacrifice, New Kingdom, $3\frac{1}{2}$" high; alabaster small Hes vase-model surmounted by figure of an Offerer applied in relief in carnelian and lapis, 3" high	50.0.0
Circular necklace composed of papyrus amulets, New Kingdom; circular coloured faience lid of a vase, $3\frac{1}{4}$" diameter	18.0.0
Green faience portrait statuette of a king in mummified form, inscribed in black, New Kingdom, $11\frac{3}{4}$" high	50.0.0
Blue faience Ankh amulet with black line inscription, $3\frac{3}{4}$" high	12.0.0
Minute green and blue faience figure of squatting Isis, $1\frac{3}{4}$" high	3.0.0
Small figure of a princess of ivory, New Kingdom, $3\frac{1}{4}$" high	20.0.0
Six Greek silver coins	2.0.0
Plaster cast of the Macgregor Obsidian Head	—
Amphora in alabaster inscribed with two cartouches, New Kingdom, 19" high	10.0.0

This listing of Carter's collection had for the most part been 'weeded' of pieces known to have originated in the tomb of Tutankhamun. A list drawn up by his executor, Harry Burton, records in addition a green-blue glass headrest, one green and two lapis coloured faience shabtis, cups of glass and faience, an ankh amulet, three gold harness ornaments, and a metal tenon (from one of the outer coffins). A number of these were study items upon which Carter had been working at the time of his death. They proved, nevertheless, something of an embarrassment to Carter's executors, who resolved to return them to Egypt forthwith. The pieces were sent via King Farouk to the Cairo Museum, where they were in due course reintegrated with the rest of the boy-king's treasures.

Copy of a letter from Etienne Drioton, Director-General of the Antiquities Service, to Phylis Walker, 30 April 1940
The Service des Antiquités is very touched by your kind and delicate thought in offering to the Egyptian Museum in Cairo, in remembrance of your lamented uncle and the memorable discoveries for which Egypt is indebted to him, the objects from his collection bearing the name of Tutankhamun

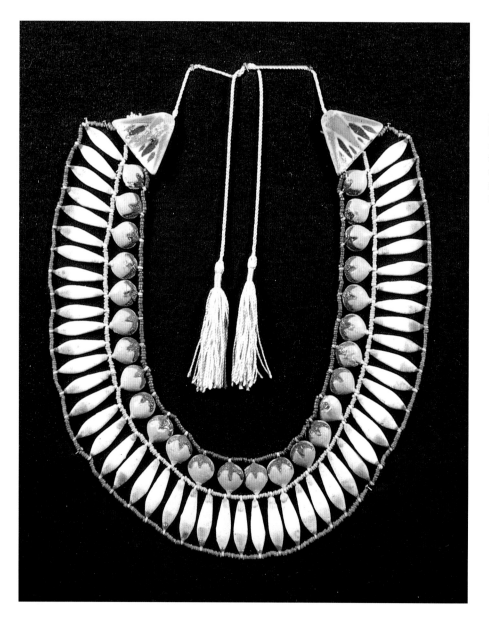

Faience collar, formerly in Carter's collection. It is composed of moulded elements representing mandrake fruits and blue lotus petals, with terminals imitating open lotus flowers. Collars composed of precisely these elements were actually worn by the ancient Egyptians and represented in wall-paintings and on coffins. Late 18th Dynasty. L. 43 cm.

A miniature vase of opaque yellow glass, from Carter's personal collection of antiquities. The techniques of early glass-making were probably introduced into Egypt from Western Asia during the 18th Dynasty, and over the next 400 years Egyptian craftsmen produced a wide range of vessels, small sculptures, jewellery, tiles and inlays in this much-prized material. Small vessels such as this one seem usually to have contained perfumes and oils. The body of the vessel has been formed by applying the molten glass to a core of clay or dung, which was afterwards removed – the usual method of fabricating such vessels in the New Kingdom. The ornamental rim was created by twining together a white and a black trail of glass which was then applied to the vessel and smoothed. The form and intense colour of this example suggest that it dates to the Ramesside Period. XRD analysis has revealed one anomaly in the use of bindheimite, rather than the usual lead antimonate, as the opacifier. H. 3.5 cm.

Large blue faience 'cinerary' urn of the Roman Period, one of the objects which was in Carter's possession at his death and which was later ceded to the Detroit Institute of Arts (p. 177). These urns display a wide variety of decoration, often incorporating wreaths of lotus petals. The spiral fluted decoration on the body and handles of this example is uncommon and seems to be relatively late (1st or 2nd century AD), but parallels are known (a similar urn is in the Louvre) and the same kind of decoration is found on vessels of glass, stone and metal. A ceramic workshop in which vessels of this general type (though without fluted ornamentation) were manufactured was discovered by Petrie at Memphis, and examples are known from many sites in Egypt. H. 23 cm.

Small figure of a seated cat in black haematite, one of the items in Carter's collection at the time of his death. It entered the possession of his niece Phylis Walker and ultimately passed to the Cleveland Museum of Art. The cat sits upon a small base in the shape of the hieroglyphic sign for 'protection', and has a loop for suspension attached to the back; in all probability it was designed as an amulet intended to provide the wearer with the protection of the goddess Bastet. Late Period. H. 4.3 cm.

... These objects will be received by us with acknowledgment, and this will be a new enrichment of the Museum to inscribe to your uncle's memory ...

Letter from Phylis Walker to Percy E. Newberry, 12 October 1946
... I feel I must write and tell you that after I left you all on Thursday I called in at Spink's, and they volunteered the information—without my having mentioned the subject first—that the objects have now gone back to Egypt by air, and should be in the hands of the King by this time.

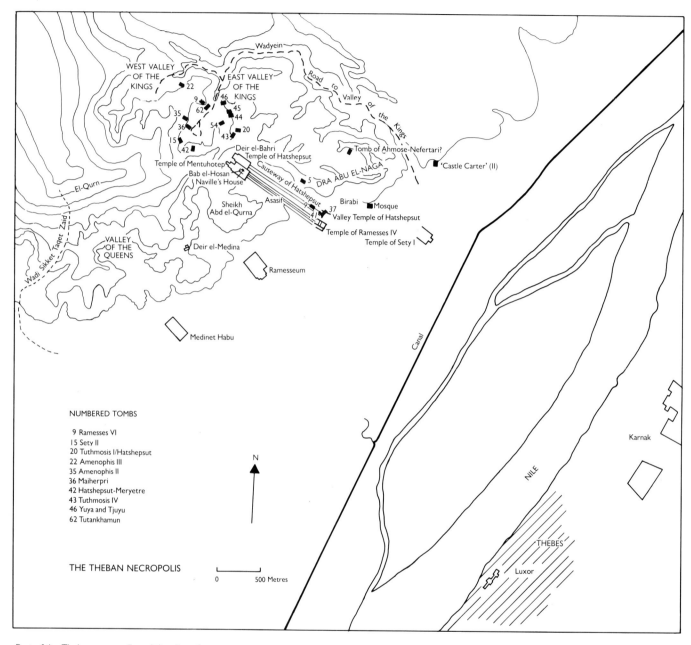

NUMBERED TOMBS

 9 Ramesses VI
15 Sety II
20 Tuthmosis I/Hatshepsut
22 Amenophis III
35 Amenophis II
36 Maiherpri
42 Hatshepsut-Meryetre
43 Tuthmosis IV
46 Yuya and Tjuyu
62 Tutankhamun

THE THEBAN NECROPOLIS

0   500 Metres

Part of the Theban necropolis and the sites of
Carter's principal excavations.

OPPOSITE Egypt and the sites associated with the
work of Howard Carter.

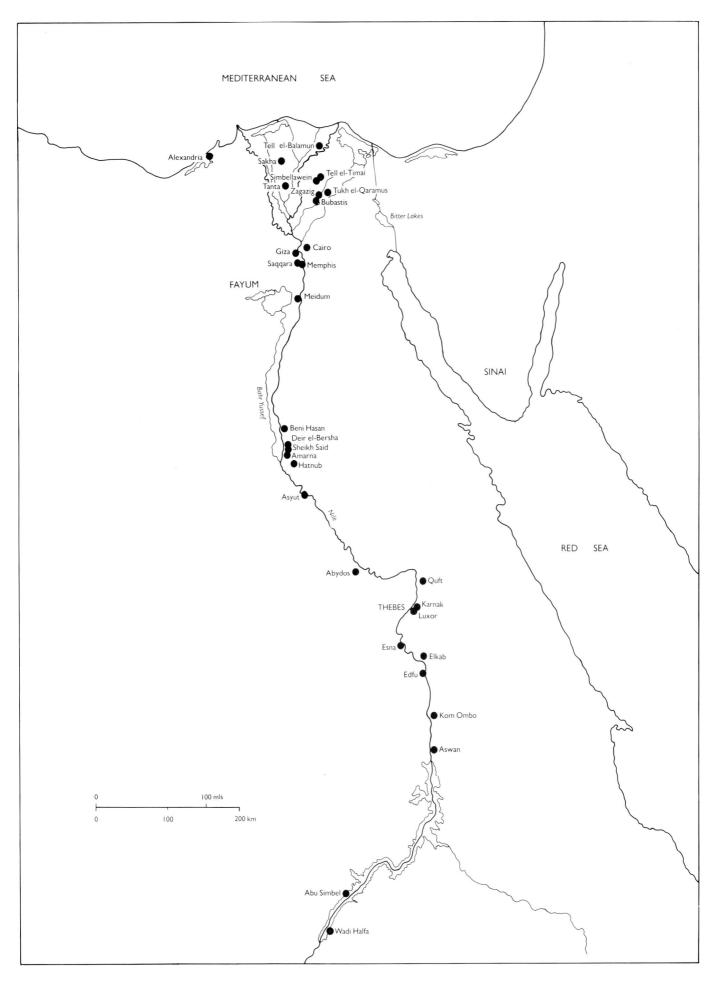

MEDITERRANEAN   SEA

Alexandria

Tell el-Balamun

Sakha

Simbellawein

Tanta

Zagazig

Tell el-Timai

Tukh el-Qaramus

Bubastis

Bitter Lakes

Cairo

Giza

Saqqara

Memphis

FAYUM

Meidum

SINAI

Bahr Yussef

Beni Hasan

Deir el-Bersha

Sheikh Said

Amarna

Hatnub

Asyut

Nile

RED   SEA

Abydos

Quft

THEBES

Karnak

Luxor

Esna

Elkab

Edfu

Kom Ombo

Aswan

0   100 mls

0   100   200 km

Abu Simbel

Wadi Halfa

Epilogue

Howard Carter died on 2 March 1939 and was buried in a simple grave at Putney Vale Cemetery, London. The inscription on the headstone reads:
HOWARD CARTER
Archaeologist and Egyptologist
May 9th, 1874–March 2nd, 1939.

Inscription on the 'Wishing Cup' (Carter Object no. 14) from the tomb of Tutankhamun
… May your spirit live, may you spend millions of years, you who love Thebes, sitting with your face to the north wind, your eyes beholding happiness.

Howard Carter had first visited Egypt as a humble epigraphic assistant, the Norfolk straw still protruding from his youthful, ungentlemanly ears. When he left for the last time it was as the most famous archaeologist in the world, an elegantly dressed connoisseur of the arts, sporting a cigarette-holder à la Lord Carnarvon and with a strongly developed taste for champagne. He had travelled a long way – and no thanks to his tact and diplomacy.

What Carter achieved he achieved because of his ability and dedication, combined with several generous helpings of good luck. By the time of his discovery of 'the Tomb' he had been living and working in Egypt for more than a quarter of a century – a quarter century which seems, with the benefit of hindsight, to have been filled with extraordinarily appropriate experience and achievement for what the future held in store. By 1922 Carter's knowledge and practical abilities had been honed to razor sharpness: the privilege of discovering Tutankhamun and the responsibility for clearing the tomb could not have been entrusted to more worthy or capable hands.

But for Howard Carter, the discovery marked the beginning of the end. Tutankhamun made him – but it would also break him. Carter had been a man sustained and driven by a dream. With the realisation of that dream, the best the future had to offer was a fading memory of the triumphs that had gone before.

In his last years Carter seems to have devoted little time to painting, though among the personal effects in Carter's possession at his death was a watercolour paint box made by the London firm of Roberson. It was retained by Harry Burton, Carter's executor, and has remained in private hands ever since. L. (closed) 21 cm.

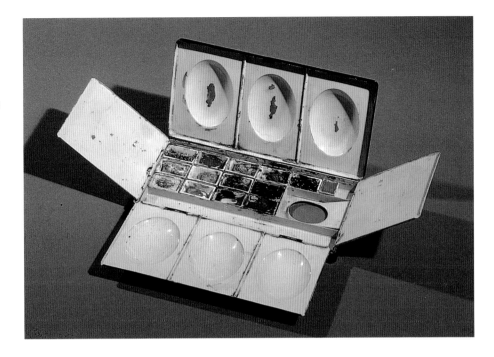

Head of a figure of Tuthmosis III from Deir el-Bahri, one of the watercolours published in Carter's *Six Portraits of the Thothmes Family*. Although Carter's paintings were much admired in their day this aspect of his achievement – like so much else – was overshadowed once public attention was focused on the tomb of Tutankhamun. The number of watercolours Carter painted is unknown and it is probable that many examples lie forgotten and neglected in private hands.

Sources of quotations

ABBREVIATIONS

ASAE	*Annales du Service des Antiquités de l'Egypte*
BM	British Museum, London
EEF/EES	Egypt Exploration Fund/Society, London
Geneva MSS	Papers preserved in the Bibliothèque publique et Universitaire, Geneva
GI	Griffith Institute, Oxford
MMA	Metropolitan Museum of Art, New York
Tut.ankh.Amen	H. Carter and A. C. Mace, *The Tomb of Tut.ankh.Amen* I (London, 1923), II and III – by Carter alone – (London, 1927 and 1933)

CHAPTER ONE

p. 10 'Much ... great man' *ASAE* 39 (1939), 53; p. 10 'I was ... miserably incomplete' GI, Carter MSS VI.2.1; p. 15 'I loved ... the lap-dog' GI, Carter MSS VI.2.1; p. 20 '[It is] to Lord ... see Egypt' GI, Carter MSS, VI.2.1; p. 20 'If you ... of mind' GI, Newberry MSS 1.21/10; p. 22 'I am ... leisure time' GI, Newberry MSS, 1.2/9; p. 22 'During the ... that country' GI, Carter MSS, VI.2.1; p. 22 '[Resolved] that ... exceeding £50' EES, Committee Minutes 16 Oct 1891; p. 23 'The complement ... following morning' GI, Carter MSS, VI.2.1; p. 24 'At Cairo ... no fools' GI, Carter MSS, VI.2.1; p. 25 'The railway ... its charm' GI, Carter MSS, VI.2.1; p. 26 'Our time ... as Blackden' EES, XII d.52; p. 27 'I have ... is splendid' GI, Newberry MSS, 1.21/23; p. 27 'I never ... mural decorations' GI, Carter MSS, VI.2.1; p. 30 'By the ... and varied' GI, Carter MSS, VI.2.1; p. 31 'There were ... the spot' GI, Carter MSS, VI.2.1; p. 32 'We crossed . . . century B.C.' GI, Carter MSS VI.2.1; p. 33 'Fraser and ... than heretofore' GI, Carter MSS, VI.2.1; p. 34 'Mr Carter ... an excavator' GI; p. 34 'Although I ... and pack' GI, Carter MSS, VI.2.1; p. 34 'While waiting ... wash up' GI, Carter MSS, VI.2.1; p. 35 'My cocoon ... examine systematically' GI, Carter MSS, VI.2.1; p. 40 'The rumour ... sky beyond' GI, Carter MSS, VI.2.1; p. 42 'As time ... rolled away' GI, Carter MSS, VI.2.1; p. 43 'The work ... in Egypt' GI, Newberry MSS, 1.8/3; p. 43 'In the ... was given' GI, Carter MSS, VI.2.1; p. 45 'The rock ... desolate solitude' GI, Carter MSS, VI.2.1; p. 45 'But hardly ... knew nothing' GI, Carter MSS, VI.2.1; p. 46 '[The papyri] ... and ashes' Egypt Exploration Fund *Archaeological Report* 1892–3, 4; p. 46 'I was ... of others' GI, Carter MSS, VI.2.1; p. 46 'I got ... me know' GI, Newberry MSS, 1.8/5; p. 47 'As for ... been cleared' GI, Newberry MSS, 1.8/9; p. 47 'I have ... Roger's eyes' GI, Newberry MSS, 1.8/7; p. 47 'I cannot ... of Brugsch' GI, Newberry MSS, 1.8/10; p. 47 'from what ... complete El-Bersheh' EES, XII f, in Archaeological Survey Papers for 1893; p. 47 '... [P.S.] Awful ... the Fund' GI, Newberry MSS, 1.8/12; p. 48 '[Following the ... work there' GI, Carter MSS, VI.2.1; p. 48 'I am ... the work' GI, Newberry MSS, 1.8/12; p. 49 'I dare ... of job' GI, Newberry MSS, 1.49/2; p. 49 'This magnificent ... my wages' GI, Carter MSS, VI.2.1; p. 54 'I have ... fine plates' EES, XVII.16; p. 54 'It is ... to do' EES, p. 54 'We had ... temple yesterday' EES, XI b2; p. 54 'Carter's manners ... all right' GI, Newberry MSS, 1.33/31; p. 54 'due possibly ... that occupation' GI, Carter MSS, VI.2.1; p. 55 'Dear Newberry ... Howard Carter' GI, Newberry MSS, 1.8/16.

CHAPTER TWO

p. 56 'telegrams were ... Deir el-Bahari' EES; p. 56 'You will ... through you' Geneva MS 2542.74; p. 56 'I have ... learning it' Geneva MS 2529.205; p. 57 'Work in ... from sebakh-digging' Egypt Exploration Fund *Archaeological Report* 1903–4, 24–5; p. 58–60 'My Dear ... at Swaffham' John Carter; p. 60 'Poor little ... with delight' MMA, Dept of Egyptian Art; p. 61 'In 1898 ... over it' GI, Carter MSS, Notebook 17, sketch IX; p. 61 'Nov. 24th ... up separately' *ASAE* 3 [1902], 115–19; p. 63 'Carter dined ... taken away' MMA, Dept of Egyptian Art; p. 66 'Some two ... next season' *ASAE* 2 [1901]. 201–2; p. 66 'I am ... being untouched' T. J. Eva; p. 66 '[On] the ... future date' *ASAE* 2 [1901], 202–4; p. 67 '[Carter] had ... very well' Geneva MS 2529.223; p. 67 'Only the ... to pieces' *ASAE* 2 [1901], 196–8; p. 69 'Last week ... present circumstances' T.J. Eva; p. 70 'Dear Mrs ... Howard Carter' BM, Dept of Egyptian Antiquities; p. 71 'We entered ... over one' MMA, Dept of Egyptian Art; p. 71 'Mr. Theo ... he accepted' GI,

Carter MSS, Notebook 16, sketch VI; p. 71 'After lunch ... the Tombs' MMA, Dept of Egyptian Art; p. 72 'We saw ... in Egypt' MMA, Dept of Egyptian Art; p. 72 'The work ... was found' GI, Carter MSS, Notebook 16, sketch VI; p. 73 'Just above ... of entry' GI, Carter MSS, Notebook 16, sketch VI; p. 73 'A few ... any further' GI, Carter MSS, Notebook 16, sketch VI; p. 74 'Leading from ... sharp knife' GI, Carter MSS, Notebook 16, sketch VI; p. 75 'Carter appeared ... blue pottery' MMA, Dept of Egyptian Art; p. 75 'We went ... unique things' MMA, Dept of Egyptian Art; p. 78 'When I ... over it' GI, Carter MSS Notebook 16, sketch VII; p. 78 'It was ... at you' GI, Carter MSS, Notebook 16, sketch VII; p. 78 'It was ... elaborately engraved' GI, Carter MSS, Notebook 16, sketch VII; p. 79 'Carter and ... the workmen' MMA, Dept of Egyptian Art; p. 79 'Newberry has ... the Museum' T.J. Eva; p. 80 'Monsieur Maspero ... much better' T.J. Eva; p. 81 'I am ... and slack' T.J. Eva; p. 81 'My Lord ... des Antiquités' GI, Carter MSS, V.107; p. 81 'Director ... des Antiquités' GI, Carter MSS, V.148; p. 83 'How is ... la Bouliniere' GI, Carter MSS, V.118; p. 84 'I am ... becoming irritating' GI, Carter MSS, V.121; p. 84 'there is ... be forgotten' GI, Carter MSS, V.124; p. 84 'A letter ... present time' GI, Carter MSS, V.125; p. 84 'I may ... is inconceivable' GI, Carter MSS, V.130; p. 84 'some 117 ozs ... in silver', Egypt Exploration Fund, *Archaeological Report*, 1904–05, 29; p. 84 'Saw much ... years ago' MMA, Dept of Egyptian Art.

CHAPTER THREE

p. 85 'I received ... no matter' GI, Newberry MSS, 1.8/26; p. 86 'Many people ... of Egyptology' Highclere Castle; p. 86 'I may ... than ever' *Tut.ankh.Amen* I, 29–30; p. 86 'Maspero has ... requisite data' Philippa Moore; p. 87 'The more ... and affection' *Tut.ankh.Amen* I, 30; p. 90 'With a ... Bahari valley' Lord Carnarvon and H. Carter, *Five years' Explorations at Thebes*, London 1912, 1–2; p. 90 'Yes! At ... pretty objects' GI, Newberry MSS, 1.8/33; p. 96 'I am ... 18th Dynasty' BM, Dept of Western Asiatic Antiquities; p. 99 'I started ... next week' Highclere Castle; p. 103 'I finished ... to him' BM, Dept of Western Asiatic Antiquities; p. 104 'Made at ... Thebes 1910' Highclere Castle; p. 104 'By noon ... Arabic style', letter in possession of Margaret Gardiner, quoted in T.G.H. James, *Howard Carter, the Path to Tutankhamun* (London, 1992), 159; p. 105 'Since my ... per mensem' GI, Newberry MSS, 1.7/97; p. 105 'I visited ... whole area' GI, Gardiner MSS, 44.26.3; p. 105 'Here at ... great heat' GI, Newberry MSS, 1.8/43; p. 106 'My dear ... turn up' GI, Newberry MSS, 1.8/54; p. 110 'My chief ... than doubled' *Tut.ankh.Amen* I, 32; p. 114 'Carter suggested ... this fashion' Highclere Castle; p. 118 'My dear ...

great worth' Highclere Castle; p. 119 'My dear ... up to?' Highclere Castle; p. 119 'My dear ... Howard Carter' Highclere Castle; p. 120 'Weigall has ... somewhat uncomfortable' GI, Newberry MSS, 1.8/35; p. 120 'Citoyen Gardiner ... my friends' GI, Newberry MSS, 1.8/35; p. 121 'I believe ... the translation' BM, Dept of Western Asiatic Antiquities; p. 121 'About 1907 ... Royal Tombs' GI, Carter MSS, Notebook 17, sketch XI; p. 122 'He professed ... my excitement' GI, Carter MSS, Notebook 17, sketch XI; p. 124 'I procured ... the floor' GI, Carter MSS, Notebook 17, sketch XI; p. 124 'The clearance ... Dynasty hypogeum' GI, Carter MSS, Notebook 17, sketch XI; p. 126 'War-work claimed ... buried there' *Tut.ankh.Amen* I, 79; p. 127 'I am ... do something' MMA, Dept of Egyptian Art; p. 127 'In these ... had vanished' BM, Dept of Western Asiatic Antiquities; p. 129 'at present ... and painting' GI, Newberry MSS, 1.8/56; p. 129 'The absence ... crawl through' *Tut.ankh.Amen* I, 79–82; p. 130 'Excitement ... was abandoned' *Tut.ankh.Amen* I, 81–82; p. 131 'My dear ... the devils!' GI, Gardiner MSS, 42.55.

CHAPTER FOUR

p. 132 'Ever since ... KV 55]' *Tut.ankh.Amen* I, 75–8; p. 134 'I entirely ... your work' MMA, Dept of Egyptian Art; p. 134 'In the ... with it?' *Tut.ankh.Amen* I, 82–5; p. 137 'The small ... something good' Nicholas Reeves; p. 138 'Have been ... at Newbury' GI, Newberry MSS, 1.8/63; p. 139 'None of ... could say?' C. Breasted, *Pioneer to the Past*, London 1948, 308–11; p. 140 'On my ... and unprecedented' Nicholas Reeves; p. 141 'My dear ... of him' GI, Gardiner MSS, cuttings; p. 142 'My dear ... believe ... intact' GI, Gardiner MSS, cuttings; p. 143 'Porch [Carnarvon] ... the workmen' St Antony's College, Oxford; p. 148 'I fancy ... leather, etc. ...' GI, Gardiner MSS, cuttings; p. 149 'Thanks ... Continental Cairo' MMA, Dept of Egyptian Art; p. 149 'Only too ... effect. Lythgoe' MMA, Dept of Egyptian Art; p. 149 'through the ... every detail' MMA, Dept of Egyptian Art; p. 151 '256, QQ ... much disintegrated' GI, Carter MSS, Tutankhamun archive; p. 154 'I worked ... his "assistance"' MMA, Dept of Egyptian Art; p. 154 'Walter [Hauser] ... with him' MMA, Dept of Egyptian Art; p. 154 'That man ... thought impossible' quoted in T.G.H. James, *Howard Carter, the Path to Tutankhamun*, London 1992, 240; p. 154 'Having a ... with me' GI, Carter MSS, Tutankhamun excavation diary, 15 November 1928; p. 154 'Gentleman Kartar ... Ahmed Kirkar' John Carter; p. 154 'Dear Sir ... Salahedeen Lautfie' John Carter; p. 154 'Poor old ... first magnitude' BM, Dept of Western Asiatic Antiquities; p. 155 '[The Society] ... should take' Report of the Thirty-fifth Ordinary General Meeting of the

EES, 1921, 7; p. 155 'This afternoon ... Eighteenth Dynasty' *The Times* 30 November 1922; p. 155 'According to ... Tutankhamen's tomb' *Yorkshire Post* 12 January 1923; p. 155 'Buxton and ... would-be visitors' H. Field, *The Track of Man. Adventures of an Anthropologist*, London 1955, 42; p. 155 'Nobody is ... M. Labouchere' John Carter; p. 156 'Pups asked ... love Eve' MMA, Dept of Egyptian Art; p. 157 'Poor Ld. ... the morning' GI, Carter MSS, Tutankhamun excavation diary, 5 April 1923; p. 157 'There was ... of them' Arthur Weigall, *Tutankhamen and Other Essays*, London 1924, 88–9; p. 157 'I cannot ... Lord Carnarvon' *Daily News* 5 April 1923; p. 158 'It has ... with contempt' *Tut.ankh.Amen.* II, xxv; p. 159 'Neither of ... the world' MMA, Dept of Egyptian Art; p. 159 'Things have ... various sorts' Margaret Orr; p. 159 'Among the ... deplorably lax' *Yorkshire Post* 29 January 1923; p. 159 'Carnarvon has ... their doings' A. H. Gardiner, *My Early Years*, privately printed 1986, 63; p. 160 'the unfortunate ... whole time' A. H. Gardiner, *My Early Years*, privately printed 1986, 63; p. 160 'Just as ... him down' C. Breasted, *Pioneer to the Past*, London 1948, 327; p. 160 'I have ... to you' MMA, Dept of Egyptian Art; p. 160 'LUXOR Wednesday ... HOWARD CARTER' *Daily News* 14 February 1924; p. 161 'Very private ... Egypt. Government ...' Museum of Fine Arts, Boston, Egyptian Dept; p. 161 'Mr. Howard ... Mr. Carter' *Daily News* 15 January 1925; p. 162 'The sarcophagus ... shining gold' C. Breasted, *Pioneer to the Past*, London 1948, 341; p. 162 'Carter and ... "solid gold"' University of Chicago, Oriental Institute, Director's Office correspondence, 1925; p. 164 'The Right ... the price' *The Times* 18 May 1923; p. 164 '1924 Contrary ... August 1926' GI, Newberry MSS, 1.8/82; p. 165 'Dear Mr. ... W. Fryzer' John Carter; p. 165 'Dear Mr. ... Belgian Ambassador' John Carter; p. 166 'Dear Sir ... truly. A.H.L.H[...] ...' John Carter; p. 166 'In recognition ... and privileges' *Yale Alumni Weekly*, vol. 33, no. 40 (4 July 1924), quoted in T.G.H. James, *Howard Carter, the Path to Tutankhamun*, London 1992, 322–3; p. 166 'By the ... add Esq.' John Carter; p. 167 'My dear ... Percy White' John Carter; p. 168 'Mr Howard ... Jeanette Leeper' John Carter; p. 168 'Dear Sir ... M. Hirose' John Carter; p. 168 'Dear Sir ... Yours respectfully' John Carter; p. 169 'I would ... publication today?' A. H. Gardiner quoted in Leonard Cottrell, *The Lost Pharaohs* London 1950, 168–9.

CHAPTER FIVE
p. 170 '(Carter) is ... own class' Archives of the Cleveland Museum of Art; p. 170 'There is ... the beautiful' Detroit Institute of the Arts, quoted by W. H. Peck, *Journal of the Society for the Study of Egyptian Antiquities* XI/2 (March 1981), p. 66; p. 170 'Solid silver ... good condition' GI, Carter MSS 'rough diary', 6 April 1922; p. 171 'Howard Carter ... studied it' Nicholas Reeves; p. 171 'Dear Mr. ... C. R. Paravicini' John Carter; p. 171 'Dear Mr. ... with stand' John Carter; p. 174 'My dear ... Frederick G. Kenyon' John Carter; p. 175 'We beg ... (Thirty-five pounds)' John Carter; p. 175 'I do ... one day' John Carter.

CHAPTER SIX
p. 179 'Sunk in ... no one', M. S. Drower quoted in H. V. F. Winstone, *Howard Carter and the discovery of the tomb of Tutankhamun*, London, 1991, 283; p. 179 'Howard Carter ... long-standing feud' Adel Sabit, *A King Betrayed* London 1989, 90; p. 180 'but I shall ... with me', Adel Sabit, *A King Betrayed*, London 1989, 99; p. 181 'Sir, Having ... Eldeen Loutfi' John Carter; p. 181 'Sir Miss ... Egypt Egypt' John Carter; p. 181 'I Howard ... thirty one'; p. 182 'Stater of ... high 10.0.0' BM, Dept of Egyptian Antiquities; p. 183 'The Service ... uncle's memory' GI, Newberry MSS, with 1.44/74; p. 185 'I feel ... this time' GI, Newberry MSS, 1.44/81.

EPILOGUE
p. 188 'May your ... beholding happiness' *Tut.ankh.Amen* I, pl. XLVI.

QUOTATIONS IN CAPTIONS
p. 67 'The two ... the same' John Carter; p. 89 'The houses ... in silence' Amelia Edwards, *A Thousand Miles up the Nile*, London 1890, 4; p. 104 '"La Maison ... desert!' John Carter; p. 114 'assuredly ... sculpture' A. H. Gardiner, *Journal of Egyptian Archaeology* 4, 1917, 1; p. 142 'the day ... see again' *Tut.ankh.Amen* I, 94; p. 146 'There before us ... blow' *Tut.ankh.Amen* I, 179; p. 146 'First Carter ... he said ...' A. H. Gardiner, *My Early Years*, privately printed 1986, 66; p. 158 'I have had ... being shaved' A. H. Gardiner, *My Early Years*, privately printed 1986, 68–9.

Sources of illustrations

Chronology

Overlapping dates usually indicate coregencies. Before the Twenty-sixth Dynasty all dates given are approximate.

FIRST DYNASTY
*c.*3100–2890 BC

SECOND DYNASTY
*c.*2890–2686 BC

THIRD DYNASTY
*c.*2686–2613 BC

FOURTH DYNASTY
*c.*2613–2494 BC

FIFTH DYNASTY
*c.*2494–2345 BC

SIXTH DYNASTY
*c.*2345–2181 BC

SEVENTH/EIGHTH DYNASTIES
*c.*2181–2125 BC

NINTH/TENTH DYNASTIES
*c.*2160–2130 BC, *c.*2125–2025 BC

ELEVENTH DYNASTY
*c.*2125–1985 BC

TWELFTH DYNASTY
*c.*1985–1795 BC

THIRTEENTH DYNASTY
*c.*1795–*c.*1650 BC

FOURTEENTH DYNASTY
*c.*1750–*c.*1650 BC

FIFTEENTH DYNASTY
*c.*1650–1550 BC

SIXTEENTH DYNASTY
*c.*1650–*c.*1550 BC

SEVENTEENTH DYNASTY
*c.*1650–1550 BC

EIGHTEENTH DYNASTY
*c.*1550–1295 BC

NINETEENTH DYNASTY
c.1295–1186 BC

TWENTIETH DYNASTY
*c.*1186–1069 BC

TWENTY–FIRST DYNASTY
*c.*1069–945 BC

TWENTY-SECOND DYNASTY
*c.*945–715 BC

TWENTY-THIRD DYNASTY
*c.*818–715 BC

TWENTY-FOURTH DYNASTY
*c.*727–715 BC

TWENTY-FIFTH DYNASTY
*c.*747–656 BC

TWENTY-SIXTH DYNASTY
664–525 BC

TWENTY-SEVENTH DYNASTY
525–404 BC

TWENTY-EIGHTH DYNASTY
404–399 BC

TWENTY-NINTH DYNASTY
399–380 BC

THIRTIETH DYNASTY
380–343 BC

PERSIAN KINGS
343–332 BC

MACEDONIAN KINGS
332–305 BC

THE PTOLEMIES
305–30

Select Bibliography

ABBREVIATIONS

ASAE   Annales du Service des Antiquities de l'Egypte (Cairo, 1900–)

JEA   Journal of Egyptian Archaeology (London, 1914–).

WORKS WHOLLY OR PARTLY WRITTEN BY HOWARD CARTER

Carnarvon, the Earl of and Carter, Howard, *Five Years' Explorations at Thebes. A record of work done 1907–1911* (Oxford, 1912).

Carter, Howard, 'Report on tomb-pit opened on the 26th January 1901, in the Valley of the Tombs of the Kings, between No. 4 and No. 28', *ASAE*, 2 (1901), 144–5, pls I–II.

Carter, Howard, 'Report on work done at the Ramesseum during the years 1900–1901', *ASAE*, 2 (1901), 193–195, pls I–II.

Carter, Howard, 'Report upon the tomb of Sen-nefer found at Biban el-Molouk near that of Thotmes III No. 34', *ASAE*, 2 (1901), 196–200, pl. I.

Carter, Howard, 'Report on the Tomb of Mentuhotep 1st at Deir el-Bahari, known as Bab el-Hoçan', *ASAE*, 2 (1901), 201–5, pls I–II.

Carter, Howard, 'Report on the robbery of the tomb of Amenothes II, Biban el Moluk', *ASAE*, 3 (1902), 115–21, pls I–II.

Carter, Howard, 'Report on general work done in the southern inspectorate', *ASAE*, 4 (1903), 43–50 and 2 pls.

Carter, Howard, 'Report of work done in Upper Egypt (1902–1903)', *ASAE*, 4 (1903), 171–180, pls I–III.

Carter, Howard, *Six Portraits of the Thothmes Family, facsimiled from the Temple of Deir el Bahari* (possibly London, 1906–7).

Carter, Howard, 'Report on the tomb of Zeser-ka-ra Amenhetep I, discovered by the Earl of Carnarvon in 1914', *JEA*, 3 (1916), 147–154, pls XVII–XXIII.

Carter, Howard, 'A tomb prepared for Queen Hatshepsuit and other recent discoveries at Thebes', *JEA*, 4 (1917), 107–18, pls XIX–XXII.

Carter, Howard, 'A tomb prepared for Queen Hatshepsuit discovered by the Earl of Carnarvon (October 1916)', *ASAE*, 16 (1916), 179–82.

Carter, Howard, 'An ostracon depicting a red jungle-fowl (the earliest known drawing of the domestic cock)', *JEA*, 9 (1923), 1–4, pl. XX, 1.

Carter, Howard, *The Tomb of Tut.ankh.amen. Statement with Documents, as to the Events which occurred in Egypt in the Winter of 1923–24, leading to the ultimate break with the Egyptian Government* (London, 1924, 'For private circulation only').

Carter, Howard, 'The reign of Tutankhamen' in Ross, E. Denison, *The Art of Egypt through the Ages* (London, 1931), 40–6.

Carter, Howard and Gardiner, A. H., 'The tomb of Ramesses IV and the Turin plan of a royal tomb', *JEA*, 4 (1917), 130–58, pl. XXX.

Carter, Howard and Legrain, Georges, 'Report of work done in Upper Egypt (1903–1904)', *ASAE*, 6 (1905), 112–29, pls I–IV.

Carter, Howard and Mace, Arthur C., *The Tomb of Tut.ankh.Amen I–III* (London, 1923–33).

Carter, Howard and Newberry, P. E., *The Tomb of Thoutmosis IV* (London, 1904).

Carter, Howard and Newberry, P. E., *The Tomb of Thoutmosis*

IV. *Catalogue générale des antiquités Égyptiennes du Musée du Caire Nos. 46001–46529* (London, 1904).

Carter, Howard and White, Percy, 'The Tomb of the Bird', *Pearson's Magazine*, Vol. 56 (July–December 1923), 433–7.

CARTER'S LIFE AND CAREER
Brunton, Guy, 'Howard Carter', *ASAE*, 39 (1939), 49–53.

Desroches-Noblecourt, C., *Tutankhamen. Life and Death of a Pharaoh* (London, 1963).

Hoving, Thomas, *Tutankhamun. The Untold Story* (New York, 1978).

James, T. G. H., 'Howard Carter and the Cleveland Museum of Art' in Turner, E. H. ed., *Object Lessons. Cleveland creates an Art Museum* (Cleveland, 1991), 66–77.

James, T. G. H., *Howard Carter. The Path to Tutankhamun* (London, 1992).

Malek, J., 'Paiuenamun, Sambehdet, and Howard Carter's survey of Tell el-Balamun in 1913', *Revue d'Égyptologie*, 36 (1985), 181–5.

Newberry, P. E. 'Howard Carter', *JEA*, 25 (1939), 67–9.

Peck, W. H., 'The discoverer of the tomb of Tutankhamun and the Detroit Institute of the Arts', *Journal of the Society for the Study of Egyptian Antiquities*, XI/2 (March 1981), 65–7.

Reeves, N., *Ancient Egypt at Highclere Castle* (Highclere, 1989).

Reeves, N., *The Complete Tutankhamun* (London, 1990).

Reeves, N., *Valley of the Kings. The decline of a royal necropolis* (London, 1990).

Reeves, N., 'Howard Carter's collection of Egyptian and Classical antiquities' in Lloyd, A. B. ed., *Greatest of Seers* (forthcoming).

Romer, J., *Valley of the Kings* (London, 1981).

Winstone, H. V. F., *Howard Carter and the discovery of the tomb of Tutankhamun* (London, 1991).

Index

Italic refers to illustrations